Hexagonie, Part 2

An Innovative Way to Teach French

Maria Rice-Jones

Brilliant
PUBLICATIONS

About the author

Maria Rice-Jones is a French national with a Masters Degree in Modern Languages from the Sorbonne University in Paris. Since 1990, she has taught French to students of primary level and above in Paris, Milan and London.

Maria Rice-Jones is also the author of *Unforgettable French: Memory Tricks to Help You Learn and Remember French Grammar* (ISBN 978-1-905780-54-9).

Unforgettable French uses memory tricks to teach and reinforce major points of French grammar from the basics up to GCSE level, to learners of all ages. It is full of tried-and-tested memory tricks based on sound and idea associations to help you to engage your memory and remember key grammatical points.

Unforgettable French is a valuable companion to *Hexagonie*, as the memory tricks in *Unforgettable French* are presented in a highly visual page-by-page format to help pupils to visualize the language better. The sheets can be enlarged to make mini-posters or used as "aide-mémoires". In addition, *Unforgettable French* includes many new memory tricks, not introduced in *Hexagonie*.

Published by
Brilliant Publications
Unit 10
Sparrow Hall Farm
Edlesborough
Dunstable
Bedfordshire LU6 2ES

Written by Maria Rice-Jones
Illustrated by Sarah Wimperis
Designed by Gloss Solutions

ISBN 978-1-905780-18-1 (This book is sold together with a CD. The individual items are not available separately.)

First published in the UK 2010.
10 9 8 7 6 5 4 3 2 1

Contents

From the author   **5**

Teaching using the Hexagonie method   **6–10**

Unit 1   **It's my life!**   **11–28**
"Je m'appelle" ("My name is")
The alphabet and accents
Nationalities
Numbers 0-20

Unit 2   **The things in my life**   **29–47**
"Qu'est-ce que c'est?" ("What is it?")
Masculine and feminine

Unit 3   **Life is beautiful!**   **48–67**
"Ce", "cet", "cette", "ces" ("This/that" and "these/those")
Fruit and vegetables
Adjectives
Clothing

Unit 4   **Life with "to have" and "to be"**   **68-90**
The verb "avoir" ("to have") in the present tense
The verb "être" ("to be") in the present tense
Asking questions with "est-ce que" and by
inverting the subject and verb
Sentences with "pas de"

Unit 5   **My life, your life, his life**   **91–110**
All the possessives
Il y a

Unit 6   **Life in action**   **111–128**
"En", "au", and "aux" ("to a country" or "in a country")
The verb "parler" ("to speak") in the present tense
À ("to" or "at")

Unit 7   **To live and work – that's life!**   **129–152**
Question words
"Habiter" ("to live") in the present tense
Types of building
"Travailler" ("to work") in the present tense
Professions

Unit 8   **To play forever**   **153–169**
To play in the playground
To play a sport
To play an instrument

Unit 9   **Time flies**   **170–193**
Numbers 20–100
Telling the time
"Commencer" ("to start") in the present tense
"Terminer" ("to finish") in the present tense
"Petit déjeuner", "déjeuner" and "dîner" ("breakfast", "lunch"
and "dinner")

Unit 10   **Let's go!**   **194–213**
"Aller à" ("to go to")
Modes of transport
Days of the week

Unit 11   **Food and drink: That's what life is all about!**   **214–240**
Food and drink
The verb "manger" ("to eat") in the present tense
The verb "boire" ("to drink") in the present tense
"Pas de" / "beaucoup de"

Unit 12   **To do everything in life**   **241–254**
The verb "faire" ("to do") in the present tense

Unit 13   **What is the weather doing?**   **255–275**
Months of the year
Seasons
Weather

Unit 14   **Describe your life!**   **276–292**
More adjectives

Unit 15   **Test yourself!**   **293–305**
Review of all the previous units in the book

Vocabulary introduced per unit   **306–313**
Photocopiable sheets   **314–316**
Tableau d'Honneur   314
Je suis désolé(e) …   315
Pas de   316
Transcript for CD   **317–323**
Answer key for worksheets   **324–329**

From the author

Hexagonie is designed for non-specialist and specialist teachers of French in primary schools. It offers a fresh and creative approach to teaching French and is presented in a logical, easy-to-follow format. Whatever their experience with the French language, Hexagonie will enable teachers to achieve material results in the classroom. The fast-paced lessons, with an emphasis on learning and using language structures, enable pupils to rapidly demonstrate the ability to communicate and converse with confidence.

I have been developing, trialing and testing the *Hexagonie* method over many years for use in my own classroom. It has now been formalized as a book at the encouragement of my pupils and colleagues. *Hexagonie* is guided by my own personal quest to challenge the "difficulties" of the French language head-on with a bold and imaginative teaching style that makes learning French easier and more accessible than is typically possible with many French schemes or textbooks. A key principle of the *Hexagonie* method is that parrot-style learning of grammatical rules and vocabulary lists should be avoided because it is laborious, and what is learned is often quickly forgotten. Instead, my approach to learning makes learning French enjoyable. It encourages children to play with words and language structures and to create their own memory techniques, which in turn help them to internalize the language, making them more efficient learners.

Hexagonie is a highly systematic "synthetic" approach to teaching French. Elements of language are carefully introduced, one step at a time, so that each unit builds on what has been learned before, creating a firm foundation.

Hexagonie integrates a wide range of interesting facts about French and the French way of life so that pupils will gain a rich insight into the culture and diversity of the country.

Hexagonie will make you see French in a different light and help you to teach more creatively and efficiently. This is what *Hexagonie* is all about.

Enjoy!

Maria

Maria Rice-Jones

Teaching using the Hexagonie method

Hexagonie is a two-part scheme for teaching French to 7-11 year olds. *Hexagonie, Part 1* is for use with pupils in Years 3 and 4 (or later, depending on when they start French) and *Hexagonie, Part 2* is for use with pupils in Years 5 and 6.

Hexagonie, Part 2 consists of:
* Book containing lesson plans and photocopiable sheets
* Audio CD

Structure of the units

There are 15 units in *Hexagonie, Part 2*. Units 1–3 recap on material covered in *Hexagonie, Part 1*. You may wish to skip these units, or selectively choose those elements you feel your pupils need to revise. As with *Hexagonie, Part 1*, each unit builds on the preceding one, so they need to be taught in order. However, it is up to you, the teacher, to decide how many lessons to split the units into. The units are subdivided so there are convenient breaking points. We haven't provided rigid lesson plans as the time available and pace in which pupils can work will differ from class to class. Each unit provides a detailed lesson plan and related photocopiable pupil sheets.

Bonjour and au revoir

We recommend that you begin each lesson with "Bonjour" and end with "Au revoir". Greeting people politely is a very important part of French culture, and taking the time to greet the children at the start of the lesson and say a formal goodbye at the end will reinforce this.

Hexagonie story

In each unit you will find a story about the imaginary land of "Hexagonie" narrated by the verb Voyager. These stories, written in English, are designed to be read aloud, either by you or by pupils, and then discussed. The imaginary land of Hexagonie gets its name from the shape of France. In fact, many French people refer to France as "l'Hexagone". The inhabitants of Hexagonie are parts of speech: nouns, verbs, etc. These fun stories reinforce key teaching points. They work in much the same way as the "memory tricks", helping to engage pupils' imaginations and encourage learning. Pupils could be encouraged to keep their copies of the stories and make them into a little booklet.

Recap on previous units

Each unit (after Unit 1) starts with a recap on what has been learned in the preceding lesson. If you split up the units into smaller segments, we recommend that you begin each lesson with a quick oral recap of what you did the lesson before.

Essential words and phrases

Each unit has a list of essential words and phrases that can be photocopied and given to children. As with the Hexagonie stories, these could be collated and made into a small booklet.

Vocabulary lists and materials needed

The vocabulary and materials needed are listed in boxes to the side of each section, so it is easy to see at a glance what vocabulary will be introduced, and what materials are needed. A full list of the vocabulary introduced in each unit is on pages 306–313. For your convenience, we have included all the words and phrases used in *Hexagonie, Part 2*, even though some were introduced in *Hexagonie, Part 1*.

Logos used in lesson plans

Each unit contains a wide variety of activities, ranging from role plays and games through to Mexican waves and listening activities. You do not need to do all the activities and you should use your professional judgement to decide which to include. Other suggestions for introducing vocabulary appear on page 9.

The following logos have been used to make the lesson plans easy to navigate:

 Role play is an excellent way of giving children the opportunity to practise speaking French.

 This logo refers to the photocopiable pupil sheets. The number of the sheet is indicated on the logo. For more information on the pupil sheets, please see page 8.

 This logo indicates that a track on the CD is required. The appropriate track number appears on the logo.

 On the board – this logo indicates when it would be beneficial to illustrate the key points being taught on the board.

 Game – this logo is used to indicate a variety of games – some paper-based, others more active.

 Memory tricks are an important part of the *Hexagonie* approach. I provide a wide range of tried and tested "memory tricks" based on sound and idea associations. They enliven and facilitate the learning process by helping pupils to learn and remember what is being taught. Wherever memory tricks are used to master tricky grammatical points or vocabulary, experience shows that what is learnt once usually sticks for good. So, whenever a teacher or pupil faces a difficulty in French, the best solution is to use or devise a memory trick – what was difficult before will suddenly seem much easier and is less likely to be forgotten.

Having posters of these tricks displayed around the classroom will help pupils to visualize the language better. *Unforgettable French*, also written by Maria Rice-Jones, in a valuable companion to *Hexagonie*. In *Unforgettable French* the memory tricks are presented in a highly visual page-by-page format, and can easily be enlarged to make attractive mini-posters for display.

Throughout the scheme, pupils (and teachers!) are encouraged to construct their own memory tricks. Creating memory tricks is all about playing with words: it is an imaginative "game" which makes learning fun and also teaches pupils how to learn more efficiently. That means not just learning something for today, but knowing how to learn something so that you remember it for life.

Pupil pages

A variety of pupil pages has been included, so that you can choose the sheet most appropriate for your pupils. The pupil pages use the following logos, to help give pupils independence and instil confidence when reading instructions.

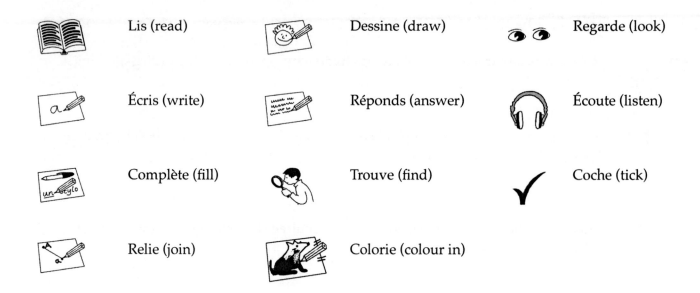

Lis (read)	Dessine (draw)	Regarde (look)
Écris (write)	Réponds (answer)	Écoute (listen)
Complète (fill)	Trouve (find)	Coche (tick)
Relie (join)	Colorie (colour in)	

Answers to the pupil sheets are given on pages 324–329.

Audio CD

The CD contains 54 tracks. A full transcript appears on pages 313–324. The oral activities on the CD model the language introduced in the scheme and provide listening activities, which gradually grow in length and complexity. Some of the listening activities are linked to specific worksheets. In addition there are seven songs, as well as instrumental versions of the tunes to allow children to sing on their own and enable you to adapt the language, see for example, 'Jean Petit qui danse', page 105. After listening to the tracks, you could ask questions to test the pupils' comprehension and give them more opportunities for speaking.

How Hexagonie relates to KS2 Framework for Languages

Hexagonie, Part 2 addresses all of the learning objectives for Years 5, and 6 for Oracy and Literacy, and many of those for Intercultural Understanding. The charts below show which objectives are addressed in each unit. As you will see, most of the learning objectives are addressed in each unit, so that pupils are given many opportunities to practise both their oral and written skills. Through doing the activities suggested in *Hexagonie*, pupils will also develop knowledge about the French language, and develop effective learning strategies for learning languages. Indeed, developing effective strategies for learning French is what *Hexagonie* is all about.

	O5.1	O5.2	O5.3	O5.4	L5.1	L5.2	L5.3	IU5.1	IU5.2	IU5.3
Unit										
1	•				•					
2	•			•	•					
3	•	•	•	•	•		•			
4	•	•	•	•	•	•	•			•
5	•		•		•	•	•	•		
6	•	•		•		•	•		•	
7	•		•		•	•	•		•	
8	•	•	•	•	•		•	•		
9	•	•	•		•	•		•		
10	•	•	•	•	•	•	•	•	•	
11	•		•		•	•	•	•	•	•
12		•	•		•	•	•			
13	•		•		•	•	•		•	
14	•	•			•	•	•			
15	•	•	•	•	•	•	•			

	O6.1	O6.2	O5.3	O6.4	L6.1	L6.2	L6.3	L6.4	IU6.1	IU6.2	IU6.3
Unit											
1					•						
2	•	•									
3	•	•									
4	•	•	•		•	•	•	•			
5	•		•		•		•	•			
6			•	•				•			
7	•		•	•	•	•	•	•	•	•	
8	•	•	•		•				•		
9			•								
10	•		•	•	•	•	•	•		•	
11	•	•	•	•	•		•	•		•	
12	•		•		•	•		•			
13	•		•	•	•	•	•	•		•	
14	•				•			•			
15		•	•	•	•	•		•			

Suggestions for introducing new vocabulary

Throughout *Hexagonie, Part 2*, the vocabulary is introduced using visual material: items from the classroom, miniatures and flashcards. The vocabulary is given as a suggestion and it is up to you, the teacher, to decide if you introduce it all.

Experience shows that pupils learn in different ways, which is why I have included a variety of learning styles – from 'engaging' activities (role play, games) through to oral and written activities. Using the vocabulary in many different ways will help pupils to remember it.

Hexagonie is primarily an oral approach to learning French. Photocopiable sheets are included to enable the children to practise what they have learned in class or at home. They contain a variety of activities ranging from drawing and matching activities through to reading and writing practice. It is intended that they should be given out only at the end of the lesson, and that you go over the language on the sheet first with the children. However, it is up to you, the teacher, to decide which sheets to give out and when, as you are the one who knows your pupils best. Remember, it is important for children to have lots of practice pronouncing words orally before seeing them in the written form.

Praising pupils

The more French your pupils hear using the language structures introduced in *Hexagonie,* the better. Here are some simple phrases using "c'est" you can use when praising children:

- C'est amusant!   It is funny!
- C'est beau!   It is beautiful!
- C'est intéressant!   It is interesting!
- C'est correct!   It is correct!
- C'est excellent!   It is excellent!
- C'est très bien!   It is very well done!
- Ce n'est pas difficile!   It isn't difficult!
- C'est magnifique!   It is magnificent!
- C'est simple!   It is simple!

Other useful French phrases

- Ce n'est pas clair!   It isn't clear!
- C'est dangereux!   It is dangerous!
- Ce n'est pas normal!   It isn't normal!
- C'est difficile!   It is difficult!
- C'est impossible!   It is impossible!
- C'est incorrect!   It is incorrect!
- C'est délicieux!   It is delicious!

It's my life!

Key teaching points/vocabulary

"Je m'appelle" ("My name is")
The alphabet and accents
Nationalities
Numbers 0–20

Bonjour, je m'appelle...

Hello, my name is...

Say "Bonjour" to the whole class, and encourage the pupils to reply "Bonjour Madame/Monsieur" in chorus.

Introduce yourself by saying twice, "Bonjour, je m'appelle Madame/Monsieur/Mademoiselle (your name)". Address a single pupil asking him/her the simple question, "Et toi?" Encourage him/her to reply, "Je m'appelle Thomas", "Je m'appelle Emma" etc. Go around the classroom asking the same question to each pupil in turn.

Perform a Mexican wave where every pupil introduces himself or herself by saying his or her name, "Je m'appelle Thomas", "Je m'appelle Emma" etc.

Congratulate the pupils with an enthusiastic "Très bien" or "Bravo".

Tell the pupils that:
"Je m'appelle" literally means "I call myself." Point out that "m' " is short for "me". "M' " is used before a verb that starts with a vowel. "Me" shows that I am introducing myself and not anybody else.

Vocabulaire

bonjour	hello
Madame	Mrs/Madam
Monsieur	Mr/Sir
Mademoiselle	Miss
je m'appelle	my name is (I am called)
Et toi?	And you?
très bien	well done
bravo	bravo

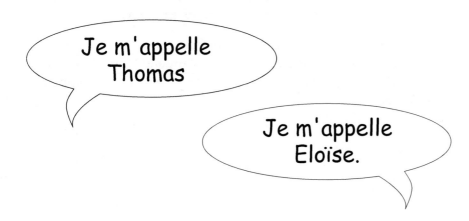

© Maria Rice-Jones and Brilliant Publications

Vocabulaire

tu t'appelles	your name is (you are called)
il/elle s'appelle	his/her name is (he/she is called)
Tu t'appelles comment?	What is your name?
Il/elle s'appelle comment?	What is his/her name?
oui	yes
non	no
moi	me

Materials

★ Pictures cut out from papers or magazines showing famous people from different countries. You could include actors, prime ministers, presidents, sport celebrities etc.
★ Sheet 1a (page 19)
★ Tableau d'Honneur (page 314)
★ Stickers (optional)

Tu t'appelles..., il s'appelle...

You are called…, he is called…

Write the following on the board underlining the letters marked below:

Je m'appelle
Tu t'appelles
Il/elle s'appelle

Ask if anyone in the class would like to guess what "Tu t'appelles" means ("Your name is" or "You call yourself"). Point out that "t' " stands for "te".

Ask the class if they can work out what "Il s'appelle" and "Elle s'appelle" mean ("His name is" and "Her name is"). Point out that "s' " before "appelle" stands for "se".

 "Te" starts with a "t", just like "tu".
In English we can find "**se**" in "il/elle s'appelle" in the words "him**se**lf" and in "her**se**lf".

Point at a pupil and ask his or her neighbour the question, "Il/elle s'appelle comment?" ("What is his/her name?"), waiting for the answer, "Il/elle s'appelle (pupil's name)". Continue with more pupils.

Always congratulate the pupils with an enthusiastic "Très bien" or "Bravo".

 Give Sheet 1a to the pupils and ask them to complete this activity in the class or at home.

 One by one, hold up the pictures of various famous people and ask the class to name each one by asking, "Il/elle s'appelle comment?" waiting for the answer, "Il/elle s'appelle (name of the famous person)". Reward the pupils who answer correctly by giving them a "Tableau d'Honneur" or a sticker.

To reinforce the use of "Il/elle s'appelle", go around the class pointing at a pupil and asking, "Elle s'appelle Mary?" The class should answer, "Oui, elle s'appelle Mary" or "Non, il s'appelle John" etc.

L'alphabet

The alphabet

Vocabulaire

l'alphabet (m)	the alphabet
une consonne	a consonant
une voyelle	a vowel
Comment ça s'écrit?	How is that spelt?
le pendu	hangman

Materials

* ★ CD, Tracks 1–3
* ★ Sheets 1b(i)–1b(ii) (pages 20–21), photocopied on to card, one per pupil or one per group
* ★ Scissors
* ★ Tableau d'Honneur (page 314)
* ★ Stickers (optional)

Sing the alphabet song in French to the tune "Twinkle, twinkle little star" (CD, Track 1) which pupils learned in Hexagonie, Part 1. Listen to it all the way through once then encourage the whole class to sing with you. An instrumental version is available on Track 2.

Note:
The last two lines of the song are as follows:

Voilà je sais mon abc	*There! I know my abc*
Alors c'est à toi maintenant.	*Now it's your turn*

Write on the board some letters in alphabetical order such as, "d, e, g, h" but omit one letter, for example, "f". Ask the pupils to tell you which letter is missing. Do the same with other strings of letters.

Listen to the names being spelt out on Track 3 on the CD then write down the names.

Names on Track 3: 1. Robert; 2. Jessica; 3. Maria; 4. Thomas; 5. Ivor

Choice of activities

Perform a Mexican wave where every pupil introduces himself or herself by saying his/her name and surname, "Je m'appelle Thomas Hamilton" and spells his/her name and so on. You might need to prompt pupils by asking, "Comment ça s'écrit?" ("How is that spelt?").

Play "le pendu" (hangman) using the names or surnames of the pupils in the class. The pupils must say the letter names in French. Use "oui" or "non" to say whether a letter is correct or not.

Give each pupil or each group of pupils a copy of Sheets 1b(i)–1b(ii) photocopied on to card. Ask them to cut the sheet up into cards. To begin with, ask them to sort the cards into two piles, one of "consonnes" ("consonants") and one of "voyelles" ("vowels"). Call out "consonne" or "voyelle" and ask the pupils to hold up a letter that belongs to the category that you asked for.

Tell the pupils to spread the letters out on their desk in front of them. Then say that you will spell out a word in French and that they will have to find the letters and line them up in front of them. When you finish spelling out the word, the pupils should be able to tell you what the word is. If you are doing this as a group activity, the groups could race each other to be the first to identify the word. When the pupils get the hang of this game, you could ask individual pupils in the class to think of a word and spell it out.

Play the television game "Countdown" (with letters only). Divide the pupils into groups of four. In each group, ask the pupils to form two opposing teams. Using Sheets 1b(i)–1b(ii) (cut into cards), put two piles on your desk, one of consonants and one of vowels. Groups take it in turn to choose nine letters, saying whether they'd like a "consonne" or "voyelle". Write the letters chosen on the board. When you have written all nine letters on the board, the game can start. In each group, the two teams have one minute to find the longest French word they can think of, using the letters chosen. After one minute, stop the game and ask each team to say its word. The winning teams are the ones who have found the longest word in their group. Reward winning teams by giving them a "Tableau d'Honneur" or a sticker. If pupils cannot think of any French words, give them suggestions, e.g. colours, numbers, greetings etc. Alternatively, if you have enough French – English dictionaries, you could give one to each group.

Vocabulaire

un accent aigu	acute accent
un accent grave	grave accent
un accent circonflexe	circumflex accent
un père	a father
une mère	a mother
un frère	a brother
une tête	a head
à	at
la maison	the house
où	where
un dîner	a dinner
un château	a castle
un hôpital	a hospital
une règle	a ruler
un éléphant	an elephant
Noël	Christmas
une télévision	a television
un téléphone	a telephone
un bébé	a baby
une école	a school
un hélicoptère	a helicopter
une étoile	a star
une cuillère	a spoon
une église	a church

Materials

★ Sheet 1c (page 22)
★ CD, Track 4

Accents

Accents

Tell the pupils that three main types of accent can be added to the letter "e":

Write this table on the board:
é   accent aigu
è   accent grave
ê   accent circonflexe

Explain to the pupils that "é" is "e accent aigu" ("e with an acute accent"). It is used to make the sound "ay" as in "télévision" and "téléphone".

Explain to the pupils that "è" is "e accent grave" ("e with a grave accent"). It is used to make the sound "eh" as in "père" (father), "mère" (mother) and "frère" (brother).

Explain to the pupils that "ê" is "e accent circonflexe" ("e with a circumflex accent"). It is used to stress the sound "eh" as in "tête" (head).

Tell the pupils that the grave accent and the circumflex accent can also be found on letters other than "e". You could write some words on the board that contain vowels with an accent such as:
à   in "à la maison" ("at the house")
ù   in "où" ("where")
â   in "château" ("castle")
î   in "dîner" ("dinner")
ô   in "hôpital" ("hospital")

Optional

You could introduce the sign called trema (¨), found in some words like Noël to indicate that the vowel before the ë must be pronounced as well as the "e".

Ask the pupils to listen to Track 4 on the CD. Each word is repeated twice. The pupils have to put the appropriate accent ("acute" or "grave") on the letters highlighted in bold on Sheet 1c.

Hexagonie story

Give each pupil a copy of Sheet 1d: "Keep your hat on". This explains a way of remembering the accents. Discuss to reinforce the points covered.

Materials
★ Sheet 1d (page 23)

De quelle nationalité es-tu?

What is your nationality?

This is a recap from Hexagonie, Part 1. Display a large map of the world. Tell the pupils that you are going to introduce different nationalities. If you have a whiteboard, you could display a map of the world with the country names written in French (search for *"carte du monde"* on Google images).

Point to a country and say, e.g. "L'Angleterre". Say "il est anglais/elle est anglaise". Repeat it twice, emphasizing the different endings. Then ask the pupils to repeat after you, "il est anglais/elle est anglaise". Now point to "La France" on the map and say "il est français/elle est française" twice, then encourage the children to repeat after you. Then point to "L'Irlande" and do the same with "il est irlandais/ elle est irlandaise".

Continue to introduce the nationalities, grouping them by their sound endings, as shown below. You may introduce as many countries as you wish, but use at least three from each category, making sure you introduce all the nationalities of your pupils.

Vocabulaire

une nationalité	a nationality
allemand(e)	German
américain(e)	American
anglais(e)	English
canadien(ne)	Canadian
chinois(e)	Chinese
écossais(e)	Scottish
espagnol(e)	Spanish
français(e)	French
gallois(e)	Welsh
indien(ne)	Indian
irlandais(e)	Irish
italien(ne)	Italian
japonais(e)	Japanese
pakistanais(e)	Pakistani
polonais(e)	Polish
portugais(e)	Portuguese
je suis…	I am
je suis désolé(e)	I am sorry
je ne sais pas	I don't know
De quelle nationalité es-tu?	What is your nationality?
De quelle nationalité est-il/elle?	What is his/ her nationality?

Materials
★ Large map of the world (ideally with countries labelled in French)
★ "Je suis désolé(e)…" (page 315)
★ Pictures of famous people

Nationalities ending with the sound "ai" in the masculine:

Country	Masculine	Feminine
L'Angleterre	anglais	anglaise
La France	français	française
L'Irlande	irlandais	irlandaise
L'Écosse	écossais	écossaise
Le Japon	japonais	japonaise
Le Pakistan	pakistanais	pakistanaise
La Pologne	polonais	polonaise
Le Portugal	portugais	portugaise

Nationalities ending with the sound "un" in the masculine:

Country	Masculine	Feminine
L'Amérique	américain	américaine
Le Canada	canadien	canadienne
L'Italie	italien	italienne
L'Inde	indien	indienne

Other nationalities:

L'Allemagne	allemand	allemande
L'Espagne	espagnol	espagnole
Le Pays de Galles	gallois	galloise
La Chine	chinois	chinoise

If you have several nationalities in your class, you could perform a Mexican wave where every pupil says his/her nationality before asking another pupil the question, "De quelle nationalité es-tu?" and so on. For example:

Thomas	"Je suis anglais, et toi Prachy, de quelle nationalité es-tu?"
Prachy	"Je suis indienne, et toi Emilia, de quelle nationalité es-tu?"
Emilia	"Je suis italienne, et toi Michaël, de quelle nationalité es-tu?" and so on.

Always praise a correct response with "Très bien Thomas" or "Bravo Prachy" to build your pupils' confidence. If a pupil does not know what to say, hold up the sheet which says "Je suis désolé(e) Madame/Monsieur, je ne sais pas" (page 315). Explain to them that it means, "I am sorry Madam/Sir, I don't know". In the early stages, hold up this card every time a pupil gets stuck. After a while the pupils will know this useful phrase by heart and will automatically use it if needed.

One by one, hold up pictures of famous people (cut out from various papers or magazines) and ask the pupils, "Il/elle s'appelle comment? De quelle nationalité est-il/elle?" Wait for the pupils to tell you, "Il s'appelle (his name) et il est français" or "Elle s'appelle (her name) et elle est américaine" etc.

Bonjour, enchanté(e)

Hello, nice to meet you.

Tell the pupils that when you meet someone for the first time in a formal situation, you must say "enchanté(e)" which is the equivalent of "How do you do?" (The masculine form is "enchanté"; the feminine form is "enchantée").

Memory trick

Ask the pupils what the English verb "to enchant" means. Can they find a memory trick such as: "to enchant" means "to delight" in English and, when you meet a person for the first time, you are delighted.

Vocabulaire

enchanté(e)	nice to meet you
je suis de...	I am from

Materials

★ Sheet 1e (page 24)
★ CD, Track 5

Put the pupils in pairs and ask them to role-play greeting someone in French in a formal situation. The conversation could go something like this. You could hand out Sheet 1e as a written prompt.

Person A:	Hello, nice to meet you.	Bonjour, enchanté(e).
	My name is…	je m'appelle …
Person B:	Answer the greeting and give your name.	Bonjour, enchanté(e), je m'appelle…
Person A:	What is your nationality?	De quelle nationalité es-tu?
Person B:	Say your nationality and ask the same question.	Je suis…, et toi, de quelle nationalité es-tu?
Person A:	Tell your nationality. Then say where you come from and ask where he/she comes from.	Je suis… . Je suis de …, et toi?
Person B:	Me, I am from…. Goodbye.	Moi, je suis de…. Au revoir.
Person A:	Goodbye.	Au revoir.

Go around the room, listening to the role-plays, correcting where necessary. Give lots of praise and encouragement.

Ask at least four pairs to perform the role-play in front of the class and reward the pupils who do well.

The dialogue on Sheet 1e can also be used as a listening/reading exercise using Track 5 on the CD.

Nombres 0–20

Numbers 0–20

Recap on numbers to 20. First count to three with your fingers "un, deux, trois". Encourage the pupils to repeat these three numbers in chorus after you. Then continue with numbers up to 20.

 To help the class, you could write the numbers 0 to 20 in figures on the board. Point at them one at a time encouraging the class to say the word in French, then write it on the board, spelling out the letters in French as you write. Then ask individual pupils to count from 1 to 20 and from 20 to 1.

Choice of activities

 Pupils pass round a bag containing cards with the numbers 0–20 on them in figures. When it is their turn, pupils pull out a card at random and say the number in French, after which they pass the bag to the next player.

 Give the pupils Sheet 1f with the song: "Un, deux, trois". Listen to this French song (CD, Track 6) and encourage the pupils to sing as it will help them to remember the numbers up to 12 in French. It is about picking cherries. An instrumental version is on Track 7.

 Give the pupils Sheet 1g and ask them to match the numbers to the words by drawing a line between them. The exercise at the bottom of the sheet practises writing the numbers 11–20.

 Give the pupils Sheet 1h and ask them to read and complete the activities. Encourage pupils to read the sums at the bottom of the page out loud in French.

Vocabulaire

un	one
deux	two
trois	three
quatre	four
cinq	five
six	six
sept	seven
huit	eight
neuf	nine
dix	ten
onze	eleven
douze	twelve
treize	thirteen
quatorze	fourteen
quinze	fifteen
seize	sixteen
dix-sept	seventeen
dix-huit	eighteen
dix-neuf	nineteen
vingt	twenty
allons dans les bois	let's go to the woods
cueillir des cerises	to pick cherries
dans mon panier neuf	in my new basket
elles seront toutes rouges	they will all be red
une comptine	a counting rhyme
une feuille	a leaf
une perle	a pearl

Materials

★ Set of cards with the numbers 1 to 20 in a bag
★ Sheets 1f–1h (pages 25–27)
★ CD, Tracks 6–7

Essential words and phrases

 At the end of this unit, give the pupils Sheet 1i to help them remember some essential words and phrases.

Materials

★ Sheet 1i (page 28)

Au revoir!

Finish the lesson by saying "Au revoir!" and by waving or shaking every pupil's hand. Expect them to reply, "Au revoir!" in chorus or individually.

Vocabulaire

au revoir	goodbye

Nom:_____   **La date:**_____

Regarde 👁👁 et lis 📖

Look and read.

> Bonjour! Je m'appelle Antony.

> Bonjour! Moi, je m'appelle Lucie.

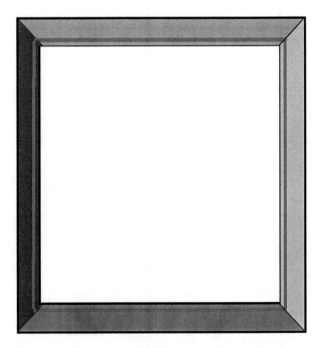

Dessine ✏ et écris ✏

Draw a picture of yourself in the frame, and then introduce yourself in French, using "Je m'appelle… ."

....

....

Moi (me)

a	b	c	d	e
f	g	h	i	j
k	l	m	n	o
p	q	r	s	t
u	v	w	y	z

a	b	c	d	e
f	g	h	i	j
l	m	n	o	p
r	s	t	w	x
a	è	i	o	é

Nom:_____   **La date:**_____

Écoute et écris

*Listen to Track 4 on the CD. Every word is repeated twice. Decide whether an **é** or an **è** is needed on the letters in bold.*

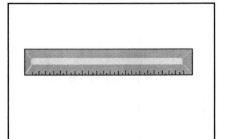

1. une **r**egle

2. un **e**lephant

3. un **b**ebe

4. un fr**e**re

5. une m**e**re

6. un p**e**re

7. une **e**cole

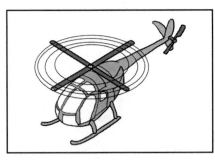

8. un h**e**licoptere

9. une t**e**levision

10. une **e**toile

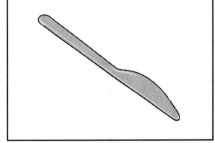

11. une cuill**e**re

12. une **e**glise

Nom:_____   **La date:**_____

Keep your hat on!

Hello, nice to meet you! I am the verb Voyager. As you can probably tell from my name, I love to travel and discover new places. I'd like to tell you about my visit to the country of Hexagonie.

On my first day, I saw all the letters of the alphabet parading in front of the royal family. My attention was drawn to the letter "e" who was obviously making an effort to impress them with her three different hats.

The first hat sloped upwards to the right (é) and was called an "acute".

The second hat sloped upwards to the left (è) and was called a "grave".

The third, which was called a "circumflex", looked as if the two sloping hats had been joined to form a cone (ê).

King Être and Queen Avoir were so impressed by the letter "e" and her hats that they asked her to come forward and introduce herself. The letter "e" showed them her hats, one by one, and each time she changed her hat, she sounded a bit different.

I quickly realized that hats were very popular in Hexagonie. The "grave" hat was also worn by the letters "a" (à) and "u" (ù). Then, all of a sudden, the letter "c" made a dramatic entrance wearing a funny dress. The dress looked a bit like a tail and was called a "cedilla" (ç). I had to stop myself from laughing out loud.

I wanted to find a way of remembering the two hats I liked the most: the "acute" and the "grave". Then the story of "a cute monkey" came to mind. It was one I had been told on an earlier trip. In the story, "a cute monkey" goes up a tree to build his house, but sadly has a grave fall. Luckily for the monkey, he does not fall into his grave because after a while he is all right. Here is a quick sketch I have done to remind me of the story:

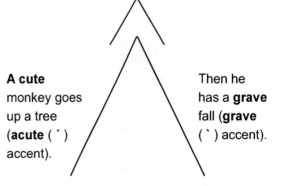

He builds his house on top of the tree.

A cute monkey goes up a tree (**acute** (´) accent).

Then he has a **grave** fall (**grave** (`) accent).

Hexagonie, Part 2   23
© Maria Rice-Jones and Brilliant Publications

Nom:_____ **La date:**_____

Lis

Read this dialogue between Luc and Susan.

Bonjour, enchanté, je m'appelle Luc.

Bonjour, enchantée, je m'appelle Susan.

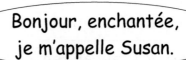

De quelle nationalité es-tu?.

Je suis anglaise, et toi, de quelle nationalité es-tu?

Je suis français. Je suis de Boulogne, et toi?

Moi, je suis de Nottingham. Au revoir.

Au revoir.

Nom:_____   **La date:**_____

Écoute

Tracks
6 & 7

Listen to this counting rhyme called "une comptine". It is about picking cherries. It will help you remember how to count up to twelve in French.

Un, deux, trois
Allons dans les bois

One, two, three
Let's go to the wood

Quatre, cinq, six
Cueillir des cerises

Four, five, six
To pick up cherries

Sept, huit, neuf
Dans mon panier neuf

Seven, eight, nine
In my new basket

Dix, onze, douze
Elles seront toutes rouges.

Ten, eleven, twelve
They will be all red.

© Maria Rice-Jones and Brilliant Publications

Nom:_____   **La date:**_____

Regarde et relie

Draw lines to match the numbers to the words.

1	quatre
13	dix-neuf
7	un
12	douze
10	huit
4	treize
16	cinq
8	seize
5	sept
19	dix

Écris

Write the following numbers in letters.

11 ....

12 ....

13 ....

14 ....

15 ....

16 ....

17 ....

18 ....

19 ....

20 ....

un	deux	trois	quatre	cinq	six	sept	huit	neuf	dix
onze	douze	treize	quatorze	quinze	seize	dix-sept	dix-huit	dix-neuf	vingt

Nom:_____ **La date:**_____

Dessine

Draw more leaves (feuilles) on the tree to make the correct number.

Seize feuilles

Dessine

Draw more pearls (perles) on the necklaces to make the correct number.

Dix-huit perles

Douze perles

Écris

Write the answers in words. Say the sums out loud in French.

$4 + 6 =$ _____ $10 + 10 =$ _____

$15 + 2 =$ _____ $20 - 13 =$ _____

$19 - 7 =$ _____ $4 - 4 =$ _____

$3 + 3 =$ _____ $5 + 8 =$ _____

$12 - 6 =$ _____ $20 - 2 =$ _____

Nom:_____   **La date:**_____

Essential words and phrases

How to greet people

Bonjour	Hello
Bonjour Madame	Hello Madam
Bonjour Monsieur	Hello Sir
Bonjour Mademoiselle	Hello Miss

Note
French people like to show who they are talking to in order to be polite. If you don't do it, it is often seen as rude.

How to introduce yourself

Je m'appelle ...	My name is ...

How to say what nationality you are

Je suis anglais(e)	I am English
Je suis indien(ne)	I am Indian

How to say you don't know

Je suis désolé(e) Madame/ Monsieur, je ne sais pas	I am sorry Madam/Sir, I don't know

Note
When a boy writes this sentence, he must write "désolé", but when a girl writes the same sentence, she must write 'désolée' with an extra "e" at the end of the word.

Saying goodbye

Au revoir	Goodbye
Au revoir Madame	Goodbye Madam
Au revoir Monsieur	Goodbye Sir
Au revoir Mademoiselle	Goodbye Miss

The things in my life

Key teaching points

"Qu'est-ce que c'est" ("What is it?")
Masculine and feminine

Bonjour, comment vas-tu?

Hello, how are you?

Say "Bonjour" to the whole class and wait for the pupils to reply "Bonjour Madame/Monsieur."

Call the register ("l'appel") in French and say whether the pupil called is "présent", "présente", "absent" or "absente". During the following lessons, when you call the register, expect every pupil to respond "présent" or "présente" when their name is called out. As these words are similar in English, the pupils will easily remember them.

Tell the pupils that at the beginning of every lesson you will ask some pupils how they are by saying "Comment vas-tu?", which means "How are you?" Tell the pupils that they have to answer, "Je vais bien merci", which means "I am well thank you". Then call out the name of a pupil and ask him/her "Comment vas-tu, Thomas/ Marie?" and wait for the pupil to reply "Je vais bien merci".

Ask for volunteers to perform a dialogue, imagining that two pupils meet and greet each other in the street, asking how the other is, for example:

Vocabulaire

Comment vas-tu?	How are you?
je vais bien merci	I am well thank you
l'appel (m)	the register
présent(e)	present
absent(e)	absent
moi aussi	me too

Bonjour, Emma!

Bonjour Thomas! Comment vas-tu?

Je vais bien merci et toi?

Moi aussi, je vais bien.

© Maria Rice-Jones and Brilliant Publications

Recap on "Je m'appelle" and "Je suis (nationalité)"

Point to a pupil and say "Je m'appelle Madame/Monsieur (your name) et je suis (your nationality), et toi?" Encourage him/her to answer with his/her name and nationality and to ask another pupil of his/her choice "et toi?" and so on.

Materials

Sheet 2a (page 36)

Hexagonie story

Give each pupil a copy of Sheet 2a: "The useful question: qu'est-ce que c'est?" which introduces "qu'est-ce que c'est". Read and discuss the points covered. You could demonstrate the memory trick for "qu'est-ce que c'est" on the whiteboard.

Qu'est-ce que c'est?

What is it?

Collect together some classroom objects. Point at one item at a time to introduce it by saying "C'est un stylo, c'est une gomme" etc. Then point to one of the objects and ask all the pupils, "Qu'est-ce que c'est?" ("What is it?") and wait for them to reply in chorus, "C'est un..." or "C'est une...."

Then ask the same question to individual pupils. If a pupil does not know the answer, encourage him or her to say "Je suis désolé(e) Madame/Monsieur, je ne sais pas" ("I am sorry Madam/Sir, I don't know"). In the early stages, hold up the sheet with this sentence written on it every time a pupil gets stuck (page 315). After a while the pupils will know this useful phrase by heart and will automatically use it if needed.

Vocabulaire

Qu'est-ce que c'est?	What is it?
un bureau	a desk
un crayon	a pencil
un stylo	a pen
un stylo plume	an ink pen
un taille-crayon	a pencil sharpener
un cahier	an exercise book
un classeur	a folder
un ordinateur	a computer
une règle	a ruler
une trousse	a pencil case
une gomme	a rubber
une fenêtre	a window
une chaise	a chair
un mur	a wall
une porte	a door
un poster	a poster
une lampe	a lamp
une table	a table
un professeur	a teacher
un élève	a pupil
un plafond	a ceiling

Materials

★ A collection of classroom objects
★ Sheets 2b(i)–2b(iv) (pages 37–40), photocopied back-to-back and cut into cards, one set for each pair of pupils
★ Je suis désolé(e)… (page 315)
★ Scissors

A useful way to remember that "un ordinateur" means "a computer" is to say that you give "orders" to the "ordinateur".

Help pupils to remember that "un classeur" is a folder by telling them that you use "un **class**eur" in the **class**. The word "**class**" appears in "**class**eur".

Put the pupils in pairs and give each pair a set of cards made from Sheet 2b(i)–2b(iv) (or ask them to cut out the cards). Ask one pupil to hold up each of the 20 cards in turn and show them one by one to his/her partner. The partner must say the French word for each item, e.g. "C'est une porte, c'est un stylo, c'est un cahier…." Walk around the room listening to the pupils, correcting as necessary, and praising them.

Les mots masculins et féminins

Masculine and feminine words

Using words the pupils already know, write two columns on the board, one containing masculine words (which take "un") and the other containing feminine words (which use "une"). In the column containing the feminine words underline the "e" in "une" and the last "e" in the word itself:

un stylo	un**e** port**e**
un cahier	un**e** trouss**e**
un bureau	un**e** chais**e**
un crayon	un**e** gomm**e**

Vocabulaire

un livre	a book
un dictionnaire	a dictionary
un verre	a glass
l'eau (f)	water
la limonade	lemonade
un cartable	a schoolbag

Materials

Classroom and household objects
Sheet 2c (page 41)

Remind pupils that "un" goes with most words that do not end in "e", but warn them that there are some exceptions.

Write "un dictionnaire" on the board. Tell the pupils that "dictionnaire" is masculine even though it ends in "e". Ask the pupils if they know of a way of remembering whether it is masculine or feminine. (The story in Unit 5 in Hexagonie, Part 1 suggests one way of remembering it.)

Explain that the best way to remember the exceptions is to use memory tricks. The best tricks are the ones that capture the imagination because they are shocking or funny. Once the pupils get the hang of memory tricks, they can start to make up their own.

Say that the way you remember it is to think that in the past only boys were allowed to go to school. Boys and men were the only ones who were allowed to open "un livre" (a book) or "un dictionnaire" (a dictionary), which is why they are masculine.

Write "une maison" (a house) on the board. Ask the pupils if anyone can think of a way of remembering that "maison" is feminine. They will probably suggest that traditionally women took care of the house.

Write "un verre" (a glass) on the board. Ask the pupils if they can think of a way of remembering that "verre" is masculine. Tell them that in the past it was only acceptable for men to drink alcohol. Women were expected to drink soft drinks, which are feminine, such as "la limonade" and "l'eau".

Write on the board: "une fleur, un téléphone, une télévision, un cartable". Put the pupils into pairs, and then ask them to work out ways of remembering whether these nouns are masculine or feminine. Ask one or two pairs to make suggestions to the whole group at the end.

Suggestions for ways to remember some exceptions:

une fleur (a flower):
Remember that flowers are usually given to women

un téléphone (a telephone):
Think of the important role of the telephone in business, typically a male domain.

une télévision (a television):
Think of women watching more television because they have not traditionally gone out to work.

un cartable (a schoolbag):
Remember that boys used to go to school for longer than girls.

Télévision is a very helpful exception to remember because all the nouns ending in "ion" (apart from "un avion" – "a plane") are also feminine. For example: une information (a piece of information), une région (a region), une question (a question).

2c

Ask the pupils to fill in the spaces with "un" or "une" in front of every noun.

Vocabulaire

un magasin	a shop
un souvenir	a souvenir
je voudrais…	I would like…
voilà	here it is/here they are
un client/ une cliente	a customer
un commerçant/ une commerçante	a shopkeeper
C'est combien?	How much is it?
s'il vous plaît	please
sur	on

Materials

CD, Track 8
Sheet 2d (page 42)

Au magasin de souvenirs

At the souvenir shop

2d

Put the pupils in pairs and ask them to role-play a conversation between a customer and a shopkeeper in a souvenir shop. The conversation could go something like this. You could hand out Sheet 2d as a written prompt.

Before starting the role-play remind the pupils that "je voudrais" means "I would like" and "voilà" can be used every time something is handed over. It is the equivalent of "here it is/here they are."

Le client/ la cliente:	Say hello Madam/ Sir.	Bonjour Madame/ Monsieur.
Le commerçant/ la commerçante:	Reply hello Madam/ Sir/ Miss.	Bonjour Madame/ Monsieur/ Mademoiselle.
Le client/ la cliente:	Say hello Madame/ Sir. Ask for a book on Paris, please.	Je voudrais un livre sur Paris s'il vous plaît.
Le commerçant/ la commerçante:	A book on Paris, very well, here it is.	Un livre sur Paris. Très bien, voilà.
Le client/ la cliente:	Ask for a French/English dictionary, please.	Je voudrais un dictionnaire français/ anglais s'il vous plaît.
Le commerçant/ la commerçante:	Here it is Sir/Madam/ Miss.	Voilà Monsieur/ Madame/ Mademoiselle.
Le client/ la cliente:	Very well, how much is it please?	Très bien, c'est combien s'il vous plaît?
Le commerçant/ la commerçante :	It is 20 euros Sir/ Madam/Miss.	C'est vingt euros Monsieur/Madame/ Mademoiselle.
Le client/ la cliente:	Say thank you very much Sir/ Madam. Goodbye.	Merci beaucoup Monsieur/Madame. Au revoir.
Le commerçant/ la commerçante :	Goodbye Sir/Madam/ Miss.	Au revoir Monsieur/ Madame/ Mademoiselle.

Go around the room, listening to the role-plays, correcting where necessary. Give lots of praise and encouragement.

Ask at least four pairs to perform the role-play in front of the class and reward the pupils who do well.

The dialogue on Sheet 2d can also be used as a listening/reading exercise using Track 8 on the CD.

Vocabulaire

la pluie	the rain
le vent	the wind
l'orage (m)	the storm
le klaxon	the horn
le chat	the cat
le chien	the dog
la cloche	the bell
le train	the train
l'avion(m)	the aeroplane
la guitare	the guitar
l'oiseau(m)	the bird
le réveil	the alarm clock
la moto	the motorbike
l'horloge(f)	the clock
c'est	it is/it's
c'est correct	it's correct

Materials

CD, Tracks 9–10
Sheets 2e(i)–2e(ii) (pages 43–44), photocopied and cut into cards
Sheet 2f (page 45)

C'est la pluie

It's the rain

Tell the pupils that you are going to introduce some words before playing a game. Hold up the card of "la pluie" (the rain) and say "C'est la pluie", encouraging the pupils to repeat "C'est la pluie". Continue with all the cards: le vent, l'orage, le klaxon, le chat, le chien, la cloche, le train, l'avion, l'hélicoptère, la guitare, l'oiseau, le téléphone, le réveil, la moto, l'horloge.

When you have introduced all the cards ask them to tell you what all these words have in common. They should say that they all make a noise.

Track 9 on the CD provides the sounds of the objects and animals that have just been introduced. Play each sound twice and then ask the class "Qu'est ce que c'est?" As a class they should reply "C'est le vent, c'est la guitare" etc.

Congratulate a correct answer with an enthusiastic "C'est correct", "Très bien" or "Bravo".

Give each pupil a copy of Sheet 2f. Ask them to look at the words on the sheet. Then play Track 10 on the CD. Each sound is played twice and then there's a pause. After hearing the sound, the pupil should fill in the space on the sheet.

Materials

Sheet 2g (page 46)

Le, la, l' et les

The

Say to the pupils that sometimes we want to be more specific and not say "a house" but "**the** house". Remind the pupils that in French, there are three ways of saying "the" about a singular word: "le", "la" and "l' ". "Le" is masculine, "la" is feminine and "l' " is used in front of a vowel. If there is more then one item, it is plural and "les" is used. If needed, you could remind the pupils about the story in Unit 6 in Hexagonie, Part 1.

Give each pupil a copy of Sheet 2g and ask them to draw lines between the words and "le", "la" or "l' ".

Essential words and phrases

| 2h |

At the end of this unit, give the pupils Sheet 2h, which will help them to remember essential words and phrases.

Resources

Sheet 2h (page 47)

Au revoir! Bonne semaine!

Say "Au revoir" to your pupils and tell them that you are going to wish them a nice week by saying "Bonne semaine". Ask them to reply "Vous aussi" ("you too"). You could say "à bientôt" which means "see you soon".

Vocabulaire

bonne semaine	have a good week
vous aussi	you too (to a group or an adult)
à bientôt	see you soon

Nom:_____   **La date:**_____

The useful question: "Qu'est-ce que c'est?"

To find out more about Hexagonie, I arranged to go on a tour of the country with a noun called Guide. We visited many towns together and admired all sorts of impressive monuments.

At the beginning of our journey, Guide kindly said that I should always ask him about things which were new to me. He taught me to say "Qu'est-ce que c'est?" which means "What is it?" At first I didn't find this easy, but luckily he helped me by pointing out that "Qu'est-ce que c'est?" has many letters in common with the word "question".

To help me remember he wrote "qu'est-ce que c'est" using different colours: "qu" in red, "est" in green, and the rest in black: "qu'est-ce que c'est?" He then divided it into two parts putting one on top of the other:

qu'est-ce que c'est?

During our travels Guide entertained me with stories about King Être and Queen Avoir. I remember the one about the day Queen Avoir was walking alone in her garden and found a snake. Now the queen had never seen a snake before and had quite a shock at the sight of the unusual creature. In a terrified voice she cried out "Qu'est-ce que c'est?" But to the snake this sounded like hissing, so he thought that the queen was just trying to be friendly. Overcoming his initial nerves, the snake slithered up to the queen with an endearing smile on his face. The queen was so enchanted that she decided to keep the snake as a royal pet. She named him "Qu'est-ce que c'est?" because it was the first thing she had said when she had seen him. The snake loved his new name given by the queen, and to this day he cannot stop repeating it as he slithers proudly through the royal garden.

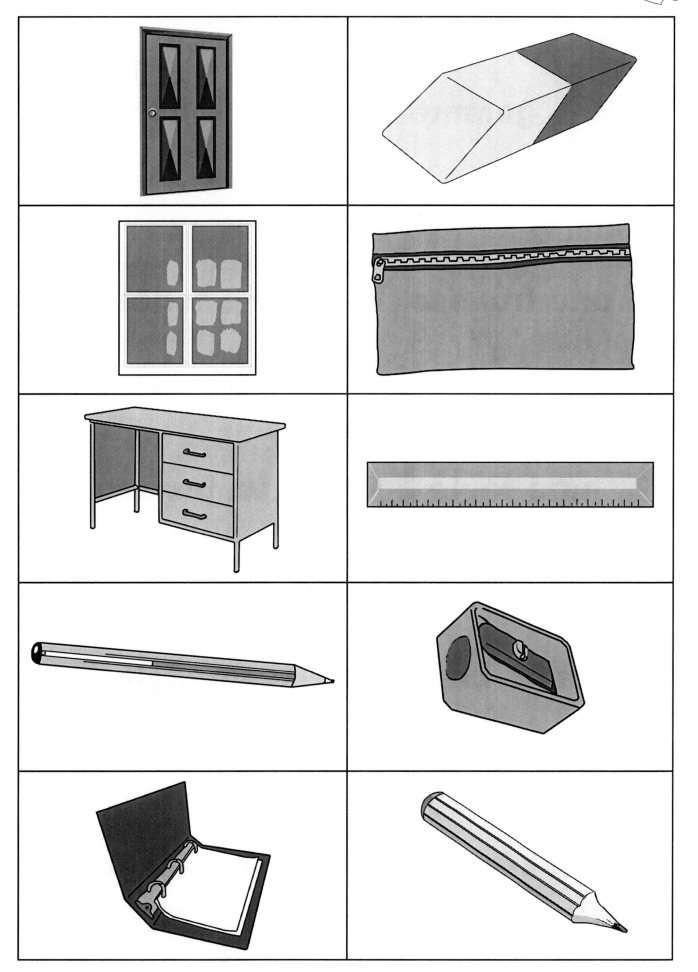

une gomme	**une porte**
une trousse	**une fenêtre**
une règle	**un bureau**
un taille-crayon	**un stylo**
un crayon	**un classeur**

un stylo plume	**un cahier**
un professeur	**une chaise**
un ordinateur	**un plafond**
une table	**une lampe**
un poster	**un élève**

Nom:_____   **La date:**_____

Lis et écris

Write "un" or "une" before each of the following words:

1. _____ ordinateur

2. _____ maison

3. _____ élève

4. _____ téléphone

5. _____ bureau

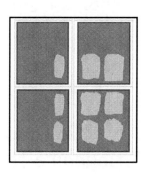

6. _____ fenêtre

7. _____ cartable

8. _____ lampe

9. _____ fleur

10. _____ cahier

11. _____ télévision

12. _____ verre

Nom:_____   **La date:**_____

Lis

Read this dialogue between a customer and a shopkeeper in a souvenir shop.

Bonjour Madame.

Bonjour Monsieur.

Je voudrais un livre sur Paris, s'il vous plaît.

Un livre sur Paris. Très bien, voilà.

Je voudrais un dictionnaire français/anglais s'il vous plaît.

Voilà Monsieur.

Très bien, c'est combien s'il vous plaît?

C'est vingt euros Monsieur.

Merci beaucoup Madame. Au revoir.

Au revoir Monsieur.

la pluie

le vent

l'orage

le klaxon

le chat

le chien

la cloche

le train

© Maria Rice-Jones and Brilliant Publications

l'avion

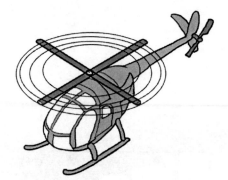

l'hélicoptère

la guitare

l'oiseau

le téléphone

le réveil

la moto

l'horloge

Nom:_____   **La date:**_____

Regarde et écris

la pluie	le vent	l'orage	le klaxon
le chat	le chien	la cloche	le train
l'avion	l'hélicoptère	la guitare	l'oiseau
le téléphone	le réveil	la moto	l'horloge

Écoute et écris

Listen to Track 10 on the CD, then write in French the name of whatever makes that sound.

1. ....   5. ....

2. ....   6. ....

3. ....   7. ....

4. ....   8. ....

Nom:_____ **La date:**_____

Lis   et relie

Match up the words with "le", "la", or "l'"

fleur

oiseau

cloche

maison

| **le** |

eau

chien

| **la** |

chat

guitare

| **l'** |

classeur

téléphone

porte

avion

Nom:_____ **La date:**_____

Essential words and phrases

How to say "How are you?" to a friend
Comment vas-tu?

How to say "How are you?" to the teacher
Comment allez-vous?

How to ask "What is it?"
Qu'est-ce que c'est?

How to say "It is…"
C'est…

How to say "It's correct"; "it's very good"
C'est correct; c'est très bien

How to say "please" to the teacher
S'il vous plaît Madame/Monsieur

How to say "please" to a friend
S'il te plaît

What to reply when the teacher wishes you a good week
"Bonne semaine"
Vous aussi (you too)

How to say "Goodbye, see you soon"
Au revoir, à bientôt

Unit 3

Life is beautiful!

Key teaching points

"Ce", "cet", "cette" and "ces" ("This/that" and "these/those")
Fruit and vegetables
Adjectives
Clothing

Vocabulaire

ce	this + masculine singular noun beginning with a consonant
cette	this + feminine singular noun beginning with a consonant or a vowel
ces	these + plural noun (masculine and feminine)
cet	this + masculine singular noun beginning with a vowel
bleu(e)	blue
vert(e)	green
noir(e)	black
jaune	yellow
rouge	red
grand(e)	tall
petit(e)	small
une couleur	a colour
ou	or
mais	but
une orange	an orange
une université	a university
une armoire	a wardrobe
un(e) ami(e)	a friend
une chambre	a bedroom
une cuisine	a kitchen
un enfant	an child
une voiture	a car
un journal	a newspaper
un cinéma	a cinema
un monument	a monument
une personne	a person
un pull-over	a jumper

Materials

★ Sheet 3a (page 59)

Bonjour

Say "Bonjour" to the whole class, waiting for the pupils to reply "Bonjour Madame/Monsieur." Call the register in French and expect every pupil to respond "présent" or "présente" when their name is called out. When you have no answer say "absent(e)". Call out the name of a pupil and ask him/her, "Comment vas-tu?" waiting for his/her answer "Je vais bien, merci." Ask other pupils how they are.

Recap on "Qu'est-ce que c'est ?"

Perform a 'Mexican wave' where a pupil points at something and ask the pupil sitting next to him/her: "Qu'est-ce que c'est?" The second pupil replies and then points at a different object and asks the pupil sitting on his/her other side, "Qu'est-ce que c'est?"

Ce, cet, cette et ces
This/that and these/those

Ce
(This/that)

Put two pens on your desk, for example, one blue and one black. Look at a pupil's pen and say, "Le stylo de Thomas est vert." Now, pick up one pen and say, "Le stylo de Thomas est vert. **Ce** stylo est bleu." Pick up the other pen and say, "**Ce** stylo est noir."

Put two notebooks on your desk, for example, one bigger than the other. Pick up the larger one and say, "**Ce** cahier est grand." Pick up the other notebook and say, "**Ce** cahier est petit." (Use hand symbols if the pupils don't understand "grand" and "petit.") Ask the pupils what they think "ce" means. They should be able to tell you it means "this".

Point at masculine objects around the room and ask individual pupils questions such as: "Est-ce que ce crayon est jaune?", "Est-ce que ce poster est grand ou petit?"

 Write on the board "ce" underneath "le" underlining the "e" and point out that "ce" (this) rhymes with the article "le" ("the").

Cette

(This/that)

Take two pencil cases and put them on your desk, for example, one yellow and one red. Look at a pupil's pencil case and say, "La trousse de Marie est bleue." Now, pick up the yellow pencil case and say "La trousse de Marie est bleue mais cette trousse est jaune." Do the same with the red pencil case, "Cette trousse est rouge." Ask the pupils some questions using feminine nouns so that they can practise saying "cette":

Est-ce que cette trousse est rouge?

Oui, cette trousse est rouge.

Est-ce que cette trousse est bleue?

Non, cette trousse est jaune.

Try to include some feminine nouns starting with a vowel such as "orange" and "école": "Est-ce que cette orange est sur la table ou sur la chaise?" Ask the pupils to tell you what word you used to say "this". Can they tell you why you didn't use "ce"? (Because "ce" is used with masculine words and "cette" is used with feminine words.)

 Write "cette" on the board. Then write a list of feminine nouns starting with a vowel and another list starting with a consonant, for example:

cette amie	cette trousse
cette école	cette chambre
cette armoire	cette cuisine
cette orange	cette maison
cette université	

Point out that all feminine singular nouns take "cette" whether they begin with a consonant or a vowel.

Cet

Write on the board:

cet avion

cet oiseau

cet éléphant

cet élève

Ask questions to give pupils practise using "cet". For example, point to a boy and ask another pupil, "est-ce que cet élève est français?" The pupil should reply, "Non, cet élève n'est pas français." Point to a picture of a child and ask, "Est-ce que cet enfant est grand ou petit?"

Ces

(These, those)

Put two or three of the same item on your desk, for example, two pens or three books. Look at a pupil's pens/books and say, "Les stylos de Jack sont bleus". Now hold up the two pens and say, "Les stylos de Jack sont bleus mais **ces** stylos sont noirs". Continue with further plural objects in the classroom using "ces". Then point at groups of objects in the classroom and ask individual pupils questions such as:

Rebecca, de quelle couleur sont ces stylos?

Ces stylos sont noirs.

Eddie, est-ce que ces stylos sont noirs?

Non, ces stylos sont bleus.

Ask the pupils what "ces" means. They should be able to tell you that it means "these".

Write on the board "ces" underneath "les" underlining the "es" in both words and point out that "ces" rhymes with "les".

Memory trick

The article "le" helps us to remember to use "ce" to say "this" or "that" in front of a masculine singular noun starting with a consonant. The "l" is simply replaced by "c". "Le" and "ce" rhyme, for example:
le stylo
ce stylo

The article "les" helps us to remember to use "ces" to say "these" or "those" in front of all plural nouns, whether they are masculine or feminine. The "l" is simply replaced by "c". "Les" and "ces" rhyme, for example:
les stylos
ces stylos

For feminine singular nouns, the article "la" doesn't help us. For all feminine, singular nouns we use "cette" to say "this" or "that", for example:
cette chaise
cette école
cette horloge

When we have a masculine singular noun that starts with a vowel we add a "t" to "ce" to make "cet", which is easier to say. For example:
cet ami
cet enfant

"Cet" and "cette" are pronounced in the same way.

3a

Ask the pupils to fill in the blanks with "ce, cet, cette ou ces". As some of the words will be new to the pupils (although understandable as they are similar to English words), e.g. "le cinéma", "le monument", "les personnes" etc, it is important to read through the words together, so that pupils hear the correct pronunciation. These new words have been used to help pupils realize that they can understand more French words that they thought they could.

Vocabulaire

un marron	a chestnut
une tomate	a tomato
un avocat	an avocado
une cerise	a cherry
un citron	a lemon
une carotte	a carrot
une salade	a lettuce
un abricot	an apricot
une olive	an olive
une banane	a banana
un chou-fleur	a cauliflower
de quelle couleur est…	what colour is…
orange	orange
marron	chestnut (brown)
blanc(he)	white
rose	pink
brun(e)	brown
gris(e)	grey

Resources

★ Fruit and vegetables of different colours
★ Sheets 3b(i)–3b(ii) (pages 60–61) photocopied, coloured in and cut into cards
★ Sheet 3c (page 62)

Fruits et légumes

Fruits and vegetables

3b (i) **3b (ii)**

Hold up the items of fruit and vegetables one at a time and say, "C'est une orange, c'est un marron, c'est un avocat, c'est un citron, c'est une cerise, c'est une salade, c'est une tomate etc". Then ask individual pupils questions about each flashcard. It is helpful to start with fruit whose colour is the same word. You could use cards made from sheets 3b(i) and 3b(ii), but they will need to be coloured in first.

Teacher:	De quelle couleur est cette orange?
Pupil:	Cette orange est orange.
Teacher:	De quelle couleur est ce marron?
Pupil:	Ce marron est marron.
Teacher:	De quelle couleur est cet avocat?
Pupil:	Cet avocat est vert.
Teacher:	De quelle couleur est ce citron?
Pupil:	Ce citron est jaune.
Teacher:	De quelle couleur est cette cerise?
Pupil:	Cette cerise est rouge.
Teacher:	De quelle couleur est cette salade?
Pupil:	Cette salade est verte.
Teacher:	De quelle couleur est cette tomate?
Pupil:	Cette tomate est rouge.
Teacher:	De quelle couleur est cette carotte?
Pupil:	Cette carotte est orange.

3c

Give the pupils a copy of Sheet 3c and ask them to fill in the blanks with "ce", "cet" or "cette", colour in the pictures and then answer the questions.

Les vêtements

Clothing

Point at different articles of clothing that the pupils are wearing and ask questions about the colour of those items.

Practise the main items of clothing by showing pictures of some famous French-speaking people (both alive and historical), for example, Zidane, Napoléon or French cartoon characters, for example, Astérix, Tintin. For example, ask the pupils, "Le pantalon de Tintin est jaune?" They should reply, "Non, le pantalon de Tintin est brun".

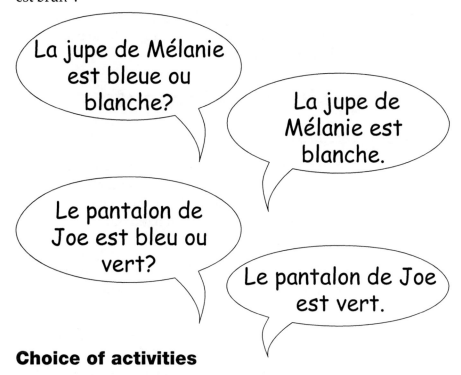

La jupe de Mélanie est bleue ou blanche?

La jupe de Mélanie est blanche.

Le pantalon de Joe est bleu ou vert?

Le pantalon de Joe est vert.

Choice of activities

Challenge the pupils to name as many items of clothing as they can think of that start with the same letter. For example, for the letter "C" they could include chaussettes, chaussures, chapeau, chemise, chemise de nuit, cravate, collant, casquette and ceinture. You could set a time limit.

Challenge the pupils to name as many items of clothing as they can think of that sound similar in French and in English. Examples could include: veste, pull-over, pyjama, costume, jean, bottes, short, robe. Some of the words the pupils will think of probably won't have the same meaning in French as in English, e.g:

"une veste" is not "a vest" but "a jacket"
"un costume" is not "a costume" but "a suit"
"une robe" is not "a robe" but "a dress"

Tell pupils these are called "false friends". Encourage pupils to think of memory tricks to remember these words.

Vocabulaire

les vêtements (m)	clothes
les bottes (f)	boots
les chaussettes (f)	socks
les chaussures (f)	shoes
une chemise	a blouse
une chemise de nuit	a nightgown
un costume	a suit
une cravate	a tie
un jean	a pair of jeans
une jupe	a skirt
une robe	a dress
un pantalon	a pair of trousers
un pyjama	a pair of pyjamas
un tee-shirt	a t-shirt
un sweat-shirt	a sweatshirt
un short	a pair of shorts
une veste	a jacket
un manteau	a coat
les accessoires (m)	accessories
des gants (m)	some gloves
un bonnet	a bonnet
un chapeau	a hat
une écharpe	a scarf
un collant	a pair of tights
une casquette	a baseball cap
une ceinture	a belt

Materials

★ Real clothes
★ Posters/pictures of cartoon characters or celebrities
★ Sheet 3d (page 63)

Put a few posters of characters (for example, Tintin) or a famous person (such as Zidane) around the room where the pupils can see them. Put the pupils into pairs. The first pupil will ask questions about the clothes and the second will answer. For example, the first pupil could ask "De quelle couleur est le chapeau/ la chemise/ la cravate/ la jupe/ le jean de (famous person's name)?" "De quelle couleur sont les chaussures/ les bottes de (famous person's name)?" Go around the class listening to their conversations. Praise pupils with an enthusiastic "Très bien" when they are doing well.

3d

Give each pupil a copy of Sheet 3d. Ask the pupils to read the description and colour in the items of clothing the correct colour.

Vocabulaire

trop	too
un vendeur/	a shop
une vendeuse	assistant
aussi	also/too

Materials

★ Sheet 3e (page 64)
★ CD, Track 11

Au magasin de vêtements

At the clothes shop

Put the pupils in pairs and ask them to role-play a conversation between a customer and a shop assistant in a clothes shop. The conversation could go something like this. You could hand out Sheet 3e as a written prompt.

Le client/ la cliente:	Say hello to the sales assistant	Bonjour Monsieur/ Madame/ Mademoiselle.
Le vendeur/ la vendeuse:	Reply hello Sir/Madam/ Miss.	Bonjour Monsieur/ Madame/ Mademoiselle.
Le client/ la cliente:	Say that you would like a black pair of trousers and a white shirt please. This pair of trousers is very nice and this shirt too.	Je voudrais un pantalon noir et une chemise blanche s'il vous plaît, Monsieur/Madame/ Mademoiselle. Ce pantalon est très joli et cette chemise aussi.
Le vendeur/ la vendeuse:	I am sorry Sir/Madam/ Miss but this shirt is not for you because it is too big.	Je suis désolé(e) Monsieur/Madame/ Mademoiselle, mais cette chemise n'est pas pour vous car elle est trop grande.
Le client/ la cliente:	And this green shirt, is it for me?	Et cette chemise verte, est-ce qu'elle est pour moi?

Le vendeur/ la vendeuse:	Yes, this shirt is perfect.	Oui, cette chemise verte est parfaite.
Le client/ la cliente:	Very well, I would like this black pair of trousers and this green shirt, please	Très bien, je voudrais ce pantalon noir et cette chemise verte, s'il vous plaît.
Le vendeur/ la vendeuse:	Thank you very much Sir/ Madam/Miss.	Merci beaucoup Monsieur/Madame/ Mademoiselle.

Go around the room, listening to the role-plays, correcting where necessary. Give lots of praise and encouragement.

Ask at least four pairs to perform the role-play in front of the class and reward the pupils who do well.

3e

The dialogue on Sheet 3e can also be used as a listening/reading exercise using Track 11 on the CD.

Track 11

Hexagonie story

3f

Give the pupils Sheet 3f. Read this with the pupils and discuss to reinforce the points covered and then say that the young nouns used lots of adjectives to describe their school. Point out the use of "ce", "cette", "cet" and "ces".

Vocabulaire

un menu	a menu
une leçon	a lesson
un uniforme	a uniform
une place	a place

Materials

★ Sheet 3f (page 65)

Vocabulaire

neuf(neuve)	new
vieux(vieille)	old
court(e)	short
long(ue)	long
gros(se)	fat
mince	thin
jeune	young
beau/belle	handsome/ beautiful
laid(e)	ugly
riche	rich
pauvre	poor

Materials

★ Pictures of people from magazines (optional)

Vocabulaire

un exercice	an exercise
un directeur/ une directrice	a headteacher
gentil(le)	kind

see also list of adjectives on pages 56–57

Materials

★ Sheet 3g (page 66)

Quelques adjectifs

Some adjectives

Point at the table and ask, "Cette table est grande ou petite?" (Use hand gestures if the pupils don't understand "grande" or "petite".) The class should answer "Cette table est grande". Now introduce other adjectives that are opposites asking the same type of question but pointing at different objects. For example, "Thomas est vieux ou jeune?" ("Thomas is old or young?") You could use pictures from magazines of people with the characteristics you wish to highlight.

neuf(neuve) ou vieux(vieille)	new or old
court(e) ou long(ue)	short or long
gros(se) ou mince	fat or thin
jeune ou vieux(vieille)	young or old
beau(belle) ou laid(e)	handsome(beautiful) or ugly
riche ou pauvre	rich or poor

Adjectifs similaires en français et en anglais

Similar adjectives in French and English

Some French adjectives are written exactly the same way as they are in English and have the same meaning, but are pronounced differently. Even if they look slightly different, it is often possible to recognize their equivalent in English quite easily. It is very empowering for pupils to realize how many French words they can understand.

 Select from the list below the adjectives you want to practise with your pupils. Write them on the board, saying them as you do so, and ask individual pupils to guess what each French adjective means. Encourage the pupils to repeat the words after you so that they can get used to sounding them out.

Français	Anglais
actif/ve	active
agressif/ve	aggressive
amusant(e)	amusing/fun
blond/e	blond
calme	calm
compétitif/ve	competitive
correct(e)	correct
courageux/se	courageous

difficile	difficult
élégant(e)	elegant
excellent(e)	excellent
extraordinaire	extraordinary
extravagant(e)	extravagant
idéal(e)	ideal
important(e)	important
impossible	impossible
incorrect(e)	incorrect
intelligent(e)	intelligent
intéressant(e)	interesting
invisible	invisible
magnifique	magnificent
moderne	modern
naturel(le)	natural
nécessaire	necessary
nerveux/se	nervous
normal(e)	normal
occupé(e)	occupied
pâle	pale
patient(e)	patient
poli(e)	polite
positif/ve	positive
possible	possible
simple	simple
sincère	sincere
spectaculaire	spectacular
strict(e)	strict
stupide	stupid
terrible	terrible
violent(e)	violent

Ask pupils questions using the adjectives. For example, show a pupil's worksheet marked with a tick and ask, "Est-ce que cet exercice est correct ou incorrect?" "Est-ce que le directeur/ la directrice est important(e)?" "Est-ce que cette école est moderne?"

Ask pupils to make up sentences about what kind of class they would like, using "je voudrais" and two adjectives, for example:

Je voudrais une classe intelligente et intéressante.
I would like an intelligent and interesting class.

Je voudrais une classe calme et gentille.
I would like a calm and kind class.

Je voudrais une classe amusante et excellente.
I would like a funny and excellent class.

 Divide the pupils into groups of four and give each group a list of four adjectives to mime in front of the class (for example, grand, gros, beau, amusant, stupide, intelligent etc). Each pupil must mime an adjective. The class guess which adjective it is.

Give Sheet 3g to the pupils and ask them to fill in the gaps with the opposite adjectives.

Resources

★ Sheet 3h (page 67)

Essential words and phrases

3h

At the end of this unit, give the pupils Sheet 3h, which will help them to remember essential words and phrases.

Au revoir! Bonne semaine! Bon week-end!

Remember always to wish the pupils a good week or weekend depending on when the lesson takes place. Wait for them to reply "Merci Madame/Monsieur, vous aussi".

Nom:_____   **La date:**_____

Écris

Write "ce", "cet", "cette" or "ces" in front of each noun

1. la voiture

    _____ voiture

2. le journal

    _____ journal

3. les enfants

    _____ enfants

4. le cinéma

    _____ cinéma

5. la télévision

    _____ télévision

6. le monument

    _____ monument

7. les personnes

    _____ personnes

8. l'école

    _____ école

9. l'oiseau

    _____ oiseau

10. les professeurs

    _____ professeurs

11. le pull-over

    _____ pull-over

12. l'avion

    _____ avion

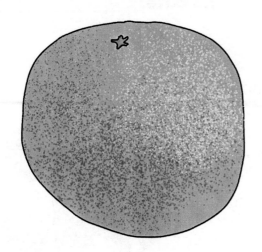

une orange

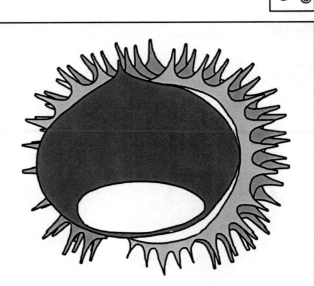

un marron

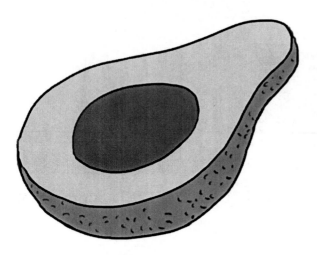

un avocat

une cerise

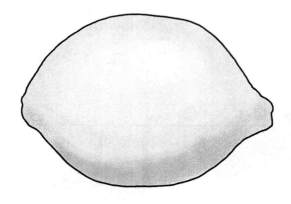

un citron

une salade

une tomate

une olive

une carotte

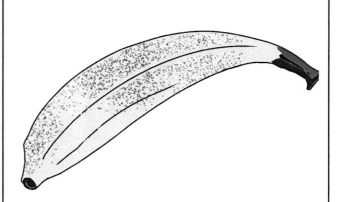

une banane

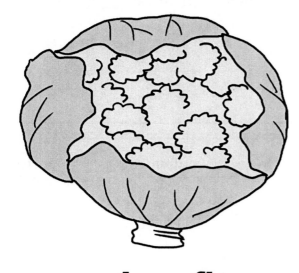

un chou-fleur

un abricot

Nom:_____   **La date:**_____

Écris et colorie

Fill in the blanks with "ce", "cet" or "cette" in the following questions. Colour in the illustrations and then answer the question.

1. De quelle couleur est _____ marron? Ce marron est_____	2. De quelle couleur est _____ cerise?  _____
3. De quelle couleur est _____ salade?  _____	4. De quelle couleur est _____ orange? 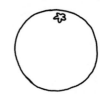 _____
5. De quelle couleur est _____ carotte?  _____	6. De quelle couleur est _____ citron? _____
7. De quelle couleur est _____ tomate? _____	8. De quelle couleur est _____ avocat?  _____
9. De quelle couleur est _____ olive? _____	10. De quelle couleur est _____ abricot? _____

Nom:_____   **La date:**_____

Lis et colorie

Read the description and colour the item of clothing.

Ce pantalon est jaune.

Ce pull-over est rose.

Cette jupe est blanche.

Ces chaussures sont noires.

Ce chapeau est bleu et orange.

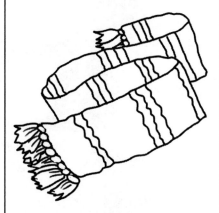

Cette écharpe est grise.

Ces chaussettes sont rouges.

Cette chemise est verte.

Ce manteau est bleu.

Nom:_____ **La date:**_____

Lis

Read this dialogue between a customer and a shop assistant in a clothes shop.

Track 11

Bonjour Monsieur.

Bonjour Madame.

Je voudrais un pantalon noir et une chemise blanche s'il vous plaît, Monsieur. Ce pantalon est très joli et cette chemise aussi.

Je suis désolé Madame, mais cette chemise n'est pas pour vous car elle est trop grande.

Et cette chemise verte, est-ce qu'elle est pour moi?

Oui, cette chemise verte est parfaite.

Très bien, je voudrais ce pantalon noir et cette chemise verte, s'il vous plaît.

Merci beaucoup Madame.

Nom:_____ **La date:**_____

The happy school

One morning in Hexagonie I saw all the little nouns on their way to school and noticed how happy they looked. I thought this seemed unusual because I hadn't enjoyed school much as a child. Then someone told me that things were different in Hexagonie because King Être and Queen Avoir worked hard to make sure that all their subjects were happy, no matter how young or old.

In the olden days, school in Hexagonie had not been much fun either, but when King Être became King he changed things. He created a new type of school where the little nouns were allowed to have whatever they wanted!

Each school day would begin with a visit to four different rooms, where the young nouns would be asked to make all sorts of choices.

The first room was for words beginning with "le" such as "le menu" (the menu). Here, for example, they would be shown different menus and asked which they wanted for lunch. To show which menu they had chosen they would point to it and, instead of just saying "le menu", they made their choice sound more special by saying "ce menu" (this menu).

The second room was for words beginning with "les". Here, they would find "les leçons" (the lessons) and would be asked to select several subjects they felt like studying that day. To show which lessons they had chosen, they would point to them and, instead of just saying "les leçons", they made their choice sound more special by saying "ces leçons" (these lessons).

The third room was for masculine words beginning with "l'" such as "l'uniforme". In Hexagonie every school has seven different uniforms so this was sometimes a difficult decision. To show which one they had chosen to wear that day, the young nouns would point to it and, instead of just saying "l'uniforme", they made their choice sound more special by saying "cet uniforme" (this uniform). They said "cet" because it sounds like the number "sept" and reminded them that they had a choice of seven uniforms.

Finally they would visit the room for words starting with "la" such as "la place". Here they would be asked in which place in the classroom they wanted to sit that day. In each classroom there were just seven seats because the number seven is considered a lucky number in Hexagonie. So when they had made their choice, they pointed at the place they wanted and said "cette place". They said "cette" because it sounds like the number "sept" and reminded them they had a choice of seven places.

If only school had been like that in my day!

Nom:_____   **La date:**_____

Lis et écris

Fill in the gaps with the opposite adjective.

1. Madame Martin n'est pas vieille, elle est _____.	2. Antoine n'est pas petit, il est _____.
3. La voiture de Marc n'est pas grande mais elle est _____.	4. L'exercice est incorrect ou _____
5. Monsieur Rousseau est mince ou _____.	6. Monsieur Martin est jeune ou _____.
7. La Seine (River Seine) est courte ou _____.	8. Le stylo n'est pas blanc, mais il est _____.

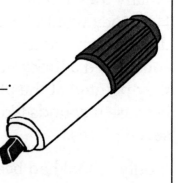

Nom:_____   **La date:**_____

Essential words and phrases

How to say "this/that" and "these/those"

le stylo	the pen	The article "le" helps us to remember to use "ce" to say "this" or "that" in front of a masculine singular noun starting with a consonant. The "l" is simply replaced by "c". "Le" and "ce" rhyme.
ce stylo	this/that pen	
les stylos	the pens	The article "les" helps us to remember to use "ces" to say "these" or "those" in front of all plural nouns, whether they are masculine or feminine. The "l" is simply replaced by "c". "Les" and "ces" rhyme.
ces stylos	these/those pens	
cette chaise	this/that chair	For feminine singular nouns, the article "la" doesn't help us. For all feminine singular nouns we use "cette" to say "this" or "that".
cette école	this/that school	
cette horloge	this/that clock	
cet ami	this/that friend	When we have a masculine singular noun that starts with a vowel, we add a "t" to "ce" to make "cet", which is easier to say. "Cet" and "cette" are pronounced in the same way.
cet enfant	this/that child	

Some common adjectives to describe a person

Grand(e) ou petit(e)	Tall or short
Vieux(vieille) ou jeune	Old or young
Gros(se) ou mince	Fat or thin
Blond(e), brun(e) ou roux(rousse)	Blond, brunette or red-head
Pauvre ou riche	Rich or poor
Beau(belle) ou laid(e)	Handsome/beautiful or ugly

Unit 4

Life with "to have" and "to be"

Key teaching points/vocabulary

The verb "avoir" ("to have") in the present tense
The verb "être" ("to be") in the present tense
Asking questions with "est-ce que" and by inverting the subject and verb
Sentences with "pas de"

Vocabulaire

Et vous?	And you? (plural and polite)
car	because (in a sentence)
je suis content(e)	I am happy
je ne suis pas fatigué(e)	I am not tired

Bonjour…

Say "Bonjour" to the whole class, waiting for the pupils to reply "Bonjour Madame/Monsieur." Call the register in French and expect every pupil to respond "présent" or "présente" when their name is called out. When you have no answer say "absent(e)". Call out the name of a pupil and ask him/her, "Comment vas-tu?" waiting for his/her answer "Je vais bien, merci." Ask other pupils how they are. Encourage the pupil to ask you "Et vous?" then answer with "Je vais bien merci." If you want you can mime how you feel and say: "Je vais bien merci car je suis content(e)" or "Je vais bien car je ne suis pas fatigué(e)."

Recap on some adjectives

Play a miming game. Ask some pupils to mime an adjective and its opposite in front of the class. For example, a pupil could mime "grand" (big) and "petit" (small) or "gros" (fat) or "mince" (thin). The class has to guess the adjectives.

Vocabulaire

Est-ce que…?	Introduces a question

Est-ce que…?

Introduces a question

Write "Est-ce que…?" and "question" on the board and underline the letters that they have in common:

Est-ce **que**…?   **Ques**tion

Remind pupils that "Est-ce que…?" introduces a question. Get them used to the sound of "Est-ce que…?" by repeating it several times with the pupils saying it after you. Tell the pupils that "Est-ce que…?" is like an alarm bell telling them to listen carefully to the question. Tell them not to worry about translating "Est-ce que…?" because the literal translation would be "Is it that…?" which does not help at all.

Explain that we write "Est-ce qu'… ?" before a vowel.
For example :

Est-ce qu'il…?
Est-ce qu'elle…?
Est-ce qu'ils…?
Est-ce qu'elles…?

You could reread the story about the "Est-ce que officers" from Hexagonie, Part 1 (Unit 7).

Avoir
To have

Est-ce que tu as…?
Do you have…?

Ask individual pupils some questions with "Est-ce que?" and the verb "avoir" that require a positive answer such as:

Teacher: Est-ce que tu as un professeur de français?
Pupil: Oui, j'ai un professeur de français.

Encourage pupils to explain their answers using "car".

Teacher: Est-ce que tu as des stylos?
Pupil: Oui, j'ai des stylos car c'est nécessaire pour l'école.

Teacher: Est-ce que tu as une trousse?
Pupil: Oui, j'ai une trousse car c'est nécessaire pour les stylos.

Est-ce qu'il/elle a…?
Does he/she have…?

Ask individual pupils some questions about a third person with "Est-ce que?" and the verb "avoir" that require a positive answer such as:

Teacher: Est-ce que Marie a un stylo bleu?
Pupil: Oui, elle a un stylo bleu.

Teacher: Est-ce que Thomas a un frère ou une sœur?
Pupil: Il a un frère et deux sœurs.

Teacher: Est-ce que Sunil a les yeux bleus ou marron?
Pupil: Il a les yeux marron.

Vocabulaire

avoir	to have
j'ai	I have
tu as	you have
il/elle a	he/she has
nous avons	we have
vous avez	you have (plural and polite)
ils/elles ont	they have
Est-ce que tu as…?	Do you have…?
Est-ce que vous avez…?	Do you have…? (plural and polite)
des	some
pour	for
une sœur	a sister
un bras	an arm
une main	a hand
un doigt	a finger
une jambe	a leg
un œil (des yeux)	an eye (eyes)
un nez	a nose
une bouche	a mouth
une épaule	a shoulder
un genou (des genoux)	a knee (knees)
un pied	a foot
un orteil	a toe
les cheveux (m)	hair
je n'ai pas de	I don't have
Est-ce qu'ils / elles ont…?	Do they have…?
une radio	a radio

Materials
★ Sheet 4a (page 80)

Est-ce que vous avez ...? Nous avons...

Do you have...? We have...

This activity recaps on parts of the body, learned in Hexagonie, Part 1 (Unit 9). Point at the pupils and at yourself as you say: "Nous avons deux bras, nous avons deux yeux, nous avons deux jambes, etc". Ask the pupils the meaning of "nous avons" (we have).

Now tell the pupils that you will ask them some questions with "vous" which means "you" when talking to a group of people. Ask them to respond in unison with "nous avons" (we have).

Teacher:	Est-ce que vous avez dix doigts ou onze doigts?
Pupils:	Nous avons dix doigts.
Teacher:	Est-ce que vous avez une jambe ou deux jambes?
Pupils:	Nous avons deux jambes.
Teacher:	Combien de bras est-ce que vous avez?
Pupils:	Nous avons deux bras.

Tell the pupils that "vous" is also used for one person when you want to be polite. Explain that when they ask you a question they must use "vous" and not "tu" as you are not their friend but their teacher and you are older than them.

Encourage at least five pupils individually to ask you a question with "vous avez" such as:

Pupil:	Monsieur/Madame, est-ce que vous avez un chien?
Teacher :	Oui, j'ai un chien.
	Non, je n'ai pas de chien.
Pupil:	Monsieur/Madame, est-ce que vous avez un frère ou une sœur?
	Monsieur/Madame, est-ce que vous avez une voiture rouge?
	Monsieur/Madame, est-ce que vous avez des enfants?

Est-ce qu'ils/elles ont...?

Do they have?

Point at two pupils and ask questions about them to the rest of the class using "ils/elles ont" (they have) and encourage the pupils to answer with "ils/elles ont".

Teacher :	Est-ce que Sunil et Marie ont des pull-overs verts?
Pupil:	Oui, ils ont des pull-overs verts.
Teacher :	Est-ce que Sunil et Marie ont des chaussures noires?
Pupil :	Oui, ils ont des chaussures noires.

 Write on the board the verb "to have" on the left with "j', tu, il/elle, nous, vous, ils/elles" and the verb "avoir" on the right. Read the words out loud as you write them. Underline the letters the English and French words have in common. Point out that all the forms of "avoir" have an "a" in them, except for "ils/elles ont".

To have		Avoir	
I	h**a**ve	j'	**a**i
you	h**a**ve	tu	**a**s
he/she	h**a**s	il/elle	**a**
we	h**a**ve	nous	**av**ons
you	h**a**ve	vous	**av**ez
they	have	ils/elles	ont

Point out that "as" (tu as) and "a" (il/elle a) are pronounced the same way, but "as" is written differently because we always use an "s" for "tu".

Why is there an "s" in "tu as"? Look at the alphabet! We use "tu" when we refer to those people who are closest to us and "s" loves the letters "t" and "u" and "s" is closest to them in the alphabet.

OPQR **S** **TU** VWXYZ

4a

Encourage pupils to make up sentences using "je, tu, il, elle, nous, vous, ils, elles" and the verb "avoir".

Sheet 4a can be used in class or as homework to reinforce the correct forms of "avoir" in the present tense.

Vocabulaire

un/une réceptionniste	a receptionist
un hôtel	a hotel
au nom de	in the name of
une réservation	a reservation
une clé	a key
une chambre	a bedroom
une douche	a shower
un passeport	a passport
des bagages (m)	some luggage
une valise	a suitcase

Materials

★ Sheet 4b (page 81)
★ CD, Track 12

Arrivée dans un hôtel en France

Arrival at a hotel in France

4b

Put the pupils in pairs and ask them to role-play someone arriving at a hotel in France. The conversation could go something like this. You could hand out Sheet 4b as a written prompt.

Le client/la cliente:	Say hello to the receptionist.	Bonjour Madame/Monsieur.
Le/la réceptionniste:	Reply hello to the hotel guest.	Bonjour Madame/Monsieur.
Le client/la cliente:	Say that you have a reservation in the name of …, please.	J'ai une réservation au nom de…, s'il vous plaît.
Le/la réceptionniste:	Here it is, you have room 18.	Voilà, vous avez la chambre dix-huit.
Le client/ la cliente:	Does the bedroom have a shower?	Est-ce que la chambre a une douche?
Le/la réceptionniste:	Yes Madam/Sir, it has a shower. Do you have a passport Madam/Sir?	Oui, Madame/Monsieur elle a une douche. Avez-vous un passeport Madame/Monsieur?
Le client/ la cliente:	Yes, here it is Madam/Sir.	Oui, voilà Madame/Monsieur.
Le/la réceptionniste:	Thank you Madam/Sir. Do you have some luggage?	Merci Madame/Monsieur. Avez-vous des bagages?
Le client/ la cliente:	Yes, I have two suitcases.	Oui, j'ai deux valises.
Le/la réceptionniste:	Very well Madam/Sir. Here you have the key.	Très-bien Madame/Monsieur. Ici vous avez la clé.
Le client/ la cliente:	Thank you very much Sir/Madam. Goodbye.	Merci beaucoup Monsieur/Madame. Au revoir.
Le/la réceptionniste:	Goodbye.	Au revoir.

Go around the room, listening to the role-plays, correcting where necessary. Give lots of praise and encouragement.

Ask at least four pairs to perform the role-play in front of the class and reward the pupils who do well.

The dialogue on Sheet 4b can also be used as a listening/reading exercise using Track 12 on the CD.

Two different ways to ask a question

Tell the pupils that there are two ways to ask a question in French. If they do not want to use "Est-ce que" all the time to form a question, they can swap the order of the subject and the verb. Demonstrate changing a sentence into a question on the board. Point out that we add a hyphen between the verb and the subject in the question. For example:

Tu as des stylos.   **As-tu** des stylos?

Give pupils other sentences and ask them to convert them into questions using this method, for example:

Tu as deux yeux.   As-tu deux yeux?

Tu as un cahier marron.   As-tu un cahier marron?

Tu as une voiture bleue.   As-tu une voiture bleue?

Explain that this method of making a question can be used with any sentence. Give some examples using other forms of "avoir". Ask them to convert some sentences into questions using both "Est-ce que...?" and swapping the order of the subject and the verb.

J'ai des stylos.	Est-ce que j'ai des stylos?	Ai-je des stylos?
Tu as des stylos.	Est-ce que tu as des stylos?	As-tu des stylos?
Il a des stylos.	Est-ce qu'il a des stylos?	A-t-il des stylos?
Elle a des stylos.	Est-ce qu'elle a des stylos?	A-t-elle des stylos?

Tell the pupils that the letter "t" in "A-t-il...?" and "A-t-elle...?" is added to ease the pronunciation between the two vowels.

Nous avons des stylos.	Est-ce que nous avons des stylos?	Avons-nous des stylos?
Vous avez des stylos.	Est-ce que vous avez des stylos?	Avez-vous des stylos?
Ils ont des stylos.	Est-ce qu'ils ont des stylos?	Ont-ils des stylos?
Elles ont des stylos.	Est-ce qu'elles ont des stylos?	Ont-elles des stylos?

Vocabulaire

pas de	not any
un rendez-vous	an appointment
le docteur	the doctor
un parapluie	an umbrella
maintenant	now
pourquoi	why
un objet	an object
un poisson rouge	a goldfish
une famille	a family
un/une cousin(e)	a cousin
un problème	a problem
une voiture	a car

Materials

★ Sheets 4c and 4d (pages 82–83)

★ "pas de" (page 316)

Pas de

Not any

Make a series of negative statements with "je n'ai pas de" stressing "pas de/pas d'":

J'ai une bicyclette mais je n'ai **pas de** voiture.
J'ai des amis anglais mais je n'ai **pas d'**amis français.
J'ai une sœur mais je n'ai **pas de** frère.

Hold up a card with "pas de" written on it (page 316) and encourage the pupils to tell you things they do not have.

> Je n'ai pas de chien.

> Je n'ai pas de chat.

> Je n'ai pas de voiture.

When French people "have" something, they care whether it is masculine or feminine because they are very interested in the things that are theirs. However, for things that do not belong to them, they see no point in saying whether it is masculine or feminine. Why bother when it is something that does not belong to them anyway? That is why, instead of using "un'", "une" after "pas" they just use a straightforward "de" and say "pas de".

Write on the board positive sentences and encourage the pupils to put them in the negative form using "pas de":

Positive sentences	Negative sentences
J'ai un frère. (I have a brother).	Je n'ai pas de frère. (I do not have a brother).
J'ai une sœur. (I have a sister).	Je n'ai pas de sœur. (I do not have a sister).
J'ai des problèmes. (I have some problems).	Je n'ai pas de problèmes. (I do not have any problems).
J'ai des amis. (I have some friends).	Je n'ai pas d'amis. (I do not have any friends).

Ask individual pupils a series of questions that require negative answers. Ask at least one question with "un", one question with "une" and one question with "des":

Teacher: Emma, est-ce que tu as une maison à Paris?
Emma: Non, je n'ai pas de maison à Paris.

Teacher: Arthur, est-ce que tu as une voiture?
Arthur: Non, je n'ai pas de voiture parce que j'ai huit ans.

Teacher: Rebecca, est-ce que tu as un parapluie maintenant?
Rebecca: Non, je n'ai pas de parapluie.

Teacher: Thomas, est-ce que Rebecca a des amis français?
Thomas: Non, elle n'a pas d'amis français.

Put the pupils into pairs. One pupil in each pair will play the interviewer and one will be the interviewee. The interviewer must ask questions to find what the interviewee does and does not have.

To help the interviewer, a list of topics to ask about could be written on the board. For example:

Animaux	**Famille**	**Vêtements**	**Objets**
un chien	une mère	un chapeau	un ordinateur
un chat	une sœur	un pull-over	un livre
un poisson rouge	un frère	un pantalon	une voiture
un cheval	un cousin	une jupe	un avion
etc	etc	etc	etc

At the end of the interview, ask the pupils to swap roles. Walk around the room listening to the pupils, correcting as necessary, and praising them.

4c

Sheet 4c reinforces the different forms of "avoir".

4d

Give the pupils Sheet 4d. Ask the pupils to read the questions and answer using "pas de". As an extension activity you could ask pupils to write (or say) the questions out again changing the way the question is asked, for example:

As-tu des enfants?   Est-ce que tu as des enfants?

Vocabulaire

être	to be
je suis	I am
tu es	you are
il/elle est	he/she is
nous sommes	we are
vous êtes	you are (plural and polite)
ils/elles sont	they are
marié(e)	married
un animal domestique	a pet
un appartement	an appartment
fatigué(e)	tired
salut	hi/hello
un parent	a parent
moderne	modern
ancien(ne)	ancient
une vue	the view
la mer	the sea
superbe	superb
j'adore	I love
ici	here
une piscine	a swimming pool
un restaurant	a restaurant
grosses bises	love (literally: big kisses)
un jardin	a garden
un garçon	a boy
une fille	a girl
un garage	a garage
divorcé(e)	divorced
une reine	a queen
un roi	a king
un président	a president
une république	a republic
depuis	since
un symbole	a symbol
une devise	a motto
liberté	freedom
égalité	equality
fraternité	fraternity (brotherhood)
un drapeau	a flag

"Être"

"To be"

Est-ce que tu es?

Are you?

Ask individual pupils some questions with "Est-ce que?" and the verb "être":

Teacher: Est-ce que tu es professeur de français?
Pupil: Non, je ne suis pas professeur de français.

Teacher: Est-ce que tu es anglais?
Pupil: Oui, je suis anglais.

Teacher: Est-ce que tu es occupé(e) maintenant?
Pupil: Oui, je suis occupé(e) maintenant.

Est-ce qu'il/elle est?

Is he/she?

Ask individual pupils some questions about a third person or an object with "Est-ce que?" and the verb "être":

Teacher: Est-ce que Marie est grande ou petite?
Pupil: Elle est petite.

Teacher: Est-ce que Thomas est français?
Pupil: Non, il n'est pas français parce qu'il est anglais.

Teacher: Est-ce que Sunil a les yeux bleus ou marron?
Pupil: Il a les yeux marron.

Teacher: Est-ce que ce stylo est bleu ou noir?
Pupil: Ce stylo est noir.

Teacher: De quelle couleur est ce crayon?
Pupil: Ce crayon est rouge.

Est-ce que vous êtes? Nous sommes....

Are you? We are...

Point at a pupil (let's say Sunil) and yourself and say:

Teacher: Sunil et moi, nous sommes anglais. Nous ne sommes pas français. Nous sommes dans la classe maintenant. Nous ne sommes pas à Paris maintenant mais nous sommes avec vous.

Ask pupils to translate what you said. They should be able to tell you that "nous sommes" means "we are."

Now tell the pupils that you will ask them some questions with "vous êtes" (you are) and ask them to answer in chorus with "nous sommes" (we are).

Teacher:	Est-ce que vous êtes avec moi maintenant?
Pupils:	Oui, nous sommes avec vous.

Teacher:	Est-ce que vous êtes espagnols?
Pupils:	Non, nous ne sommes pas espagnols.

Teacher:	Pourquoi est-ce que vous êtes avec moi maintenant?
Pupils:	Nous sommes avec vous maintenant parce que nous sommes à l'école.

Explain that "vous" is used for one person as well as for a group of people, when you want to be polite. Explain that when they ask you a question they must use "vous" and not "tu" as you are not their friend but their teacher and you are older than them.

Encourage at least five pupils individually to ask you a question with "vous êtes" such as:

Pupil:	Monsieur/Madame, est-ce que vous êtes grand(e)?
Teacher :	Oui, je suis grand(e).

Pupil:	Monsieur/Madame, est-ce que vous êtes docteur?
	Monsieur/Madame, est-ce que vous êtes français(e)?
	Monsieur/Madame, pourquoi est-ce que vous êtes avec nous maintenant?

Est-ce qu'ils/elles sont?

Are they?

Ask individual pupils some questions about some objects in the class with "ces" (these/those) and "ils sont", "elles sont":

Teacher:	Est-ce que ces chaises sont modernes ou anciennes?
Pupil:	Elles sont modernes.

Teacher:	Est-ce que ces stylos sont sur la table ou sur la chaise?
Pupil:	Ils sont sur la table.

Teacher:	Est-ce que ces fenêtres sont grandes ou petites?
Pupil:	Elles sont grandes.

Write on the board the verb "être" with "je, tu, il/elle, nous, vous, ils/elles".

To be		Être	
I	am	je	suis
you	are	tu	es
he/she	is	il/elle	est
we	are	nous	sommes
you	are	vous	êtes (plural and polite)
they	are	ils/elles	sont

Vocabulaire (cont.)

un homme	a man
une femme	a woman
une monarchie	a monarchy
vrai	true
faux	false

Materials

★ Sheets 4e–4i (pages 84–88)
★ CD, Tracks 13–15

Tell the pupils that the verb "être" for "tu es" is pronounced in the same way as in 'il/elle est' but is written differently.

Why is there an "s" in "tu es"? Look at the alphabet! We use "tu" when we refer to those people who are closest to us and "s" loves the letters "t" and "u" and "s" is closest to them in the alphabet.

OPQR *S* TU VWXYZ

"Ils sont" (they are) and "ils ont" (they have) can be confusing for some pupils. One way of remembering that "sont" belongs to "être" is to point out that all the forms of "être" have an "s" in them.

Je _suis_
Tu e_s_
Il/Elle e_st_
Nous _somme_s
Vous ête_s_
Ils/Elles _s_ont

Choice of activities

Give the pupils Sheet 4e. Ask them to read through the top of the sheet and then join up the words. For the activity at the bottom of the sheet, ask the pupils to fill in the gaps with the correct form of the verb "être".

Sheet 4f uses both "avoir and "être", so pupils will need to read the sentences and questions carefully. At the top of the sheet they need to write in the correct forms of "être" and "avoir". At the bottom they need to answer the questions.

On this sheet the pupils must read the postcard that Marie has sent her friend Brigitte, and tick to show if the statements are true or false. Pupils can listen to this postcard being read out loud on Track 13 on the CD.

Ask pupils to read this passage about La famille Durand and to answer the questions. Pupils can listen to this passage being read out loud on Track 14 on the CD.

Ask pupils to read this passage about France and to answer the questions. Pupils can listen to this passage being read out loud on Track 15 on the CD.

Hexagonie story

Give the pupils Sheet 4j: "The power of love," the next Hexagonie story. Ask the pupils to read the story or ask one pupil to read it out loud. Discuss to reinforce the points covered.

> **Materials**
> ★ Sheet 4j (page 89)

Essential words and phrases

At the end of this unit, give the pupils Sheet 4k, which will help them to remember essential words and phrases.

> **Materials**
> ★ Sheet 4k (page 90)

Au revoir! Bonne semaine! Bon week-end!

Remember always to wish the pupils a good week or weekend. Wait for them to reply "Merci Madame/Monsieur, vous aussi."

Nom:_____ **La date:**_____

Regarde 👀 et relie

tu •   • avez

Luc •   • a

nous •   • ai

j' •   • as

Emma et Louis •   • ont

vous •   • a

Marie •   • avons

Regarde 👀 et écris

Find the right word from the list and write it next to the verb form that it takes.

j'	tu	il	elle	nous	vous	ils	elles

1. _____ avons un chien.

2. _____ ai une idée.

3. _____ ont des enfants.

4. _____ a trois frères.

5. _____ avez un chat.

6. _____ as 10 ans.

7. _____ a une radio.

8. _____ ont un ordinateur.

Nom:_____ **La date:**_____

Lis

Read this dialogue between a guest arriving at a hotel in France and the receptionist.

Bonjour Madame.

J'ai une réservation au nom de Roberts, s'il vous plaît.

Bonjour Monsieur.

Est-ce que la chambre a une douche?

Voilà, vous avez la chambre dix-huit.

Oui, Monsieur elle a une douche.

Oui, voilà Madame.

Oui, j'ai deux valises.

Avez-vous un passeport Monsieur?

Merci Monsieur. Avez-vous des bagages?

Merci beaucoup Madame. Au revoir.

Très bien Monsieur. Ici vous avez la clé.

Au revoir.

Nom:_____ **La date:**_____

Lis et complète

Fill in the gaps with the correct form of the verb "avoir".

ai	as	a	avons	avez	ont

1. J' _____ des chaussures.

2. Tu _____ un frère et une sœur.

3. Nous _____ un rendez-vous avec le
docteur.

4. Est-ce que vous _____ un ordinateur?

5. Est-ce qu'elle _____ un chien ou
un chat?

6. J' _____ deux bananes.

7. Ils _____ un cahier.

8. Je n' _____ pas d'oranges.

Nom:_____ **La date:**_____

Lis et écris

Read and then write down your answer using "pas de"

1. As-tu des enfants? Pourquoi?

___Non,_____

2. Est-ce que tu as un parapluie maintenant? Pourquoi?

___Non,_____

3. As-tu une voiture? Pourquoi?

___Non,_____

4. As-tu un ordinateur orange? Pourquoi?

___Non,_____

5. Est-ce que tu as une maison en France? Pourquoi?

___Non,_____

Nom:_____   **La date:**_____

Regarde 👀 et relie 📝

tu •   • es

Pierre •   • est

nous •   • suis

je •   • êtes

Pierre et Martine •   • sommes

vous •   • est

Marie •   • sont

Regarde 👀 et écris 📝

Find the right word from the list and write it next to the verb form that it takes.

je	tu	il	elle	nous	vous	ils	elles

1. _____ sommes frères.

2. _____ suis brune.

3. _____ sont vieux.

4. _____ est belle.

5. _____ êtes mariés.

6. _____ es petit.

7. _____ est blond.

8. _____ sont sœurs.

Nom:_____   **La date:**_____

Regarde 👁👁 et complète ✎

Fill in the gaps with the correct form of the verbs "avoir" and "être" in the present tense:

1. J'_____ des chaussures car je n' _____ pas de bottes.
2. Tu _____ content car tu _____ un frère et une sœur.
3. Ils _____ malades car ils _____ fatigués.
4. Elle _____ très occupée parce que la directrice _____ malade.
5. Nous _____ un rendez-vous avec le docteur mais il _____ absent.
6. Est-ce que vous _____ français ou anglais?
7. Est-ce que vous _____ un ordinateur?
8. Est-ce qu'elle _____ un chat ou un chien?
9. Est-ce qu'ils _____ grands?
10. Est-ce que tu _____ des animaux?

Lis 📖 et écris ✎

Read and then write down your answer.

1. Est-ce que tu as les yeux bleus, verts ou marron?

   _____

2. Est-ce que tu es brun(e) blond(e) ou roux/rousse?

   _____

3. Est-ce que tu es petit(e)?

   _____

4. Est-ce que tu as un animal domestique?

   _____

5. Est-ce que tu as un appartement ou une maison?

   _____

6. Est-ce que tu as une Rolls-Royce? Pourquoi?

   _____

7. Est-ce que tu as un passeport italien? Pourquoi?

   _____

8. Est-ce que tu as un ordinateur rouge?

   _____

Nom:_____   **La date:**_____

Lis and coche ✓

Read the following postcard and tick to show if the following statements are "vrai" (true) or "faux" (false).

Track
13

Salut Brigitte!

En ce moment, je suis avec mes parents à Deauville. Nous sommes dans un grand hôtel moderne. Ma chambre est très grande et confortable et la vue sur la mer est superbe. J'adore être ici car il y a aussi une piscine et un excellent restaurant. Et toi, où es-tu maintenant?

Grosses bises,

À bientôt!

Ton amie

Marie

Brigitte Leleu

15, rue du Parc

Beauville

France

	Vrai	Faux
1. Marie est à Deauville avec l'école.	☐	☐
2. L'hôtel est très vieux.	☐	☐
3. La chambre de Marie est très grande.	☐	☐
4. Marie aime la vue.	☐	☐
5. Il n'y a pas de piscine à l'hôtel.	☐	☐

Nom:_____ **La date:**_____

Lis et écris

Read the text below and answer the questions.

La famille Durand

Monsieur et Madame Durand sont français. Ils sont mariés et ils ont quatre enfants. Ils ont deux garçons (André et Luc) et deux filles (Estelle et Céline). André a 14 ans, Luc a 13 ans, Estelle a 10 ans et Céline a 7 ans. Monsieur Durand a 45 ans et Madame Durand a 42 ans. Ils ont une grande maison avec un grand jardin pour les enfants et un garage pour la voiture.

---

1. Est-ce que Monsieur et Madame Durand sont mariés ou divorcés?

   _____

2. Combien d'enfants ont-ils?

   _____

3. Quel âge a Céline?

   _____

4. Est-ce que Monsieur et Madame Durand ont une petite maison?

   _____

5. De quelle nationalité sont Monsieur et Madame Durand?

   _____

6. Est-ce que la famille Durand a un chat?

   _____

Vocabulaire

un jardin	a garden	un garçon	a boy	un garage	a garage
une voiture	a car	une fille	a girl	marié(e)	married
un enfant	a child	une maison	a house	divorcé(e)	divorced

© Maria Rice-Jones and Brilliant Publications

Nom:_____   **La date:**_____

Lis et écris

Read the text below and answer the following questions.

La France

En France, il n'y a pas de reine ou roi, mais il y a le Président de la République.
La France est une République depuis la Révolution de 1789.

  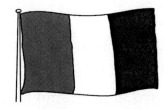

| "Marianne" est le symbole de la République Française. | La devise de la France est "liberté, égalité, fraternité". | Le drapeau français est: bleu, blanc, rouge. |

---

1. Est-ce qu'il y a un roi ou une reine en France?

   _____

2. Est-ce que le symbole de la République Française est un homme ou une femme?

   _____

3. Est-ce que la France est une monarchie ou une république?

   _____

4. De quelle couleur est le drapeau français?

   _____

5. Quelle est la devise de la France?

   _____

Aussi!

En ce moment, qui est le président de la République Française?

_____

Vocabulaire

une reine	a queen	un symbole	a symbol	un drapeau	a flag
un roi	a king	une devise	a motto	un homme	a man
un président	a president	liberté	freedom	une femme	a woman
une république	a republic	égalité	equality	une monarchie	a monarchy
depuis	since	fraternité	fraternity (brotherhood)	en ce moment	at the moment

Nom:_____   **La date:**_____

The power of love

Despite their royal status, King Être and Queen Avoir were just like any other couple in many ways. They liked the fact that they were different from each other, but also knew the importance of having some things in common.

Let me tell you about some of their differences first. King Être is the king of all verbs and for this reason he likes to be seen wearing his crown (Ê). Because the inhabitants of Hexagonie call him "**S**uperking", King Être has decided always to use the letter "**s**" when he describes himself or other people. Therefore, when he talks about himself he says "je **suis**"(I am). When he describes one other person he says "tu e**s**" (you are – if it is a dear friend), "vous ête**s**" (you are – when he talks to a person in a formal way), "il e**st**" (he is) or "elle e**st**" (she is). When he describes more than one person he uses longer words but still with an "**s**": he says "nous **s**omme**s**" (we are), "vous ête**s**" (you are) or "ils **s**ont/elles **s**ont" (they are).

Queen Avoir's name starts with the first letter of the alphabet because she is the first lady. So when she talks about the things she or her subjects have, she likes using her initial "**a**". For example, to say "I have", she will say "j'**ai**". When she is talking about one other person she says "tu **a**s" (you have – if it is a dear friend), "vous **a**vez" (you have – when she talks to a person in a formal way), "il **a**" (he has) or "elle **a**" (she has). And if she is talking about more than one person there are times when she also prefers to use "**a**": for example "nous **a**vons" (we have) and "vous **a**vez" (you have).

Now let me tell you about their similarities. Soon after they were married, King Être and Queen Avoir were pleased to notice that, despite their many differences, there was one sound that they already shared. This was the sound (eh). Queen Avoir makes this sound when she says: "j'ai" (I have) and King Être when he says: "tu es" (you are), "il est" (he is) and "elle est" (she is). This was an encouraging start, but it still left many differences. It was therefore agreed that from then on Queen Avoir would try to sound more like her husband when she talks about "ils" and "elles". That is why she now says "ils/elles ont" (they have) which looks and sounds very similar to the King's "ils/elles sont" (they are) – but without the "s" at the beginning – which is the King's special letter that only he can use.

© Maria Rice-Jones and Brilliant Publications

Nom:_____ **La date:**_____

Essential words and phrases

What to say when you want to ask a question:
Est-ce que... ?

The verb "avoir" (to have)

I have	j'ai
you have	tu as
he/she has	il/elle a
we have	nous avons
you have	vous avez (plural and polite)
they have	ils/elles ont

The verb "être" (to be)

I am	je suis
you are	tu es
he/she is	il/elle est
we are	nous sommes
you are	vous êtes (plural and polite)
they are	ils/elles sont

How to say "I don't have any"

Je n'ai pas de chat.	I do not have any cat.
Je n'ai pas de voiture.	I do not have any car.
Je n'ai pas d'ordinateur.	I do not have any computer.
Je n'ai pas de problèmes.	I do not have any problems.

My life, your life, his life

Key teaching points/vocabulary

All the possessives
Il y a

Bonjour...

Say "Bonjour" to the whole class, waiting for the pupils to reply "Bonjour Madame/Monsieur". Call the register in French and expect every pupil to respond "présent(e)" when their name is called out. When you have no answer say "absent(e)". Call out the name of a pupil and ask him/her, "Comment vas-tu?" waiting for his/her answer "Je vais bien, merci." Ask other pupils how they are. Encourage the pupil to ask you "et vous?" then answer with "Je vais bien merci."

Recap on "avoir" and "être"

Ask the pupils to recite with you in chorus the different forms of the verbs "avoir" and "être'":

Avoir	Être
j'ai	je suis
tu as	tu es
il/elle a	il/elle est
nous avons	nous sommes
vous avez	vous êtes
ils/elles ont	ils/elles sont

Recite each verb at least three times.

Ask questions using "avoir" and "être", for example:
    David et Charles, est-ce que vous avez une voiture?
    Charlotte, est-ce que nous sommes dans l'école?

Do a quick-fire activity where you tell pupils which pronoun to use, which verb and subject, for example: Maria, give me a sentence with "tu", the verb "avoir" and "un chien"; Jonathan, give me a sentence with "il", the verb "être" and "l'école".

Vocabulaire

mon	my (masculine singular) and any singular noun starting with a vowel
ma	my (feminine singular) starting with a consonant
mes	my (plural)
un cheval	a horse
un grand-père	a grandfather
une grand-mère	a grand-mother
un lapin	a rabbit
un exercise	an exercise

Materials

★ Sheet 5a (page 101)
★ Simple French/English dictionary for pupils

Mon, ma, mes

My

Remind the pupils that "my" is said in three different ways in French: "mon, ma, mes".

Mon

"Mon" is used with masculine singular nouns:

mon chien   mon père

and with any singular noun (both masculine and feminine) starting with a vowel:

mon ami   mon école

 Thinking of "**mon**sieur" which means "my + sir" will help you to remember "mon".

Ma

"Ma" is used with feminine singular nouns starting with a consonant:

ma chaise   ma mère

 Thinking of "**ma**dame" which means "my + dame" will help you to remember "ma". Note that "ma" rhymes with "la".

Mes

"Mes" is used with any plural noun:

Masculine plural		**Feminine plural**	
mes chiens	mes amis	mes gommes	mes amies

 Note that "mes" rhymes with "les".

 Give the pupils Sheet 5a, where they have to write "le", "l' ", "la" or "les" before 20 nouns in the top space. Pupils will have encountered all these words in Hexagonie, Part 1, but may need to check their meaning in a dictionary. If they do, you will need to show them how to use one and you may need to point out that (m) means that it is a masculine word and (f) means that it is a feminine word. Go through the sheet with them to ensure that they have the correct answer. Then ask the pupils to write "mon", "ma" or "mes" in front of the same 20 nouns on the second line under the pictures.

Ton, ta, tes

Your

Point at something masculine (such as "un stylo" or "un cahier") that belongs to you and describe its colour, for example, "Mon stylo est bleu." Point at a pupil's pen and say, "De quelle couleur est ton stylo?" Emphasize the word "ton". Wait for the pupil to reply, "Mon stylo est noir." Do the same with other objects, for example, "De quelle couleur est ton pantalon?" Wait for the pupil to reply, "Mon pantalon est brun."

Remind pupils that "your" when talking to a friend is said in three different ways in French: "ton, ta, tes".

Ton rhymes with "mon" and is used with masculine singular words and for any noun starting with a vowel (masculine or feminine).

Ta rhymes with "ma" and is used with feminine singular words starting with a consonant.

Tes rhymes with "mes" and is used for plural words.

Ask pupils about members of their family, for example, "Quel âge a ta sœur?" Wait for the pupil to reply, "Ma sœur a huit ans." Ask other pupils questions, for example:

Est-ce que tes parents sont français?
Est-ce que ta mère a un uniforme scolaire?
Quel est ton nom?
Quel est ton prénom?
Est-ce que ta leçon de français est le matin?

"Une leçon" is feminine. Note that it ends in "on" just like "maison", which is also feminine.

Ask the pupils to perform a Mexican wave where one pupil asks another a question about his family or about something that he owns, for example, "Est-ce que ton pull-over est bleu?" The pupil replies, "Non, mon pull-over n'est pas bleu. Mon pull-over est vert" or "Oui, mon pull-over est bleu." The second pupil then asks the next pupil a question.

Give the pupils Sheet 5b and ask them to answer the questions.

Vocabulaire

ton	your (masculine singular) and any singular noun starting with a vowel
ta	your (feminine singular) starting with a consonant
tes	your (plural)
une leçon	a lesson
en face de	opposite
un uniforme scolaire	a school uniform
le matin	the morning
en général	in general
un prénom	a first name
un nom	a surname
quel/quelle/ quels/quelles	which/what

Materials

★ Sheet 5b (page 102)

Vocabulaire

son	his/her (masculine singular) and any singular noun starting with a vowel
sa	his/her (feminine singular) starting with a consonant
ses	his/her (plural)
une poupée	a doll
une peluche	a stuffed toy
un lit	a bed
d'origine	originally from
un poster	a poster
le cadet/la cadette	the youngest
un hamster	a hamster
un écureuil	a squirrel
un oiseau (oiseaux)	a bird (birds)
une poule	a chicken
un animal (animaux)	an animal (animals)
une adresse	an address

Materials

★ Sheet 5c–5d (pages 103–104)
★ Sheet 5j (page 110)
★ CD, Tracks 16–18

Son, sa, ses

His/her

Remind the pupils that "his" and "her" are said in the same way in French: "son" (his, her), "sa" (his, her) and "ses" (his, her).

 Son rhymes with "mon" and is used with masculine singular words and for any noun starting with a vowel (masculine or feminine).

Sa rhymes with "ma" and is used with feminine singular words starting with a consonant.

Ses rhymes with "mes" and is used for plural words.

 Give pupils Sheet 5j and go through it with them making sure that they understand when to use "mon", "ma" and "mes" etc.

 Give pupils sheet 5c on the possessives. Ask them to fill in the gaps with the right possessive.

  These three tracks are French children talking about their lives. Listen to the tracks first before giving the pupils the sheets (this is probably best done one at a time). Talk about the passages. How much did they understand? Were there any words or phrases they would like you to explain? Translate these, then play the extract(s) again several times. When the children are familiar with the passage(s), ask them questions to check their understanding (this can be done either in English or French).

Give the pupils Sheet 5d. Three passages are written with some gaps to fill in. Tell the pupils that they are going to listen to the passages again and they must fill the gaps with the missing words. Play the tracks as many times as necessary.

The missing words from Sheet 5d are highlighted below in bold.

 Bonjour, je **m'appelle** Adeline, je suis française et j'ai **dix** ans. Mes parents **sont** français. Je n'ai pas de frère ou de **sœur**. Ma maison **est** grande. Dans **ma** chambre, il y a **mon** bureau avec **mes** livres, **mes** stylos et **mes**

cahiers. Sur **mon** lit, il y a **ma** poupée, Lucie, et **mes** peluches. Mon ordinateur n'est pas dans **ma** chambre. Il est dans le bureau de **ma** mère.

Bonjour, je **m'appelle** Camel et je **suis** français d'origine algérienne. Mes parents sont algériens. Mon appartement n'est pas très grand **mais** il est confortable. Dans ma chambre, il y a mon ordinateur, **mes** posters et **mon** lit. J'**ai** quatre frères. Moi, je suis le cadet de la **famille** et j'ai neuf ans.

Bonjour, je **m'appelle** Manon, je suis française et j'ai neuf ans. J'ai des animaux à la **maison**: **mon** hamster qui s'appelle "Tony", **mon** chien qui s'appelle "Joker", mon **poisson** rouge qui s'appelle "Kity" et **mes** deux chats qui s'appellent "Félix" et "Lily". Dans mon jardin j'**ai** des animaux: des écureuils, **des** oiseaux et mes **cinq** poules.

Vocabulaire

il danse	he dances
ainsi	that's the way
un corps	a body
le clair	the light
la lune	the moon
prête-moi	give me
une plume	a fountain pen
écrire	to write
un mot	a word
mort(e)	dead
une chandelle	a candle
je n'ai plus de feu	I don't have any light
ouvre-moi	open for me
pour l'amour de Dieu	for the love of God
il répondit	he replied
va chez la voisine	go to the (female) neighbour
je crois qu'elle y est	I think she's there
une cuisine	a kitchen
on bat le briquet	someone lit a match

Materials

★ Sheet 5e–5f (pages 105–106)
★ CD, Tracks 19–22

Chansons françaises

French songs

Listen to the song on Track 19 of the CD, "Jean Petit qui danse". Point out the usage of "son" and "sa". Sing the song and encourage pupils to join in with you. The words to the song are on Sheet 5e and Track 20 is an instrumental version. You could alter the words to include other parts of the body, e.g. son épaule (his shoulder), sa jambe (his leg) or son corps (his body). Act out the song as you sing it.

Listen to the song on Track 21 on the CD, "Au clair de la lune". This is one of the most famous French songs for children. It was written in the 17th century. Some pupils may be familiar with the tune as it is a popular tune when learning to play an instrument. A Pierrot is a type of clown who has a white face and a black cap.

Point out the usage of some possessives in the song.

Au clair de la lune, mon ami Pierrot	In the light of the moon, Pierrot my friend
Prête-moi ta plume, pour écrire un mot.	Give me your pen to write something down.
Ma chandelle est morte, je n'ai plus de feu.	My candle's dead, I don't have any light.
Ouvre-moi ta porte, pour l'amour de Dieu.	Open your door, for the love of God.
Au clair de la lune, Pierrot répondit:	In the light of the moon, Pierrot replied:
Je n'ai pas de plume, je suis dans mon lit.	I don't have a pen, I'm in my bed,
Va chez la voisine, je crois qu'elle y est,	Go to the neighbour's, I think she's there,
Car dans sa cuisine, on bat le briquet.	For in her kitchen, someone lit a match.

Sing the song and encourage pupils to join in with you. The words to the song are on Sheet 5f and Track 22 is an instrumental version.

Notre/nos, votre/vos, leur/leurs

Our, your, their

Give a pupil of your choice a pen the same colour as yours (let's say, a blue pen). Then point at this pupil and yourself and, talking to the rest of the class, say:

> Teacher: Nos stylos ne sont pas verts mais nos stylos sont bleus.

You could say more sentences using "nos" (our) introducing items shared by yourself and the chosen pupil such as: un pull-over, un pantalon, une chaise, etc.

> Teacher: Notre pantalon n'est pas bleu mais notre pantalon est noir.

After "notre", introduce "votre" (your for a group). Give two other pupils one red pen and ask them questions with "votre" encouraging them to answer with "notre":

> Teacher: De quelle couleur est votre stylo?
> Pupils: Notre stylo est rouge.

> Teacher: De quelle couleur est votre pull?
> Pupils: Notre pull est bleu.

> Teacher: Est-ce que votre école est grande ou petite?
> Pupils: Notre école est petite.

Tell the pupils that "our" is said in two ways in French: "notre" in front of a singular noun (notre maison: our house) and "nos" in front of a plural noun (nos livres: our books).

Tell the pupils that "your" (for a group of people) is said in two ways in French "votre" in front of a singular noun (votre maison: your house) and "vos" in front of a plural noun (vos livres: your books).

Give a pupil of your choice (let's say Thomas) two blue pens like yours. Then give two other pupils two red pens and say:

Point at yourself and Thomas and say:
> Teacher: Nos stylos ne sont pas verts mais nos stylos sont bleus.

Point at the two other pupils:
> Teacher: De quelle couleur sont vos stylos?
> Pupils: Nos stylos sont rouges.

Point at the two other pupils:
> Teacher: De quelle couleur sont vos chaussures?
> Pupils: Nos chaussures sont noires.

Point at the two other pupils:
> Teacher: Est-ce que vos parents sont ici maintenant ?
> Pupils: Non, nos parents ne sont pas ici.

Vocabulaire

notre	our (masculine and feminine singular)
nos	our (plural)
votre	your (masculine and feminine singular)
vos	your (plural)
leur	their (masculine and feminine singular)
leurs	their (plural)
un jumeau une jumelle	a twin
une école mixte mixte	a co-educational school
cent	a hundred
quelquefois	sometimes

Materials

★ Sheet 5g (page 107)
★ Pictures/photos of people (optional)
★ CD, Track 23

Now ask two or three pupils to face the class and say sentences about them with the possessives "leur" (their) in front of a singular noun and "leurs" (their) in front of a plural noun:

Teacher: Les chaussures de Luke sont bleues, les chaussures de Rebecca sont bleues. Leurs chaussures sont bleues. Leur pantalon est bleu et leur chemise est blanche.

Then ask questions to the rest of the class about this group such as:

Teacher: De quelle couleur est leur pantalon?
Pupils: Leur pantalon est bleu.

Teacher: De quelle couleur sont leurs chaussures?
Pupils: Leurs chaussures sont bleues.

If you prefer, you could show the pictures of some people and you could talk about them with "leur" and "leurs". Then you could ask the pupils some questions about them with "leur" and "leurs".

After you have introduced "notre/nos", "votre/vos" and "leur/leurs" you could tell the pupils that when they talk to you, they have to use the possessive "votre/vos" which are polite forms of "your" and used when talking to someone older than you or who is not your friend. You could ask them some questions about yourself encouraging the pupils to answer with "votre/vos":

Teacher: De quelle couleur est ma chemise?
Pupils: Votre chemise est verte.

Teacher: Où est mon stylo?
Pupils: Votre stylo est sur la table.

Teacher: De quelle couleur sont mes chaussures?
Pupils: Vos chaussures sont noires.

Teacher: Où sont mes livres?
Pupils: Vos livres sont sur la table.

 Write this table on the board:

	With all singular nouns	**With all plural nouns**
our	notre	nos
your	votre	vos
their	leur	leurs

Recap on when to use "notre/nos", "votre/vos" and "leur/leurs".

When something plural is possessed, tell the pupils that all the words that show possession end in "s" and that all of them, apart from "leurs", have three letters "mes, tes, ses, nos, vos".

Give the pupils Sheet 5g and introduce the new vocabulary. Pupils may be able to guess the correct meanings of the new words from the word clues. Listen to the passage being read on CD Track 23.

Ask them to fill in "notre" or "nos" and then answer the questions.

Hexagonie story

Play the "Hexagonie love song" on Track 24 and ask the pupils to listen carefully for the possessives used. The words appear on sheet 5h and there is an instrumental version on Track 25.

5h

Vocabulaire

la vie	life
la joie	joy
un sujet	a subject
notre peuple (m)	our people
si formidable	so great
admirable	admirable
à l'infini	forever
bel	beautiful
tout	all

Materials

★ Sheet 5h (page 108)
★ CD, Tracks 24–25

Il y a

There is/are

Point to some items in the classroom such as the door, the windows, etc, and say:

Teacher: Ici (here), ici (here), ici (here), ici il y a une porte.
            Ici, il y a trois fenêtres.
            Ici, il y a un tableau.
            Ici, il y a un professeur et vingt élèves.

Ask the pupils to tell you what "il y a" means. They will certainly be able to work out that it means "there is" and "there are".

Ask individual pupils questions with "il y a" such as:

Teacher: Combien de fenêtres est-ce qu'il y a ici?
            Est-ce qu'il y a un tableau rouge ici?
            Combien d'élèves est-ce qu'il y a ici?

Vocabulaire

il y a	there is/ there are
chez moi	at my house
chez toi	at your house
un salon	a sitting room
une salle à manger	a dining room
une entrée	an entrance hall
une chambre	a bedroom
une salle de bains	a bathroom
une cave	a cellar
un grenier	a loft (attic)
une ville	a town
des magasins (m)	shops
une banque	a bank
un parc	a park
une mairie	a town hall
une gare	a train station

Vocabulaire cont.

il y a	there is/are
un cinéma	a cinema
un théâtre	a theatre
un musée	a museum
une bibliothèque	a library

Materials

★ Sheet 5i (page 109)
★ Blank sheets of paper and pencils

Materials

★ Sheet 5j (page 110)

Ask the pupils to write "Chez moi" (at my house) at the top of a blank piece of paper and to draw a quick plan of their ideal house. Remind them how we say the different rooms in the house such as: une cuisine, une salle à manger, une chambre, une salle de bains etc.

Divide pupils into pairs and ask them to take turns pretending to show their friend around their ideal house: "Chez moi il y a…." Encourage partners to ask questions such as: "Pourquoi est-ce qu'il y a trois salles de bains chez toi?" "Combien de chambres est-ce qu'il y a chez toi?"

Ask at least three pupils to talk about their ideal house in front of the rest of the class.

Remember to always give a lot of praise: "C'est très bien!," "Bravo!"

Give the pupils a copy of Sheet 5i and ask the pupils to describe where they live.

Essential words and phrases

At the end of this unit, give the pupils sheet 5j, which will help them to remember essential words and phrases.

Au revoir! Bonne semaine! Bon week-end!

Remember always to wish the pupils a good week or weekend. Wait for them to reply "Merci Madame/Monsieur, vous aussi".

Nom:_____   **La date:**_____

Regarde et écris

On the top lines write "le", "la", "l'" or "les". Check with your teacher that you have answered them all correctly, then write "mon", "ma" or "mes" on the bottom lines.

1. __le__ père

__mon__ père

2. _____ mère

_____ mère

3. _____ sœur.

_____ sœur

4. _____ frère

_____ frère

5. _____ chien

_____ chien

6. _____ chat

_____ chat

7. _____ école

_____ école

8. _____ cheval

_____ cheval

9. _____ amis

_____ amis

10._____ ordinateur

_____ ordinateur

11._____ professeurs

_____ professeurs

12._____ vêtements

_____ vêtements

13._____ grand-père

_____ grand-père

14._____ grand-mère

_____ grand-mère

15._____ cousin

_____ cousin

16._____ cousine

_____ cousine

17._____ exercices

_____ exercices

18._____ lapin

_____ lapin

19._____ uniforme

_____ uniforme

20._____ livres

_____ livres

© Maria Rice-Jones and Brilliant Publications

Nom:_____   **La date:**_____

Lis et écris

Read the questions and write down the answers. Use full sentences.

1. Quel est ton prénom?

   Mon prénom est _____

2. Quel est ton nom?

   _____

3. De quelle nationalité est ta mère?

   _____

4. De quelle nationalité est ton père?

   _____

5. De quelle couleur sont tes chaussures?

   _____

6. Où est ton professeur de français maintenant?

   _____

7. En général, est-ce que ta leçon de français est intéressante?

   _____

8. Est-ce que ton uniforme scolaire est élégant?

   _____

9. Qu'est-ce qu'il y a en face de ton école?

   Il y a _____

10. Qu'est-ce qu'il y a maintenant dans ta trousse?

    Il y a _____

Nom:_____   **La date:**_____

Lis

MON is used with:

All masculine singular nouns

mon stylo (my pen)	mon chien (my dog)	mon ami (my male friend)
ton stylo (your pen)	ton chien (your dog)	ton ami (your male friend)
son stylo (his/her pen)	son chien (his/her dog)	son ami (his/her male friend)

All singular nouns (feminine and masculine) starting with a vowel

mon ami (my male friend)	mon exercice (my exercise)	mon amie (my female friend)
ton ami (your male friend)	ton exercice (your exercise)	ton amie (your female friend)
son ami (his/her male friend)	son exercice (your exercise)	son amie (his/her female friend)

MA is only used with:

Singular feminine nouns starting with a consonant

ma trousse (my pencil case)	ma voiture (my car)	ma mère (my mother)
ta trousse (your pencil case)	ta voiture (your car)	ta mère (your mother)
sa trousse (his/her pencil case)	sa voiture (his/her car)	sa mère (his/her mother)

MES is used with:

All plural nouns

mes stylos (my pens)	mes amis (my friends)	mes chaussures (my shoes)
tes stylos (your pens)	tes amis (your friends)	tes chaussures (your shoes)
ses stylos (his/her pens)	ses amis (his/her friends)	ses chaussures (his/her shoes)

Complète

Fill in the gaps with the right possessive:

_____ adresse (my address)	_____ école (her school)
_____ prénom (your name)	_____ maison (my house)
_____ nom (his surname)	_____ maison (your house)
_____ parents (your parents)	_____ grand-mère (his grandmother)
_____ frères (my brothers)	_____ grand-mère (her grandmother)

Nom:_____   **La date:**_____

Écoute et écris

Listen to the CD and then fill in the gaps.

Bonjour, je _____ Adeline, je suis française et j'ai _____ans. Mes parents _____ français. Je n'ai pas de frère ou de _____. Ma maison est grande. Dans _____ chambre, il y a _____ bureau avec _____ livres, _____ stylos et _____ cahiers. Sur _____ lit, il y a _____ poupée Lucie et _____ peluches. Mon ordinateur n'est pas dans _____ chambre. Il est dans le bureau de _____ mère.

Bonjour, je _____ Camel et je _____ français d'origine algérienne. Mes parents _____ algériens. Mon appartement n'est pas très grand _____ il est confortable. Dans ma chambre il y a mon ordinateur, _____ posters et _____ lit. J'_____ quatre frères. Moi, je suis le cadet de la _____ et j'ai neuf ans.

Bonjour, je _____ Manon, je suis française et j'ai neuf ans. J'ai des animaux à la _____ : _____ hamster qui s'appelle "Tony", _____ chien qui s'appelle "Joker", mon _____ rouge qui s'appelle "Kity" et _____ deux chats qui s'appellent "Félix" et "Lily". Dans mon jardin _____ des animaux: des écureuils, _____ oiseaux et mes _____ poules.

Nom:_____   **La date:**_____

Jean Petit qui danse

Little Jean who dances

Jean Petit qui danse	Little Jean who dances
Jean Petit qui danse	Little Jean who dances
De son doigt il danse	With his finger he dances
De son doigt il danse	With his finger he dances
De son doigt, doigt, doigt,	With his finger, finger, finger,
De son doigt, doigt, doigt,	With his finger, finger, finger,
Ainsi danse Jean Petit!	Thus dances Little Jean!

Jean Petit qui danse	Little Jean who dances
Jean Petit qui danse	Little Jean who dances
De sa main il danse	With his hand he dances
De sa main il danse	With his hand he dances
De sa main, main, main,	With his hand, hand, hand
De son doigt, doigt, doigt,	With his finger, finger, finger
Ainsi danse Jean Petit!	Thus dances Little Jean!

Jean Petit qui danse	Little Jean who dances
Jean Petit qui danse	Little Jean who dances
De son bras il danse	With his arm he dances
De son bras il danse	With his arm he dances
De son bras, bras, bras,	With his arm, arm, arm
De sa main, main, main,	With his hand, hand, hand
De son doigt, doigt, doigt,	With his finger, finger, finger
Ainsi danse Jean Petit!	Thus dances Little Jean!

Nom:_____ **La date:**_____

Au clair de la lune

By the light of the moon

Au clair de la lune, mon ami Pierrot

Prête-moi ta plume, pour écrire un mot.

Ma chandelle est morte, je n'ai plus de feu.

Ouvre-moi ta porte, pour l'amour de Dieu.

Au clair de la lune, Pierrot répondit:

Je n'ai pas de plume, je suis dans mon lit.

Va chez la voisine, je crois qu'elle y est,

Car dans la cuisine, on bat le briquet.

Nom:_____   **La date:**_____

Lis et écris

Read the text below then fill in the gaps with "notre" or "nos".

> Je m'appelle Dany.

> Et je m'appelle Laura.

Nous sommes jumelles. _____ yeux sont bleus, et _____ cheveux sont bruns.

Nous sommes dans une école qui est dans un petit village en Normandie. _____ école est une école mixte. Dans _____ école, il y a dix professeurs et deux cents (200) élèves. Dans _____ classe, nous sommes vingt-cinq élèves, seize filles et neuf garçons. _____ professeur est une femme très gentille qui s'appelle Madame Moreau.

Dans _____ classe, il y a cinq ordinateurs et une télévision. Sur les murs de _____ classe, il y a des posters sur les différentes régions de France. _____ leçons sont intéressantes mais quelquefois elles sont trop longues.

Réponds aux questions

Answer the following questions with "leur" or "leurs":

1. De quelle couleur sont les yeux de Dany et Laura?

   _____

2. Est-ce que leur école est à Paris?

   _____

3. Combien de garçons est-ce qu'il y a dans leur classe?

   _____

4. Est-ce que leur prof est gentille?

   _____

5. Qu'est-ce qu'il y a sur les murs de leur classe?

   _____

Nom:_____ **La date:**_____

Chanson d'amour d'Hexagonie

Hexagonian love song

While I was in Hexagonie there was a song that I often heard being played on the radio. It was written in honour of the King and Queen.

Oh, oh, ma reine, mon amour,
ma vie et toutes mes joies.

C'est moi ta reine, ton amour,
ta vie et toutes tes joies.

Son amour, sa vie, ses joies
Son amour, sa vie, ses joies.

Nous aimons tous nos sujets,
notre peuple si formidable.

Vous aimez tous vos sujets,
votre amour est admirable.

Toutes leurs joies à l'infini
C'est leur bel Hexagonie.

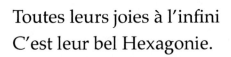

Nom:_____ **La date:**_____

Lis 📖 et dessine ✏️

Draw a simple map of where you live (your road and its surroundings) or the main street of where you live.

ma ville

Vocabulaire

des magasins	shops	une mairie	a town hall	un cinéma	a cinema
une piscine	a swimming pool	une gare	a train station	un théâtre	a theatre
une banque	a bank	un cinéma	a cinema	un musée	a museum
une école	a school	une église	a church	une bibliothèque	a library

Écris ✏️

Write three sentences describing where you live.

Example

Dans ma ville, il y a des magasins mais il n'y a pas de piscine. Il y a une bibliothèque et un musée. Il n'y a pas de cinéma.

_____

_____

_____

_____

© Maria Rice-Jones and Brilliant Publications

Nom:_____ **La date:**_____

Essential words and phrases

How to say something belongs to you

	Masculine singular		Feminine singular		Masculine plural		Feminine plural	
	Starting with a consonant	Starting with a vowel	Starting with a consonant	Starting with a vowel	Starting with a consonant	Starting with a vowel	Starting with a consonant	Starting with a vowel
my	mon père	mon ami	ma mère	mon école	mes parents	mes amis	mes sœurs	mes amies
your	ton père	ton ami	ta mère	ton école	tes parents	tes amis	tes sœurs	tes amies
his/her	son père	son ami	sa mère	son école	ses parents	ses amis	ses sœurs	ses amies
our	notre père	notre ami	notre mère	notre école	nos parents	nos amis	nos sœurs	nos amies
your	votre père	votre ami	votre mère	votre école	vos parents	vos amis	vos sœurs	vos amies
their	leur père	leur ami	leur mère	leur école	leurs parents	leurs amis	leurs sœurs	leurs amies

Life in action

Key teaching points/vocabulary

"En", "au" and "aux" ("To a country" or "in a country")
The verb parler ("to speak") in the present tense
À ("to" or "at")

Bonjour...

Say "Bonjour" to the whole class, waiting for the pupils to reply
"Bonjour Madame/Monsieur." Call the register in French and expect
every pupil to respond "présent(e)" when their name is called out.
When you have no answer say "absent(e)". Call out the name of a
pupil and ask him/her, "Comment vas-tu aujourd'hui?" waiting for
his/her answer "Je vais bien, merci." Ask other pupils how they are.
Encourage the pupil to ask you "et vous?" then answer with "Je vais
bien merci" or "je suis content(e) aujourd'hui." Encourage them to
use a variety of adjectives in their reply.

Vocabulaire
aujourd'hui   today

Recap on the possessives

Perform a Mexican wave, where one pupil asks another a question
using a word indicating possession such as:

> Eddie, de quelle couleur est mon pantalon?

> Ton pantalon est bleu.

> Lucy, de quelle nationalité est ton père ?

> Mon père est français

Vocabulaire

en vacances	on holiday
en Afghanistan	in/to Afghanistan
en Algérie	in/to Algeria
en Allemagne	in/to Germany
en Amérique	in/to America
en Angleterre	in/to England
en Belgique	in/to Belgium
au Brésil	in/to Brazil
au Canada	in/to Canada
en Chine	in/to China
au Danemark	in/to Denmark
en Écosse	in/to Scotland
en Espagne	in/to Spain
aux États-Unis	in/to the United States of America
en Égypte	in/to Egypt
en France	in/to France
au Gabon	in/to Gabon
en Grèce	in/to Greece
en Inde	in/to India
en Irak	in/to Iraq
en Irlande	in/to Ireland
en Israël	in/to Israel
en Italie	in/to Italy
au Japon	in/to Japan
en Malaisie	in/to Malaysia
au Maroc	in/to Morocco
en Martinique	in/to Martinique
au Népal	in/to Nepal
au Pakistan	in/to Pakistan
aux Pays-Bas	in/to the Netherlands
au Pays de Galles	in/to Wales
en Pologne	in/to Poland
en Russie	in/to Russia
au Sénégal	in/to Senegal
en Suisse	in/to Switzerland
en Tunisie	in/to Tunisia
au Venezuela	in/to Venezuela
un pays	a country

Materials

★ Travel brochures or postcards (optional)
★ Cards with the countries listed in Vocabulaire written on them in French
★ Cards with family members written on them

En France

In/to France

Hold up a travel brochure or the flashcard for France and say to the class, "je suis en vacances en France avec ma famille" (I am on holiday in France with my family). Emphasize "en France". Then pick up the card for England and say, "je suis en vacances en Angleterre." Again, emphasize "en Angleterre". Then pick up the flashcard for Brazil, and say, "je suis en vacances au Brésil." Continue for all the countries that are on flashcards: "en Espagne" (in/to Spain), "aux États-Unis" (in/to United States) and "en Allemagne" (in/to Germany), etc.

 Give each pupil Sheet 6a, where they will find out how to say "in" (or "to") before a country. Ask them if they know why we say "en" for some countries and why with others we say "au". They might come up with a helpful memory trick. Otherwise tell them the one below.

 When a country ends in "e", you use "en" before it. "En" also starts with "e", for example, en France (in/to France), en Italie (in/to Italy), en Angleterre (in/to England), en Irlande (in/to Ireland), en Belgique (in/to Belgium), en Espagne (in/to Spain).

When a country ends in a letter other than "e", you say "au", for example, au Brésil (in/to Brazil), au Maroc (in/to Morocco), au Canada (in/to Canada), au Venezuela (in/to Venezuela).

However when a country starts with a vowel, regardless of what letter it ends in, you say "en" to make it easier to pronounce, for example, en Irak (in/to Iraq), en Afghanistan (in/to Afghanistan).

When a country is plural, you say "aux", for example, aux États-Unis (in/to the United States).

 You will need three sets of cards: one with countries written on them (in French), one with family members and one with number of days/weeks. Give each child one card from each set, for example: Écosse, parents, trois jours. Make sure each country is not repeated more than twice. Then perform a Mexican wave where each pupil says where he/she is on holiday, with whom and for how long:

Lucy: Je suis en Écosse avec mes parents pour trois jours, et toi George?

George: Moi, je suis en vacances au Canada avec ma famille pour deux semaines, et toi Emma?

Note:
Pays de Galles is just one country so we use "au" even though it has an "s" at the end.

6b

Give sheet 6b to the pupils. It gives a list of countries without the words "en", "au" or "aux" in front of them. Ask the pupils to remember the memory tricks and to fill in the gaps.

Materials cont.

★ Cards with number of days/weeks written on them
★ Sheets 6a–6b (pages 119–120)

À Paris

In/to Paris

Tell the pupils that in French we say "to London" and "in London" in the same way: "à Londres". Tell them that before every town in the world we say "à". Ask them to find a memory trick to remember this. If they don't have any suggestions then tell them the one below.

Memory trick

London is "a" city, Wimbledon is "a" town, Rome is "a" city, etc. A town or city is usually smaller than a country. That's why we put a small letter in front of it and the first letter of the alphabet will do. Tell the pupils to remember to put a grave accent on the 'à'.

Give each group a piece of paper with the names of two or three countries and three capitals to choose from for each. Each group has to find out the right capital for the countries indicated on the piece of paper. The countries and the capitals could be as follows:

France	Paris/ Bruxelles/Lisbonne
Belgique	Berlin/Bruxelles/Bern
Canada	Madrid/Ottawa/ Delhi
Allemagne	Bern/ Bruxelles/ Berlin
Chine	Beijing/Tokyo/Ottawa
Irlande	Edimbourg/Dublin/ Bern
Espagne	Madrid/Rome/Lisbonne
Italie	Lisbonne/Rome/ Madrid
Brésil	Montevideo/Brasilia/Bern
Japon	Beijing/Tokyo/ New Delhi
États-Unis	Londres/ Washinghton/Dublin
Irak	Bern/Bagdad/ Brasilia
Inde	Beijing/New Delhi/ Lisbonne
Écosse	Edimbourg/Londres/ Dublin
Suisse	Bruxelles/Bern/ Berlin
Angleterre	Londres/Dublin/Edimbourg

Perform a Mexican wave where each pupil says where he/she is on holiday, indicating the capital in the country such as:

Matt: Je suis en vacances à Edimbourg en Écosse, et toi Ivor?

Ivor : Moi, je suis en vacances à Ottawa au Canada, et toi Emma?

Remember to always encourage the pupils and to praise them.

Vocabulaire

à Londres	in/to London
à Paris	in/to Paris
à Madrid	in/to Madrid
à Rome	in/to Rome
à Edimbourg	in/to Edinburgh
un lion	a lion
une île	an island
une canne	a cane
une tour	a tower
lourd(e)	heavy
la peau	the skin
quand	when
un pari	a bet

Materials

★ CD, Track 26
★ Sheets 6c (page 121), photocopied on to card

© Maria Rice-Jones and Brilliant Publications

Vocabulaire

parler	to speak
je parle	I speak
tu parles	you speak
il/elle parle	he/she speaks
nous parlons	we speak
vous parlez	you speak (plural and polite)
ils/elles parlent	they speak
beaucoup	a lot
un peu	a little
avec	with
combien	how many
une langue	a language
parce que	because

Materials

★ Sheets 6d (page 122), photocopied on to card

★ Tableau d'Honneur (page 314)

★ stickers (optional)

Sheet 6c will help pupils to learn the location of some towns in France and to practise their listening skills. They need to find the French town which sounds exactly like each of the following words shown on the sheet. Pupils can listen to the place names and words on the CD on Track 26.

Parler

To speak

Est-ce que tu parles...? Oui, je parle.../ Non, je ne parle pas...

Do you speak… ? Yes, I speak…/No, I don't speak…

Tell the pupils the languages that you speak by saying sentences such as:

Teacher: Je parle deux langues. Je parle français et anglais. Je parle anglais avec ma famille et je parle français avec mes amis français. Je ne parle pas espagnol avec vous parce que je suis professeur de français.

Then ask individual pupils questions with the verb "parler" such as:

Teacher: Est-ce que tu parles anglais chez toi?

Pupil: Oui, je parle anglais chez moi car je suis anglaise.

Here below are some examples of questions:

Teacher: Combien de langues est-ce que tu parles?
Avec qui est-ce que tu parles français?
En général, est-ce que tu parles beaucoup ou peu avec tes parents?

Est-ce qu'il/elle parle...?

Does he/she speak…?

Ask individual pupils questions about their parents:

Teacher: Est-ce que ton père parle français?
Est-ce que ta mère parle italien avec ton père?
Est-ce que ta mère parle beaucoup avec toi?

Est-ce qu'ils/elles parlent... ?

Do they speak...?

Ask individual pupils questions about their parents or about other people:

Teacher: Est-ce que tes parents parlent français?
Quelle langue parlent les Français?
Quelle langue parlent les Italiens?
Quelle langue parlent les Irlandais?

Tell the pupils that the verb "parler" when conjugated with "je, tu, il/elle" and "ils/elles" is pronounced in the same way but is not always written in the same way.

Write the verb "parler" with "je, tu, il/elle" and "ils/elles", pointing out the different endings and ask the pupils to colour them in red:

je   parl **e**
tu   parl **es**
il/elle   parl **e**
ils/elles   parl **ent**

Est-ce que vous parlez...? Nous parlons.....

Do you speak...?/ We speak...?

Tell the pupils : "Vous et moi, nous parlons français en ce moment. Nous ne parlons pas italien maintenant." Then ask questions to the class encouraging the pupils to answer in chorus with "nous parlons":

Teacher: Est-ce que vous parlez anglais?
Pupils: Oui, nous parlons anglais.

Teacher: Quelle langue est-ce que vous parlez maintenant?
Pupils: Nous parlons français maintenant (car nous avons une leçon de français avec vous).

Then encourage individual pupils to ask you questions with "vous parlez":

Pupil: Combien de langues est-ce que vous parlez?
Pourquoi est-ce que vous parlez français?

Read Sheet 6d on the verb "parler" in the present tense with the class and discuss the different forms of "parler" with them. Remind them, if necessary, that "ils" is used for groups of men or a mixed group of men and women, and that "elles" is used for just groups of women. Also, point out that the "nt" of "Ils parlent" and "Elles parlent" is not pronounced, so they sound the same as "Il parle" and "Elle parle".

Explain that, in French, most verbs ending in "er" use these same endings and that "je parle" can mean "I am speaking" or "I do speak" as well as "I speak".

Put the pupils in pairs. One pupil will ask his/her partner questions that use the verb "parler". For example, "Est-ce que tu parles italien?" "Quelle langue est-ce que tu parles avec tes parents?" "Est-ce que ton père parle français?" Then ask some pupils to introduce their partner to the rest of the class. To do this they will use "Il parle…" or "Elle parle…" statements, for example, "Ellie parle anglais" or "Robin ne parle pas italien". Reward the pupils who do well with a "Tableau d'Honneur" or a sticker.

Vocabulaire

danser	to dance
une boum	a dancing party
skier	to ski
penser	to think
cuisiner	to cook
regarder	to watch
jouer	to play
chanter	to sing
le tennis	tennis
écouter	to listen to
téléphoner	to telephone
dessiner	to draw

Materials

★ Tableau d'Honneur (page 314)
★ stickers (optional)
★ Sheets 6e(i)–6e(ii) (pages 123–124), photocopied back-to-back and cut into cards, one set for each group
★ Sheets 6f (page 125), cut into cards, one set for each group
★ Sheet 6g (page 126)

More "er" verbs

Hold up the card (made from Sheets 6e(i)–6e(ii)) showing a dancer and say "danser: elle danse". Ask the class to guess what it means. They may remember the song "Jean Petit qui danse". Then encourage them to say sentences in French using "danser", for example, "Je danse avec mes amis à la boum" (I dance with my friends at the dancing party).

Then hold up another card for example, of a man skiing and say: "skier: il skie: skier". Again ask the pupils to tell you what it means. Then encourage the pupils to make up sentences using "skier", for example, "Je skie en vacances avec mes parents". Always congratulate a good sentence with an enthusiastic "Très bien", "C'est correct" or "Bravo". Reward the pupils who do well with a "Tableau d'Honneur" or a sticker.

Continue with the rest of the cards, miming the verbs if necessary, to help pupils to guess the word. Ask questions to encourage them to use all the forms of the verb, for example:

Teacher: Est-ce que ta mère cuisine dans le salon?
Est-ce que vous jouez au tennis maintenant?
Est-ce qu'elles chantent bien?

They could remember "jouer" by thinking that it is "a joy" to play.

"Penser": think about the English adjective "pensive". In "**pen**ser" there is "**pen**" and in "**think**" there is "**ink**".

Stress that all these verbs end in "er" and so have the same endings for "je, tu, il/elle, nous, vous, ils/elles" as "parler".

Show the pupils the words on cards 6e(i) – 6e(ii). Can they pronounce them correctly and tell you what they mean?

You will need one set of Sheets 6e(i)–6e(ii), photocopied back-to-back and cut into cards, one for each group, and one set of Sheet 6f, cut into cards, for each group. Divide the pupils into groups. One person from each group needs to come to the board, turn over the top card from each set, read the cards and then put them on the bottom of the piles, then write the correct verb form on the board and go back to their group (e.g. if she picked "tu" and "chanter" she would write "tu chantes"). The next person in the group then can go up to take their turn. The first team to finish is the winner. Deduct points for incorrectly conjugated verbs or misspellings.

Give the pupils Sheet 6g. Ask them to choose the verb for each sentence and write it in the correct form.

Other useful "er" verbs to introduce are "écouter" (to listen to), "téléphoner" (to telephone) and "dessiner" (to draw). Mime the actions and say what you are doing, e.g: "Je parle au téléphone. Je téléphone." Can they guess what "je téléphone" means?

Je voudrais parler avec...

I would like to speak to...

Write some French names on the board, e.g. Laure, Lucie, Charlotte, Sophie, Nathalie, Pierre, Luc, Jacques, etc. Explain that although some of the names are spelled like English names, they are pronounced differently. Read through the list and ask pupils to repeat the names after you.

Tell the pupils that you want them to divide into pairs and role play making a telephone call to a French friend. Unfortunately their French friend won't be there as he/she is on holiday in a different country. The conversations should go something like this:

Person A: Bonjour Madame/Monsieur. Je suis .... Je voudrais parler avec ... s'il vous plaît.

Person B: Je suis désolé/Madame/Monsieur mais ... n'est pas là aujourd'hui car il/elle est en/au/aux ....

Pupils might find it helpful to have Sheet 6a, which lists a variety of countries, available for reference. Encourage them to take turns and to have two or three goes in each role. Go round the room, praising pupils' efforts and correcting pronunciation where necessary. You could ask two or three pairs to demonstrate their pretend telephone conversation in front of the class.

Materials
★ Sheet 6a (page 119) - optional

Materials
★ Sheet 6h (page 127)

Hexagonie story

Give the pupils Sheet 6h. Read it with them and discuss to reinforce the points covered.

Materials
★ Sheet 6i (page 128)

Essential words and phrases

At the end of this unit, give the pupils Sheet 6i, which will help them to remember essential words and phrases.

Au revoir! Bonne semaine! Bon week-end!

Remember always to wish the pupils a good week or weekend. Wait for them to reply "Merci Madame/Monsieur, vous aussi".

Nom:_____   **La date:**_____

Regarde 👁 👁

Les pays

The countries

en Angleterre	au Canada	aux États-Unis
en Allemagne	au Brésil	aux Pays-Bas
en Belgique	au Maroc	
en Chine	au Népal	
en France	au Japon	en Israël
en Italie	au Pakistan	en Afghanistan
en Inde	au Gabon	en Irak
en Irlande	au Pays de Galles	
en Écosse	au Sénégal	
en Espagne	au Vénézuela	
en Russie		
en Tunisie		
en Algérie		
en Suisse		
en Martinique		
en Pologne		

Memory trick

When to use "en" before a country:
When a country ends in "e", you use "en" before it. "En" also starts with "e", for example, en Franc<u>e</u> (in/to France).

When a country starts with a vowel, regardless of what letter it ends in, you say "en" to make it easier to pronounce, for example, en Irak (in/to Iraq).

When to use "au" before a country:
When a country starts with a consonent and ends in a letter other than "e", you say "au", for example, au Brésil (in/to Brazil).

When to use "aux" before a country:
When a country is plural, you say "aux", for example, aux États-Unis (in/to the United States).

Nom:_____   **La date:**_____

Regarde et écris

Look and then fill in the gaps using "en", "au" or "aux". Remember the memory tricks.

1. _____ Angleterre
2. _____ France
3. _____ Pays-Bas
4. _____ Allemagne
5. _____ Danemark
6. _____ Belgique
7. _____ Grèce
8. _____ Italie
9. _____ Égypte
10. _____ Israël

1. _____ Amérique
2. _____ États-Unis
3. _____ Canada
4. _____ Brésil
5. _____ Venezuela
6. _____ Martinique

1. _____ Russie
2. _____ Inde
3. _____ Malaisie
4. _____ Chine
5. _____ Japon
6. _____ Népal
7. _____ Pakistan

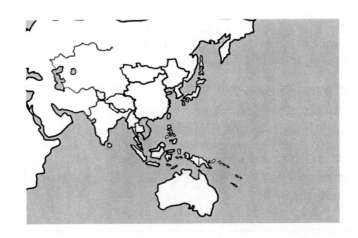

Nom:_____ **La date:**_____

Régarde et réponds

Find the French town which sounds exactly like each of the following words. You can listen to the words on the CD.

lion (lion)
sounds like the town:

_____

l'île (island)
sounds like the town:

_____

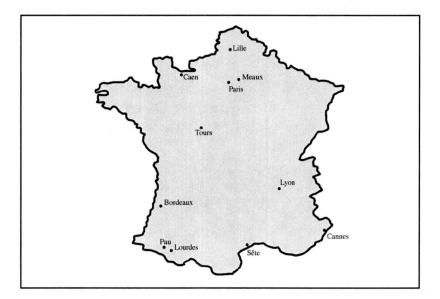

canne (cane)
sounds like the town:

_____

tour (tower)
sounds like the town:

_____

7

sept (seven)
sounds like the town:

_____

the red wine, Bordeaux,
sounds like the town:

_____

lourde (heavy)
sounds like the town:

_____

mot

mot (word)
sounds like the town:

_____

peau (skin)
sounds like the town:

_____

quand (when)
sounds like the town:

_____

pari (bet)
sounds like the town:

_____

Nom:_____   **La date:**_____

"Parler" in the present tense

Parl/ er

je	parl	e	I speak I am speaking I do speak
tu	parl	es	you speak you are speaking you do speak
il elle	parl	e	he/she speaks he/she is speaking he/she does speak
nous	parl	ons	we speak we are speaking we do speak
vous	parl	ez	you speak you are speaking you do speak
ils elles	parl	ent	they speak they are speaking they do speak

The letters "ons" at the end of "nous parlons" are found in 'nous'.

"Tu parles" has an "s" because "s" is close to "t" and "u" in the alphabet.

These are all pronounced the same way:
je parle   tu parles
il/elle parle   ils/elles parlent

Hexagonie, Part 2

penser	**skier**
regarder	**cuisiner**
jouer	**danser**
parler	**chanter**

je	**tu**
il	**elle**
nous	**vous**
ils	**elles**

Nom:_____ **La date:**_____

Regarde et écris

What are these people doing? Underneath each picture write the correct verb (from the list below) with one of the following endings: e,es,e,ons,ez,ent

1. Elle _____ .

2. Elles _____ beaucoup.

3. Il _____ au tennis.

4. Elle _____ .

5. Nous _____ .

6. Il _____ la télévision.

7. Je _____ bien.

8. Je _____ à mes vacances.

9. Vous _____ avec nous.

| skier | penser | parler | cuisiner | regarder | danser | jouer | chanter |

Nom:_____   **La date:**_____

The verbs' outfits

The verbs are Hexagonie's busiest inhabitants by far and, if it wasn't for all their hard work, nothing would ever get done. Many verbs ended in "er" like me, Voyager.

It was amazing to see how active the verbs were. What surprised me most was how often they changed the outfits they wore. Each time an "er" verb was next to a different subject, such as "je", "tu", "il", "elle", "nous", "vous", "ils" and "elles", it changed outfit – always making sure that it was perfectly suited to the occasion.

One of the "er" verbs I liked the best was called Madame Parler (to speak). She was very chatty and only too happy to show me all her different outfits.

When seen with a single subject such as "je", "il" and "elle", Madame Parler told me that she would choose a simple outfit. She just took off her final "r" and ended with an "e" (je parle, il parle, elle parle). However, with "tu" she liked to add a special letter, because "tu" was a close friend. She chose the letter "s" as it was close to "t" and "u" in the alphabet (tu parles).

When seen with plural subjects such as "nous", "vous", "ils" and "elles", Madame Parler liked to wear more sophisticated outfits. With "nous" (nous parlons) she chose to wear the outfit "ons" as it had letters in common with "nous". With "vous" (vous parlez), Madame Parler wore the letter "z" which reminded

her of the "z" sound Queen Avoir made when she pronounced the "vous" in "vous avez". And finally, with "ils" and "elles" she wore the outfit "nt" (ils/elles parlent), which is similar to the one King Être wears with "ils" and "elles" in "ils/elles sont" and Queen Avoir wears with "ils" and "elles" in "ils/elles ont."

Now I have heard that some people find these verbs tiring with all their changes of outfit – but not me. I just admire their great sense of fashion!

Nom:_____   **La date:**_____

Essential words and phrases

The "er" verbs in the present tense

Get rid of the ending "er" and replace it with the following endings:

Parl/er (to speak)

je	parl	**e**
tu	parl	**es**
il/elle	parl	**e**
nous	parl	**ons**
vous	parl	**ez**
ils /elles	parl	**ent**

How to say that you are going to a country

Use "en" before countries ending in "e"

En France	in/to France
En Angleterre	in/to England
En Écosse	in/to Scotland
En Italie	in/to Italy
En Espagne	in/to Spain

Use "en" before countries starting with a vowel

En Israël	in/to Israel
En Irak	in/to Iraq
En Afghanistan	in/to Afghanistan

Use "au" before countries not ending in "e"

Au Maroc	in/to Morocco
Au Canada	in/to Canada

Use "aux" before countries ending in "s"

Aux États-Unis	in/to the United-States
Aux Pays-Bas	in/to the Netherlands

To live and to work – that's life!

Bonjour...

Say "Bonjour" to the whole class, waiting for the pupils to reply "Bonjour Madame/Monsieur." Call the register in French and expect every pupil to respond "présent(e)" when their name is called out. When you have no answer say "absent(e)". Call out the name of a pupil and ask him/her, "Comment vas-tu?" waiting for his/her answer "Je vais bien, merci." Ask other pupils how they are. Encourage the pupil to ask you "et vous?" then answer with "Je vais bien merci" or "je ne suis pas fatigué(e) aujourd'hui." Encourage pupils to answer with an adjective.

Recap on the verbs ending in "er" in the present tense

Write on the board three or four "er" verbs learnt in the previous chapter: parler, skier, penser, cuisiner, regarder, danser, jouer, chanter. With the pupils' help, write some of them in the present tense with all the endings (e, es, e, ons, ez, ent) in red or underlined.

Perform a Mexican wave where the first pupil asks another pupil of his/her choice a question using one of the verbs written on the board. The second pupil answers and asks another question and so on.

Emma:	Thomas, est-ce que tu danses maintenant?
Thomas:	Non, je ne danse pas maintenant. Jack, est-ce que tu cuisines maintenant?
Jack:	Non, je ne cuisine pas maintenant parce que ce n'est pas possible.

Vocabulaire

habiter	to live
un(e) adulte	an adult
à la campagne	in the country
près	near
un village	a village
étudier	to study
aimer	to like/love

Materials

★ CD, Track 27
★ Sheets 7a–7b (pages 138–139)

Habiter

To live

Track 27 uses the verb "habiter" (to live) which was first introduced in Hexagonie, Part 1. Tell the pupils that they will listen to a track on the CD of a French man talking about himself and that he will use the same verb many times. Ask the pupils to listen and tell you which one it is and its meaning. You may need to play the track several times.

Je parle français parce que je suis français. J'habite dans une maison qui a un grand salon, une petite cuisine, une assez grande salle à manger, une salle de bains et trois chambres. Je n'habite pas avec mes parents car maintenant je suis adulte. Mes parents habitent avec leur chien "Rex" dans un appartement. Ils n'habitent pas dans une grande ville mais à la campagne près d'un petit village.

The passage on Track 27 on the CD also appears on Sheet 7a, in case you would like your pupils to see a printed copy.

Write "j'habite" on the board and point out that we use an abbreviated form of "je" because the "h" in "habite" is silent.

Ask the pupils questions about the French man on the CD. For example:

Teacher: Où est-ce qu'il habite?
Est-ce qu'il habite avec ses parents?

Then ask individual pupils questions about themselves such as:

Teacher: Où est-ce que tu habites? Avec qui? Dans un appartement ou dans une maison?
Où habite ta grand-mère?
Où habite … (another child in the class)?
Où habitent tes grands-parents?
Est-ce que le Président de la République française habite à Paris ou à New York?

Ask pupils to ask everyone on their table or in their group a question about where someone lives. Ask some pupils to report back to the rest of the class the answers they received.

Stress that "habiter" ends in "er" and so will have the same endings as "parler" and the other verbs learned in Unit 6.

Remind pupils of two other "er" verbs that were introduced in Hexagonie, Part 1: "étudier" (to study – highlight the similar ending sound in "j'étudie" and "study") and "aimer" (to like/love). You could recite the different conjugations of these verbs as a group: "j'étudie, tu étudies, il/elle étudie, nous étudions, vous étudiez, ils/elles étudient". Then ask for volunteers to do it by themselves.

Give Sheet 7b to the pupils and ask them to write in red the present tense endings for the verbs shown.

Hexagonie story

Give each pupil Sheet 7c and read it to the class. Talk to the pupils about the story. It is very empowering for learners to realize how many French words they already know because they are similar to their English equivalent.

Vocabulaire

accepter	to accept
refuser	to refuse
adorer	to adore
détester	to detest/ hate
commencer	to start/ commence
terminer	to terminate/ end
inviter	to invite
donner	to give
désirer	to desire

Materials

★ Sheets 7c (page 140)

Types de bâtiment

Types of building

Select two buildings you want to introduce. Hold up one picture at a time and tell the class the building illustrated on it, e.g. if you are holding up a farm, say "C'est une ferme" and repeat twice. Then show another one (e.g. une tente – a tent) and say "C'est une tente" and repeat twice. Then show the first picture and the second and wait for the pupils to repeat "C'est une ferme. C'est une tente." Continue until you feel that pupils can remember most of the types of building.

When pupils are familiar with all the words, ask questions, for example:

Est-ce que tu habites dans une maison ou un appartement?

Qui habite dans le Palais de Buckingham à Londres? (you could show a picture of Buckingham Palace).

Est-ce que cet immeuble est grand ou petit?

En vacances, où habites-tu? Est-ce que tu habites dans une tente, une caravane ou un hôtel?

Où est cette cabane? (show a picture of a tree house). Cette cabane est dans un arbre.

You could link this activity to work in geography.

Vocabulaire

une tente	a tent
un hôtel	a hotel
une ferme	a farm
une caravane	a caravan
un château	a castle
un palais	a palace
un chalet	a chalet
un immeuble	a building
un pavillon	a villa
un igloo	an igloo
une cabane	a hut/shack
une cabane pour enfants	a playhouse
une cabane dans un arbre	a tree house
un arbre	a tree
populaire	popular
un type	a type
on trouve	one finds
souvent	often
une habitation	a dwelling
confortable	comfortable
extérieur(e)	exterior
individuel(le)	individual
préférer	to prefer

Materials

★ Pictures of different types of buildings (as listed in the Vocabulaire list)
★ Sheet 7d (page 141)
★ Sheets 7e(i)–(ii) (pages 142–143)
★ CD, Track 28

Give each pupil Sheet 7d and ask the pupils to fill in the gaps with "l' ", "le" or "la" in front of the words. If the pupils are unsure, remind them that most feminine words end in "e" and that words starting with a vowel need "l' ".

These sheets introduce pupils to the main types of house in France. You can listen to this passage on Track 28 on the CD. Ask pupils: "Quelle maison est-ce que tu préfères? Pourquoi?" (Which house do you prefer? Why?)

Vocabulaire

travailler	to work
chaque	each
un jour	a day
pendant	during
si	if
malade	ill

Materials

★ CD, Track 29
★ Sheets 7a (page 138)
★ Sheets 7f–7g (pages 144–145)

Travailler

To work

Tell the pupils that they will listen to a track on the CD of a French woman talking and that she will use the same verb many times. Ask the pupils to listen and tell you which one it is and its meaning. You may need to play the track several times.

Je suis professeur et je travaille dans une école mixte. Je travaille chaque jour avec des élèves. Il y a trente élèves dans ma classe. Je ne travaille pas pendant le week-end car je suis occupée avec ma famille.

The passage on Track 29 on the CD also appears on Sheet 7a, in case you would like your pupils to see a printed copy.

Discuss what the French woman says to ensure that the pupils understand everything. You will need to explain the new words "chaque", which means "each", and "pendant", which means "during".

To remember that "pendant" means "during", remember that in "during" there is "ring". However, the French do not use the equivalent word, but use a "pendant", which is another piece of jewellery.

All the letters in "**chaque**" are in "**each**".

Ask individual pupils questions about their families such as:

Teacher: Est-ce que tes parents travaillent?
Est-ce que tu travailles? Pourquoi?
Est-ce que ta mère travaille avec ton père?
Est-ce que ton père travaille beaucoup?
Est-ce que tes parents travaillent pendant le week-end?
Si ton père est malade, est-ce qu'il travaille?

Divide the class into pairs and ask them to ask each other questions about their family using the verb "travailler".

 Ask pupils to answer the questions on Sheet 7f with full sentences, either as homework or during the lesson.

 Give each pupil Sheet 7g and ask them to fill in the correct form of the verbs indicated and "à", "au", "en" or "aux".

Les professions

Jobs

 Sheets 7h(i) – 7h(iv) can be made into cards for 16 professions. If they are not the professions you would choose for your class, we recommend that you make your own cards using pictures downloaded from the internet. A list of professions is given in the Vocabulaire box.

Select two professions you want to introduce. Hold up one card at a time and tell the class the profession illustrated on it, e.g. if you are holding up a builder, say "C'est un maçon" and repeat twice. Then show another one (e.g. un routier – a lorry driver) and say "C'est un routier" and repeat twice. Show both pictures and wait for the pupils to repeat "C'est un maçon. C'est un routier." Continue until you feel that pupils can remember most of the professions.

 The following memory tricks can be used to help pupils remember some professions:

French	English	Memory trick
un pompier	fireman	A fireman uses a **pump** (une **pomp**e) to put out fire, so the French word for fireman is "**pomp**ier".
un routier	lorry driver	The word "**rout**e" means "road" and "un **rout**ier" (lorry driver) drives on a lot of **rout**es.
un professeur/ une prof	a teacher	"**Profess**eur" is similar to the word **profess**ion.
un facteur/ une factrice	a postman	A postman brings **fact**s, so he is called "le **fact**eur".

Vocabulaire

un acteur/ une actrice	an actor/ actress
un/une architecte	an architect
un/une avocat(e)	a lawyer
un barman	a barman
un bijoutier/ une bijoutière	a jeweller
un boulanger/ une boulangère	a baker
un boucher	a butcher
un caissier/ une caissière	a check-out assistant
un chauffeur de taxi	a taxi driver
un chef	a chef
un coiffeur/ une coiffeuse	a hairdresser
un/une commerçant(e)	a shopkeeper
un/une comptable	an accountant
un conducteur de bus/ une conductrice de bus	a bus driver
un couturier/ une couturière	a dressmaker
un cuisinier/ une cuisinière	a cook
un danseur/ une danseuse	a dancer
un/une dentiste	a dentist
un docteur	a doctor
un/une électricien(ne)	an electrician
un/une étudiant(e)	a student
un facteur/ une factrice	a postman/ a postwoman

Vocabulaire (cont.)

un fermier/ une fermière	a farmer
un/une fleuriste	a florist
une hôtesse de l'air	an air hostess
un infirmier/ une infirmière	a nurse
un jardinier/ une jardinière	a gardener
un/une journaliste	a journalist
un maçon	a builder
un/une mécanicien(ne)	a mechanic
un/une musicien(ne)	a musician
un/une opticien(ne)	an optician
un/une pharmacien(ne)	a pharmacist
un/une photographe	a photographer
un/une peintre	a painter
un/une pilote	a pilot
un plombier	a plumber
un policier/ une policière	a policeman/ woman
un professeur/ une prof	a teacher
un/une réceptionniste	a receptionist
un routier	a lorry driver
un/une scientifique	a scientist
un serveur/ une serveuse	a waiter/ waitress
un soldat	a soldier
un vendeur/ une vendeuse	a sales person
un/une vétérinaire	a vet

Materials

★ Sheets 7h(i)–(iv) (pages 146–149), photocopied back-to-back and cut up into cards, one set for each group
★ Sheet 7i (page 150)

French	English	Memory trick
un infirmier/ une infirmière	a nurse	A person who is **infirm** is weak or ill, and needs "un **infirm**ier" (nurse) to look after them.
un maçon	a builder	A builder builds houses, "**maisons**". The word "**maison**" helps us find "**maçon**".
un/une comptable	an accountant	"Un **comp**table" (accountant) counts. The verb 'to count' in French is "**comp**ter".
un serveur/ une serveuse	a waiter/ a waitress	"Un **serve**ur" (waiter) **serve**s customers.
un cuisinier/ une cuisinière	a cook	"Un **cuisin**ier" (cook) cooks in the kitchen. "Un **cuisin**ier **cuisin**e dans la **cuisin**e."
un/une commerçant(e)	a shopkeeper	"Un **commerç**ant" (shopkeeper) does **commerc**e.
un vendeur/ une vendeuse	a sales person	"Un **vend**eur" (sales person) is a "**vend**or".
un/une étudiant(e)	a student	"É**tud**iant" has many letters in common with "s**tud**ent".
un/une pharmacien(ne)	a pharmacist	Very similar to the English word.
un fermier/ une fermière	a farmer	Very similar to the English word.
un/une mécanicien(ne)	a mechanic	Very similar to the English word.
un policier/ une policière	a policeman	Very similar to the English word
un docteur	a doctor	Very similar to the English word

Point to yourself and say, "Moi, je suis professeur/prof." Talk about other people's profession, e.g: "Mon père est pompier et ma mère est infirmière." Point out that we don't say "un" or "une", we just say "Je suis docteur" or "Je suis infirmier."

We can only be one person at a time, so it would be useless to say "un/une" before the profession.

Write professions on small sticky labels and stick one on each pupil's back. Pupils have to try to find out their profession by asking each other yes or no questions, e.g: "Est-ce que je suis routier?" The other pupil will reply "Oui, tu es routier" or "Non, tu n'es pas routier."

Remind pupils that for some jobs we have two words in English, one for feminine and one for masculine, e.g. actor/actress, waiter/waitress. Explain that in French there are different forms for many jobs. Where a job ends in an "e" the word stays the same, but we change "un" to "une". Write some examples on the board:

un scientifique	une scientifique
un vétérinaire	une vétérinaire
un dentiste	une dentiste
un pilote	une pilote
un architecte	une architecte

For jobs ending in "ier" in the masculine form (e.g. "fermier"), we add an accent grave to the "e" before the "r" as well as adding an "e" to make the feminine form:

un infirmier	une infirm**ière**
un fermier	une ferm**ière**
un policier	une polic**ière**

For jobs ending in "ien" in the masculine form (e.g. "pharmacien"), we need to double the "n" before adding the "e" to make the feminine form:

un pharmacien	une pharmacie**nne**
un électricien	une électricie**nne**

For jobs ending in "eur" in the masculine form (e.g. "facteur"), we have to change the "eur" to "rice" or to "euse" to make the feminine form:

un facteur	une fact**rice**
un conducteur	une conduct**rice**
un serveur	une serv**euse**
un danseur	une dans**euse**

This rule does not apply to "docteur" which does not change and stays as "un docteur" in the feminine form. Another job which does not change is "professeur". For a female teacher we say "une prof" as "professeur" always remains masculine.

Give the pupils Sheet 7i and ask them to fill in the blanks with the appropriate profession. At the bottom of the sheet they need to write down the feminine professions.

7i

Vocabulaire

un beau-père	a step-father
un demi-frère	a half-brother
passer	to pass (time)
partager	to share
agréable	agreeable/ happy
bien sûr	of course
vraiment	really
qui	who
même	same/also
amusant	amusing
ensemble	together
adorable	adorable

Materials

★ Sheet 7j (page 151)
★ CD, Track 30

J'habite à Paris

I live in Paris

Listen twice (or as many times as necessary) to what Matthieu, a young French boy who lives in Paris, says about himself.

Je m'**appelle** Matthieu. J'**ai** neuf ans et j'**habite** à Paris. J'**habite** dans un assez grand appartement, dans un immeuble moderne avec ma mère, mon beau-père, mon grand frère Bruno qui **a** onze ans et mon demi-frère Grégoire qui **a** cinq ans. Mes parents **sont** divorcés. Mon père **est** professeur et même mon beau-père **est** professeur et ma mère **travaille** dans un restaurant près de la maison. En général, je **passe** mes vacances chez mes grands-parents à Nice. Je **partage** ma chambre avec mon frère Bruno. Nous **passons** des moments très agréables ensemble car nous **avons** un ordinateur pour deux et nous **jouons** souvent avec l'ordinateur. Et bien sûr, chaque jour, nous **jouons** un peu avec Grégoire qui **est** vraiment adorable et amusant. Et toi?

Now give the pupils Sheet 7i with the text written out. Ask a pupil to read the text. New words are listed at the bottom of the sheet.

Then ask the pupils to underline with a highlighter all the verbs in the text (in bold in the passage, above). Ask them to write every verb in the present tense with "je, tu, il/elle, nous, vous, ils/elles" on a piece of paper. Afterwards write the correct forms on the board and ask pupils to check their work.

Ask individual pupils questions about the text in French, such as:

    De quelle nationalité est Matthieu?
    Quel âge a Matthieu?
    Est-ce que Matthieu a des frères ou des soeurs?
    Est-ce que ses parents sont divorcés?
    Est-ce que sa maman travaille? Où?
    Où habite Matthieu? Avec qui?
    Est-ce qu'il partage sa chambre? Avec qui?
    Où habitent ses grands-parents?
    Est-ce que Matthieu joue avec Grégoire?
    Où est-ce qu'il passe ses vacances?

Put the pupils in pairs and ask them to pretend that they have gone to a youth club in Paris and have met Matthieu and his brother Bruno. (If some pupils would prefer, they could pretend to meet a French girl.) One person should pretend to be Matthieu (or another French person at the youth club) and the other should play themselves.

Tell them they need to find out the following information about each other (you could write this list on the board):

Name
Nationality
Where they live
How old they are
How long the English person is going to be in Paris
Why they are there (because their parents are working in Paris "en ce moment" (at the moment))
What jobs their parents do

After a while, they should swap roles. Go round the room, listening to the role-plays, correcting where necessary. Give lots of praise and encouragement.

Ask some pairs to perform the role-play in front of the class and reward pupils who do well.

Materials
★ Sheet 7k (page 152)

Essential words and phrases

At the end of this unit, give the pupils Sheet 7k, which will help them to remember essential words and phrases.

Au revoir! Bonne semaine! Bon week-end!

Remember always to wish the pupils a good week or weekend. Wait for them to reply "Merci Madame/Monsieur, vous aussi".

Nom:_____ **La date:**_____

Lis et écoute

Je parle français parce que je suis français. J'habite dans une maison qui a un grand salon, une petite cuisine, une assez grande salle à manger, une salle de bains et trois chambres. Je n'habite pas avec mes parents car maintenant je suis adulte.

Mes parents habitent avec leur chien "Rex" dans un appartement. Ils n'habitent pas dans une grande ville mais à la campagne près d'un petit village.

Je suis professeur et je travaille dans une école mixte. Je travaille chaque jour avec des élèves. Il y a trente élèves dans ma classe. Je ne travaille pas pendant le week-end car je suis occupée avec ma famille.

Nom:_____   **La date:**_____

Lis et complète

Put these verbs in the present tense. Write the endings in red.

	habit	**er**	
j'	habit	____	I live, I am living
tu	habit	____	you live, you are living
il /elle	habit	____	he/she lives, he/she is living
nous	habit	____	we live, we are living
vous	habit	____	you live, you are living
ils/elles	habit	____	they live, they are living

	étudi	**er**	
j'	étudi	____	I study, I am studying
tu	étudi	____	you study, you are studying
il /elle	étudi	____	he/she studies, he/she is studying
nous	étudi	____	we study, we are studying
vous	étudi	____	you study, you are studying
ils/elles	étudi	____	they study, they are studying

	dans	**er**	
je	dans	____	I dance, I am dancing
tu	dans	____	you dance, you are dancing
il /elle	dans	____	he/she dances, he/she is dancing
nous	dans	____	we dance, we are dancing
vous	dans	____	you dance, you are dancing
ils/elles	dans	____	they dance, they are dancing

	pens	**er**	
je	pens	____	I think, I am thinking
tu	pens	____	you think, you are thinking
il /elle	pens	____	he/she thinks, he/she is thinking
nous	pens	____	we think, we are thinking
vous	pens	____	you think, you are thinking
ils/elles	pens	____	they think, they are thinking

Nom:_____   **La date:**_____

Some "er" verbs

All sorts of verbs lived in Hexagonie. Some were very popular like "Monsieur Jouer" (to play), and others were unpopular, such as "Madame Pleurer" (to cry). Some others were naughty like "Monsieur Crier" (to shout) and some were considerate like "Madame Aider" (to help).

Some verbs even looked quite similar to verbs I had met before in other countries. It was as if they came from the same family and were cousins.

Why don't I introduce some to you to see if you can recognize them as well?

There was **Madame Accepter** (to accept) who did not like **Monsieur Refuser** (to refuse) because she was always nodding, while he was always shaking his head.

There was the adorable **Madame Adorer** (to adore) who was always blowing kisses to everyone and everything, while **Monsieur Détester** (to detest) hated everyone and everything.

There was **Madame Commencer** (to commence/start) who always started the conversation, while **Monsieur Terminer** (to terminate/end) loved to end it.

There was **Madame Danser** (to dance) who danced all the time when **Monsieur Inviter** (to invite) invited her.

There was **Monsieur Donner** (to donate/to give) who was very generous with **Madame Désirer** (to desire) who was always wishing for something.

I am quite sure you could recognize these verbs. There are many more like them that I will introduce in later stories.

Nom:_____ **La date:**_____

Regarde et complète

Fill in the gaps with "l'", "le" or "la". Remember the rules for deciding whether something is masculine or feminine.

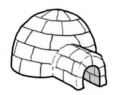

1. _____ igloo

2. _____ château

3. _____ cabane

4. _____ hôtel

5. _____ tente

6. _____ palais

7. _____ ferme

8. _____ pavillon

9. _____ église

10. _____ chalet

Nom:_____   **La date:**_____

Les maisons en France (1)

Houses in France

Il y a beaucoup de types de maisons en France.

À Paris, il y a beaucoup d'immeubles Haussmaniens.

Un pavillon est une maison individuelle confortable avec un jardin et un garage. En général, on trouve ces pavillons à l'extérieur des grandes villes.

Il y a beaucoup de châteaux viticoles sur la Loire.

Les maisons alsaciennes sont typiques en Alsace.

Nom:＿＿＿＿＿＿＿＿＿＿＿＿＿＿＿＿＿ **La date:**＿＿＿＿＿＿＿＿＿＿＿

Les maisons en France (2)

En Normandie, une maison-cour est une ferme qui est souvent une maison d'habitation.

Il y a beaucoup de chalets Savoyards dans les Alpes.

Les maisons basques sont typiques dans le Pays Basque.

En Provence, on trouve le mas provençal.

Quelle maison est-ce que tu préfères? Pourquoi?

Nom:_____   **La date:**_____

Réponds aux questions

Answer these questions.

1. Est-ce que tu parles français avec ta famille? Pourquoi?

   _____

2. Avec qui parles-tu beaucoup?

   _____

3. Quand tu parles français, est-ce que tu penses en anglais?

   _____

4. En ce moment, est-ce que tu regardes la télévision? Pourquoi?

   _____

5. Est-ce que tes parents parlent français?

   _____

6. Est-ce que notre école est grande ou petite?

   _____

7. Est-ce que tu habites dans une maison ou un appartement?

   _____

8. Où habitent tes grand-parents?

   _____

9. Est-ce que tes parents travaillent? Où?

   _____

10. Est-ce que ta mère cuisine bien? Et ton père?

   _____

11. Est-ce que tu cuisines pour tes parents? Pourquoi?

   _____

12. Maintenant, est-ce que tu penses à tes parents?

   _____

Nom:_____   **La date:**_____

Regarde 👁👁 et écris

Write the correct form of the verb in brackets in the first blank and then write "à", "au", "aux" or "en" in the second blank.

1. J' _____ _____ Canada. (habiter)

2. Il _____ _____ France. (travailler)

3. Nous _____ avec nos amis _____ Allemagne. (parler)

4. Vous _____ _____ Italie. (skier)

5. Je _____ espagnol _____ Espagne. (parler)

6. Elles _____ dans un restaurant _____ Paris. (cuisiner)

7. Ils _____ beaucoup _____ États-Unis. (travailler)

8. Elle _____ _____ Japon. (étudier)

9. Tu _____ avec tes parents _____ Écosse. (habiter)

© Maria Rice-Jones and Brilliant Publications   *This page may be photocopied for use by the purchasing institution only.*

une vétérinaire	**un docteur**
un plombier	**un soldat**
un maçon	**une prof**
une infirmière	**un policier**

un pompier	**une pharmacienne**
une factrice	**un fermier**
un routier	**une conductrice de bus**
une scientifique	**une serveuse**

Nom:_____   **La date:**_____

Regarde 👁 👁 et écris

Read the clues and fill in the blanks with the appropriate job.

fermier   professeur   docteur   serveuse   vétérinaire   conductrice de bus

1. Mon père travaille avec les animaux de la ferme.
    Il est_____ .

2. Sa mère travaille avec les personnes malades.
    Elle est _____ .

3. Ton père travaille à l'école avec les élèves.
    Il est _____ .

4. Ta mère travaille dans un restaurant.
    Elle est _____ .

5. Son père travaille avec les animaux malades.
    Il est _____ .

6. Ma mère travaille dans un bus.
    Elle est _____ .

Écris

Write the feminine for the following professions and highlight the ones that are identical in the masculine and feminine.

1. pharmacien   pharmacie**nn**____
2. infirmier   infirmièr____
3. fermier   fermièr___
4. pilote   pilot___
5. serveur   serv**eus**___
6. scientifique   scientifiqu___
7. policier   policièr___
8. dentiste   dentist___
9. vétérinaire   vétérinair___
10. facteur   fact**ric**___
11. électricien   électricie**nn**___
12. danseur   dans**eus**___

Nom:_____   **La date:**_____

Écoute et lis

Listen to Track 30 on the CD to find out about Matthieu.

Je m'appelle Matthieu. J'ai neuf ans et j'habite à Paris. J'habite dans un grand appartement, dans un immeuble moderne avec ma mère, mon beau-père, mon grand frère Bruno qui a onze ans et mon demi-frère Grégoire qui a cinq ans. Mes parents sont divorcés. Mon père est professeur et même mon beau-père est professeur et ma mère travaille dans un restaurant près de la maison. En général, je passe mes vacances chez mes grands-parents à Nice. Je partage ma chambre avec mon frère Bruno. Nous passons des moments très agréables ensemble car nous avons un ordinateur pour deux et nous jouons souvent avec l'ordinateur. Et bien sûr, chaque jour, nous jouons un peu avec Grégoire qui est vraiment adorable et amusant. Et toi?

Vocabulaire

un immeuble	a building	nous passons	we spend (time)	bien sûr	of course
moderne	modern			nous jouons	we play
mon beau-père	my step-father	agréable	agreeable/ happy	vraiment	really
mon demi-frère	my half-brother			amusant	amusing
près	near	je partage	I share		
je passe	I spend (time)	ensemble	together		

Nom:_____   **La date:**_____

Essential words and phrases

How to say some useful linking words

si

(if)

Both "si" and "if" have two letters and one in common. However, if you write the letter "f" by hand, it can look like an "s" and in French the word starts with "s".

même

(same)

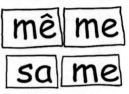

"Même" and "same" both contain four letters. They share the same final two letters "me". These letters are repeated twice in the French word "même". This helps us to remember that "même" means "same" as the same two letters are repeated twice.

même

(even)

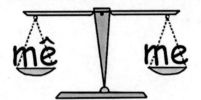

Both "même" and "even" contain four letters, with two letters in common. We could say that the French word "même" means "even", because if we imagine putting the word on a scale, it would be "even" (balanced).

même si

(even if)

pendant

(during)

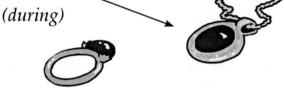

In the word "du**ring**" there is "**ring**". However, the French do not use the equivalent word, but they use a "pendant" which is another piece of jewellery.

souvent

(often)

When you write the letter "f" by hand, it can look like an "s" and "s" is the first letter of the French word "souvent". S**ou**v**en**t has the letters **o**, **e**, **n** and **t** in common with **often**.

en ce moment

(at the moment)

en ce mom**en**t

To remember that we say "en" before "ce moment", remember that "**en**" is already in "mom**en**t": **en** ce mom**en**t.

chaque

(each)

All the letters in "**each**" are in "**cha**qu**e**".

To play forever

Key teaching points/vocabulary

To play in the playground
To play a sport
To play an instrument

Bonjour...

Say "Bonjour" to the whole class, waiting for the pupils to reply
"Bonjour Madame/Monsieur." Call the register in French and expect
every pupil to respond "présent(e)" when their name is called
out. When you have no answer say "absent(e)". Call out the name
of a pupil and ask him/her, "Comment vas-tu?" waiting for his/
her answer "Je vais bien, merci." Ask other pupils how they are.
Encourage the pupil to ask you "Et vous?" then answer with "Je vais
bien merci" or "je vais bien parce que je suis content(e)." Always try
to use some adjectives that the pupils already know and encourage
pupils to do the same.

Recap on "er" verbs

Say to the pupils that they will recap on "er" verbs by
filling in Sheet 8a. Read the sheet together to practise
pronunciation.

Resources

★ Sheet 8a (page 162)

Jouer à un jeu dans la cour de l'école

To play a game in the school playground

The aim of introducing the verb "jouer" is to practise "à la", "à l'",
"au" and "aux" after it. Depending on the interests of your class,
practise the verb "jouer" with playground games or sports or both.

If you choose playground games, hold up a picture of a game, for
example a girl who is playing hopscotch and say, "Elle joue à la
marelle." then ask questions to the class about this game:

Teacher: Dans votre pays, est-ce que les écoliers jouent à la
            marelle?
Pupil: Oui, les écoliers jouent à la marelle./Oui, nous jouons
            à la marelle./Non, nous ne jouons pas à la marelle.

Teacher: Est-ce que c'est un jeu amusant?
Pupil: Oui, c'est un jeu amusant. /Non, ce n'est pas un jeu
            amusant.

Vocabulaire

un jeu	a game
un écolier	a pupil
la récréation	break time
une cour	a playground
Je joue à la marelle	I play hopscotch
Je joue à la corde à sauter	I play with the skipping rope
Je joue à l'élastique	I play French elastic (French skipping)
Je joue aux billes	I play marbles
Je joue aux cartes	I play cards
Je joue à cache-cache	I play hide and seek
À quoi est-ce que tu joues?	What are you playing?

© Maria Rice-Jones and Brilliant Publications

Materials

★ Pictures of people playing the games listed in the Vocabulaire list
★ Sheets 8b–8c (pages 163–164)
★ Tableau d'honneur (page 314)

Then introduce some more games and ask more questions:

Teacher: Est-ce que tu joues à l'élastique pendant la récréation?
Pupil: Non, je ne joue pas à l'élastique.

French elastic or French skipping is a common playground game in France. It is played using a long (3 metre) piece of elastic (2–5 mm wide) tied into a loop. Instructions on how to play are given on Sheet 8b.

Teacher: Pendant la récréation, est-ce que tu joues aux billes?
Pupil: Oui, je joue aux billes.

Teacher: Avec qui est-ce que tu joues dans la cour?
Pupil: Je joue avec mon ami(e).

Teacher: Pourquoi est-ce que tu joues au ballon pendant la récréation?
Pupil: Je joue au ballon parce que j'aime ça.

Then pass pictures of the various playground games around the class. One pupil holds up a picture. The teacher asks him/her "À quoi est-ce que tu joues?" (What do you play?), encouraging him/her to answer, "Je joue aux cartes" or "Je joue au ballon." Carry on with the pupils asking and answering the question.

Write on the board:

Je joue **à + la** corde à sauter.	=	Je joue **à la** corde à sauter.
Je joue **à + l'**élastique.	=	Je joue **à l'**élastique.
Je joue **à + le** football.	=	Je joue **au** football.
Je joue **à + les** cartes.	=	Je joue **aux** cartes.

Ask the pupils why they think "à le" changes into "au" and "à les" changes into "aux". They might say that it is because "à le" and "à les" are too difficult to say. However, as pupils commonly make the mistake of saying and writing "à le" and "à les", we have designed a memory trick to help.

The world is divided in two: there are men and women. In the same way, the French language is divided in two: there are masculine and feminine nouns. Now, let us imagine a French woman complaining about how men are untidy and never help around the home, and saying that she wishes she could change men. Well, in French, at least, the male word can get changed since "à le" becomes "au". Remember that in the word "les" there is "le", so "à les" changes into "au + x = aux".

Use the pictures showing different games. Point at a flashcard and then ask one of the pupils if they play that game. For example, if you are holding the card with the elastic on it, ask "Christine, est-ce que tu joues à l'élastique?" Wait for the pupil to respond, "Oui, je joue à l'élastique" or "Non, je ne joue pas à l'élastique". Then show another game, such as "les cartes" and encourage him/her to ask another pupil of if he/she plays that game, "David, est-ce que tu joues aux cartes?" You could do this as a Mexican wave. Continue until every pupil has been asked a question.

Give each pupil a copy of Sheet 8c. Ask them to fill in the gaps with "à la", "à l'", "au" or "aux".

Jouer à un sport

To play a sport

Hold up a picture of a sport, for example a boy playing football, and say: "Il joue au football." Then ask the class questions about the game:

Teacher: À l'école, est-ce que vous jouez au football?
Pupils: Oui, nous jouons au football./ Non, nous ne jouons pas au football.

Teacher: Est-ce que c'est un sport amusant?
Pupils: Oui, c'est un sport amusant./ Non, ce n'est pas un sport amusant.

Then introduce some more sports and ask more questions:

Teacher: Pendant la récréation, est-ce que tu joues au tennis?
Pupil: Non, je ne joue pas au tennis pendant la récréation car ce n'est pas possible.

Then pass the pictures around the class. One pupil holds up a picture. Another pupil asks the pupil holding the picture, "À quoi est-ce que tu joues?" (What are you playing?) the first pupil should reply, "Je joue au hockey" or "Je joue au basket."

Write at least four examples of ball sports on the board. For example:

Je joue au football.	I play football.
Je joue au rugby.	I play rugby.
Je joue au hockey.	I play hockey.
Je joue au cricket.	I play cricket.
Je joue au basket.	I play basketball.
Je joue au tennis.	I play tennis.
Je joue au ping-pong.	I play table tennis.
Je joue au golf.	I play golf.
Je joue au volleyball.	I play volleyball.
Je joue au badminton.	I play badminton.

Vocabulaire

je joue au football	I play football
je joue au rugby	I play rugby
je joue au hockey	I play hockey
je joue au cricket	I play cricket
je joue au basket	I play basketball
je joue au tennis	I play tennis
je joue au ping-pong	I play table tennis
je joue au badminton	I play badminton
Levez la main	Raise your hand
quand	when
le lundi	every Monday

Materials

★ Pictures of people playing the sports listed in the Vocabulaire list
★ Sheet 8d (page 165)
★ Tableau d'honneur (page 314)
★ Stickers (optional)

Ask the pupils why we always say "au" in front of all these sports. You could repeat the previous memory trick and add the following one.

We say "au" before a sport which involves a ball. Remember that a ball is round like the letter "o". We say the sound "o" before the sport, but write "au": "Je joue au tennis."

Draw a table on the board entitled "Les sports" with two columns. In the first column, write the name of a sport. Then tell the class that you are going to do a survey of the sports that they play. Tell them, for example, "Levez la main si vous jouez au football" ("Put your hand up if you play football"). You may need to mime putting your hand up. Count the number of hands (in French) and write the number on the board.

Then encourage a pupil who plays that sport, "Thomas, quand est-ce que tu joues au football?" "Avec qui est-ce que tu joues au football?" "Pourquoi est-ce que tu joues au football?" Encourage all the pupils to listen carefully as you will check later to see if they remember the answers by asking them questions such as: "Est-ce que Thomas joue au football avec son père?" "Est-ce que Thomas joue au football pendant la semaine ou pendant le week-end?" etc. Then do the same with other sports.

Les Sports

Football	23
Hockey	12
Rugby	14
Basket	1
Tennis	16
Ping-pong	5
Cricket	14

Divide the class into pairs. Say that now they must interview each other about the sports that they play. Ask each pupil to write down five questions to ask the interviewee. Once they have their list of questions, they interview their partner. Once they have asked all their questions, they swap roles. Walk around the class listening to the conversations and award a "Tableau d'Honneur" or a sticker to pairs that are working well.

A sample role play:

Est-ce que tu joues au tennis?
Oui, je joue au tennis.

Quand est-ce que tu joues au tennis?
Je joue au tennis le lundi.

Avec qui est-ce que tu joues au tennis?
Je joue au tennis avec mon frère Eddie.

Est-ce que tu joues au hockey?
Non, je ne joue pas au hockey.

Où est-ce que tu joues au rugby?
Je joue au rugby à l'école.

Tell the pupils that you will choose the best ones to present to the rest of the class.

Give each pupil a copy of Sheet 8d and ask them to fill in the gaps with "à la", "à l' ", "au" or "aux". Ask what do all the sentences have in common? Which memory trick does this sheet remind you of?

Famous sports people
Ask the pupils to find out about some famous French sportsmen and sportswomen, such as Yannick Noah, Thierry Henry, Zidane, Alain Prost, Marie-Josée Pérec, Jeannie Longo, Michel Platini, etc. During the following lesson, ask some pupils to present, in English or in French, their famous French player in front of the entire class.

Jouer d'un instrument musical

To play an instrument

Write "Je joue de" on the board. Say that in French if you want to say that you play a musical instrument you use "Je joue de". Then write on the board:

Je joue **de + la** guitare. = Je joue **de la** guitare.
Je joue **de + l'**orgue. = Je joue **de l'**orgue.
Je joue **de + le** piano. = Je joue **du** piano.
Je joue **de + les** percussions. = Je joue **des** percussions.

Ask the pupils why they think "de le" changes into "du" and "de les" changes into "des". They might say that it is because "de la" and "de les" are too difficult to say. However, as pupils commonly make the mistake of writing and saying "de le" and "de les", we have designed a memory trick to help.

Vocabulaire

je joue d'un instrument musical	I play a musical instrument
le piano	the piano
l'orgue (m)	the organ
la guitare	the guitar
le violon	the violin
la clarinette	the clarinet
la flûte	the flute
la flûte à bec	the recorder
la trompette	the trumpet
l'accordéon (m)	the accordion
les percussions	percussion instruments

Materials

★ Sheet 8e (page 166)
★ Tableau d'honneur (page 314)
★ Stickers (optional)

The world is divided in two: there are men and women. In the same way, the French language is divided in two: there are masculine and feminine nouns. Now, let us imagine a French woman complaining about how men are untidy and never help around the home, and saying that she wishes she could change men. Well, in French, at least, the male word can get changed since "de le" becomes "du".

Ask pupils what sort of instrument they play, encouraging them to respond. If they don't recognize the name of the instrument, try miming it.

| Teacher: | Est-ce que tu joues du violon? |
| Pupil: | Oui, je joue du violon./ Non, je ne joue pas du violon. |

Teacher:	Est-ce que tu joues du piano?
	Est-ce que tu joues de la guitare?
	Est-ce que tu joues de la clarinette?
	Est-ce que tu joues de la flûte?
	Est-ce que tu joues de l'orgue?
	Est-ce que tu joues de la trompette?
	Est-ce que tu joues des percussions?

If they do not play an instrument they should say, "Je ne joue pas d'instruments."

Draw a table on the board entitled "Les instruments de musique dans notre classe" with two columns. In the first column, write the name of a musical instrument. Then tell the class that you are going to do a survey of the instruments that they play. Tell them, "Levez la main si vous jouez de la guitare" ("Put your hand up if you play the guitar"). You may need to mime putting your hand up. Count the number of hands (in French) and write the number on the board. Then encourage a pupil who does not play that instrument to ask a question to a pupil who does, for example: "Emma, quand est-ce que tu joues de la guitare?" "Pourquoi est-ce que tu joues de la guitare?" Encourage all the pupils to listen carefully as you will check later if they remember the answers by asking them questions such as: "Est-ce qu'Emma joue de la guitare le mercredi?" "Est-ce qu'Emma joue de la guitare pendant la semaine ou pendant le week-end?", etc. Then do the same with other instruments.

Les instruments

Piano	5
Flûte	12
Guitare	3
Violon	6

Divide the class into pairs. Say that now they must interview each other about the instruments that they play. Ask each pupil to write down five questions to ask the interviewee. Once they have made their list of questions, they should interview the pupil. Once they have asked all their questions and listened to the answers, they should swap roles. Walk around the class listening to the conversations and award a "Tableau d'Honneur" or a sticker to pairs that are working well.

An example role play:

Est-ce que tu joues du piano?
Oui, je joue du piano.

Quand est-ce que tu joues du piano?
Je joue du piano chaque jour.

Où est-ce que tu joues du piano?
Je joue chez moi.

Est-ce que tu joues du piano avec un professeur à l'école?
Non, je joue du piano avec ma mère.

Est-ce que tu joues des percussions?
Non, je ne joue pas des percussions.

Walk around the classroom listening to the conversations. Reward the pupils by giving them a "Tableau d'Honneur" or a sticker.

Give each pupil a copy of Sheet 8e and ask them to fill in the gaps with the names of the instruments.

Famous musicians

Ask the pupils to find out about famous French composers such as Berlioz, Bizet, Camille Saint-Saëns, Erik Satie or French musicians and singers such as Jean-Jacques Goldman, Edith Piaf and Chantal Goya (who sings songs for children). Why don't you listen to some French music in the class?

Hexagonie story

Give each pupil a copy of Sheet 8f. Read it and discuss with the pupils the points covered.

Materials
★ Sheet 8f (page 167)

Materials

★ CD, Track 31
★ Sheet 8g (page 168)

J'aime le sport

I like/love sports

Listen to Track 31 on the CD, which is a conversation between two children: Isabelle and Bruno. You may follow along using Sheet 8g if you so wish. Here is a translation of the conversation.

Bruno:	Hello Isabelle.	Bonjour Isabelle.
Isabelle:	Hello Bruno.	Bonjour Bruno.
Bruno:	How are you today?	Comment vas-tu aujourd'hui?
Isabelle:	I am very well, and you?	Je vais très bien, et toi?
Bruno:	Me too. Do you love sports?	Moi aussi. Est-ce que tu aimes le sport?
Isabelle:	Yes, of course!	Oui, bien sûr!
Bruno:	In general what do you play at your school?	En général, à quoi est-ce que vous jouez à ton école?
Isabelle:	Boys play football but they don't play rugby and girls play volleyball.	Les garçons jouent au football mais ils ne jouent pas au rugby et les filles jouent au volleyball.
Bruno:	In my school, boys play football, rugby and cricket and the girls play badminton.	Dans mon école, les garçons jouent au football, au rugby et au cricket et les filles jouent au badminton.
Isabelle:	Would you like to play tennis with me?	Est-ce que tu voudrais jouer au tennis avec moi?
Bruno:	Why not?	Pourquoi pas?

Ask pupils questions about the conversation to ensure understanding.

Divide the pupils into pairs and ask them to devise a role-play along the lines of the one they have just heard, with one of them pretending to be a French child and the other playing an English child. Go round the class, listening to their role plays, correcting where necessary and giving lots of praise.

Essential words and phrases

At the end of this unit, give the pupils Sheet 8h, which will help them to remember essential words and phrases.

Materials

★ Sheet 8h (page 169)

Au revoir! Bonne semaine! Bon week-end!

Remember always to wish the pupils a good week or weekend. Wait for them to reply "Merci Madame/Monsieur, vous aussi."

Nom:_____ **La date:**_____

Regarde et écris

Look at each picture then find the correct verb to match it from the list below. Use the correct form of the verb.

regarder, cuisiner, écouter, parler, danser, chanter, jouer, dessiner, téléphoner

Il ....

Elle ....

Ils ....

Il ....

Elle ....

Elles ....

Ils ....

Il ....

Elles ....

Nom:_____   **La date:**_____

L'élastique

French elastic or French skipping

You will need:	a really long, thin piece of elastic (about 3 metres long), tied together to make a loop
	3 players

How to play:

1. Two players stand inside the loop so that they stretch it relatively taut around their ankles.

2. The third player must jump and land as follows:

Jump 1: Land with left foot outside the elastic loop and right foot inside.	Jump 2: Land with both feet together inside the elastic loop.

Jump 3: Land with both feet outside the elastic loop.	Jump 4: Land sideways to the elastic, with the left foot on top of one elastic and the right foot on top of the other.
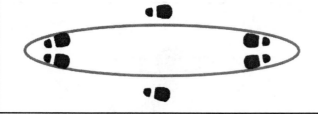	

3. After a player manages to do all the jumps successfully, the elastic is raised to knee level and the jumps are repeated. Then it is raised to thighs, waists, and the real challenge, chests!

4. If a player doesn't manage to do a jump, play passes to one of the players holding the elastic, who tries to outdo the previous player.

Nom:_____   **La date:**_____

Regarde et écris

Look at the pictures and then fill in the gaps with "à la", "à l' ", "au" or "aux".

Je joue…… cartes.

Je joue……. marelle.

Je joue…… élastique.

Je joue……ballon.

Je joue…… billes.

Je joue…… corde.

Nom: _____   **La date:** _____

Regarde et écris

Find the missing word.

Il joue _____ football.

Il joue _____ rugby.

Elle joue _____ tennis.

Il joue _____ basket.

Il joue _____ golf.

Ils jouent _____ ping-pong.

Il joue _____ cricket.

Il joue _____ hockey.

Elles jouent _____ volleyball.

Nom:_____ **La date:**_____

Regarde et écris

Look at the pictures and fill in the gaps.

Elle joue du

_____.

Il joue du

_____.

Il joue de la

_____.

Ils jouent de la

_____.

Elle joue de la

_____.

Ils jouent de la

_____.

Il joue des

_____.

Il joue de la

_____.

Elle joue de

l'_____.

Vocabulaire

le piano	the piano	la flûte	the flute	les percussions	percussion
la trompette	the trumpet	la flûte à bec	the recorder		instruments
la clarinette	the clarinet	l'accordéon	the accordion		
la guitare	the guitar	le violon	the violin		

Nom:_____   **La date:**_____

Jouer's lucky day

King Être and Queen Avoir asked the joyful verb "Jouer" (to play) to entertain all the guests with games and music at their midsummer party. The party was a real success and finished very late in the night.

Jouer returned home absolutely exhausted. Unfortunately, the following day he had to wake up very early to play a football match. So he set up his alarm clock and went to bed. When the alarm clock rang, Jouer turned it off, but fell back to sleep straight away. He woke up a few hours later, only to realize that he had missed the match. He felt dreadful and called his best friend "Gagner" (to win), who told him not to worry as the match had been cancelled because of the very bad weather. Jouer felt so relieved that he invited all the players to come to his house to play. The players were very excited to go to Jouer's house because Jouer had lots of games in his house.

Jouer was very proud of his unusual house, which he had designed himself. As he really liked playing with balls, he made the house in the shape of the letter "O" which reminded him of the shape of a ball. The house was round, like a big letter "O", with round windows and round doors, and in front of it stood a big round statue displaying all of his favourite types of balls. On the statue was engraved a very long list of all the ball sports Jouer liked to play. Before each sport he wrote the word "au" because it sounded like "O" which reminded him of a ball. This is what you could read: "je joue au tennis, au golf, au rugby, au football, au cricket, au volleyball," and the list went on and on. How impressive!

All the players were happy to see Jouer and fortunately had no idea he had overslept. They all played together for hours and in the end, what could have been a dreadful day for Jouer turned out to be a lucky one.

Nom:_____   **La date:**_____

Lis  et écoute 🎧

Read and listen to the following conversation between two children:
Isabelle and Bruno.

Bonjour Isabelle

Bonjour Bruno,

Comment vas-tu aujourd'hui?

_____

Je vais très bien, et toi?

Moi aussi. Est-ce que tu aimes le sport?

Oui, bien sûr!

_____

En général, à quoi est-ce que vous jouez à ton école?

Les garçons jouent au football mais ils ne jouent pas au rugby et les filles jouent au volleyball.

Dans mon école, les garçons jouent au football, au rugby et au cricket et les filles jouent au badminton.

_____

Est-ce que tu voudrais jouer au tennis avec moi?

Pourquoi pas?

Nom:_____   **La date:**_____

Essential words and phrases

How to say you play a sport

Most sports are masculine and we need to say "jouer au" in front of them:

Je joue **au** tennis.	I play tennis.
Je joue **au** football.	I play football.
Je joue **au** golf.	I play golf.
Je joue **au** cricket.	I play cricket.
Je joue **au** rugby.	I play rugby.

How to say you play an instrument

jouer de + le	=	jouer **du**
jouer de + la	=	jouer **de la**
jouer de + l'	=	jouer **de l'**
jouer de + les	=	jouer **des**

Je joue **de la** flûte.	I play the flute.
Je joue **de la** clarinette.	I play the clarinet.
Je joue **de la** guitare.	I play the guitar.
Je joue **de la** flûte à bec.	I play the recorder.
Je joue **du** violon.	I play the violin.
Je joue **du** piano.	I play the piano.
Je joue **de l'**accordéon.	I play the accordion.
Je joue **de l'**orgue.	I play the organ.
Je joues **des** percussions.	I play percussions.

Unit
9

Time flies

Key teaching points/vocabulary

Numbers 20–100
Telling the time
"Commencer" ("to start") in the present tense
"Terminer" ("to finish") in the present tense
"Petit déjeuner", "déjeuner" and "dîner" ("breakfast", "lunch" and "dinner")

Bonjour

Say "Bonjour" to the whole class, waiting for the pupils to reply "Bonjour Madame/Monsieur." Call the register in French and expect every pupil to respond "présent(e)" when their name is called out. When you have no answer say "absent(e)". Call out the name of a pupil and ask him/her, "Comment vas-tu?" waiting for his/her answer "Je vais bien, merci." Ask other pupils how they are. Encourage the pupil to ask you "et vous?" then answer with "Je vais bien merci" or "Je vais bien aujourd'hui car je ne suis pas fatigué(e)." Encourage pupils to use adjectives in their replies.

Recap the verb "jouer" in the present tense

Give each pupil a minute or two to think of a question they can ask using the verb "jouer". Then perform a Mexican wave where one pupil asks another a question using "jouer". After the second pupil has answered, the second pupil asks another student of his or her choice another question.

> Est-ce que tu joues au tennis?

> Oui, je joue au tennis chaque mardi

Les nombres 20–30

Numbers

Test pupils on the numbers 0 to 20 using cards. Hold up a number then wait for the class to say the number out loud.

Then hold up the following numbers on flashcards and ask the pupils to repeat them after you.

20	vingt
21	vingt et un
22	vingt-deux
23	vingt-trois
24	vingt-quatre
25	vingt-cinq
26	vingt-six
27	vingt-sept
28	vingt-huit
29	vingt-neuf
30	trente

Tell the pupils that you are going to call out numbers between one and thirty by saying, "Montrez-moi le numéro...". When the pupils hear a number, they must write that number down on a mini-whiteboard or a piece of paper and hold it up.

Ask the pupils to count up to 30 together as a class. Ask for volunteers to count to 30 by themselves.

Vocabulaire

les nombres	the numbers
vingt	twenty
vingt et un	twenty one
vingt-deux	twenty two
vingt-trois	twenty three
vingt-quatre	twenty four
vingt-cinq	twenty five
vingt-six	twenty six
vingt-sept	twenty seven
vingt-huit	twenty eight
vingt-neuf	twenty nine
trente	thirty
Montrez-moi	Show me
le numéro	the number

Materials

★ Cards with the numbers 0 to 30
★ Mini-whiteboards or several pieces of paper for each pupil

Encore des nombres

More numbers

Hold up the card of 30 and say "trente" to the class. Say the number again, then encourage the class to repeat it back to you. Repeat for the following numbers:

30	trente
40	quarante
50	cinquante
60	soixante
70	soixante-dix
80	quatre-vingts
90	quatre-vingt-dix

Then hold up the cards in a random order and ask the pupils to say the number.

Vocabulaire

trente	thirty
quarante	fourty
cinquante	fifty
soixante	sixty
soixante-dix	seventy
quatre-vingts	eighty
quatre-vingt-dix	ninety
cent	one hundred
zéro	zero

Materials

★ Cards for numbers 30, 40, 50, 60, 70, 80 and 90

Write the following numbers on the board underlining the parts of each word that are the same, as shown below:

3	<u>tr</u>ois	30	<u>tr</u>ente
4	<u>quatre</u>	40	<u>quar</u>an<u>te</u>
5	<u>cinq</u>	50	<u>cinq</u>uante
6	<u>six</u>	60	so<u>ix</u>ante

Explain that the numbers 70, 80 and 90 are made up of other smaller numbers.

70 (soixante-dix) is made up from
60 (soixante) + 10 (dix)

80 (quatre-vingts) is made up from
4 (quatre) x 20 (vingt)

90 (quatre-vingt-dix) is made up from
4 (quatre) x 20 (vingt) + 10 (dix)

Call out different numbers at random between 1 and 30 as well as 40, 50 and 60 by saying, "Montrez-moi le numéro..." and ask the pupils to write the number on a mini-whiteboard or a piece of paper and hold it up.

Vocabulaire

trente et un	thirty-one
trente-deux	thirty-two
trente-trois	thirty-three
zéro	zero

Materials

★ Sheet 9a (page 183)

Encore plus de nombres

Even more numbers

Once the pupils are familiar with the numbers 1 to 30 plus the tens they will soon be able to count up to 99.

31	trente et un
32	trente-deux
33	trente-trois

Ask the pupils if they can guess how to say 34 in French. If they say "trente-quatre" congratulate them with an enthusiastic "Bravo" or a "Très bien". Say that the same pattern is used all the way through to 70. For example,

41	quarante et un
42	quarante-deux
49	quarante-neuf
51	cinquante et un
56	cinquante-six
61	soixante et un
68	soixante-huit

Count with the pupils from 30 to 69.

To say 71 though, you have to say "soixante et onze" (60 + 11). For example:

70	soixante-dix	(60 + 10)
71	soixante et onze	(60 + 11)
72	soixante-douze	(60 + 12)
73	soixante-treize	(60 + 13)

Count with the pupils from 70 to 79.

From 80 to 99, you have to say "quatre-vingts" plus a number. For example,

80	quatre-vingts	(4 x 20)
81	quatre-vingt-un	(4 x 20 + 1)
82	quatre-vingt-deux	(4 x 20 + 2)
88	quatre-vingt-huit	(4 x 20 + 8)
89	quatre-vingt-neuf	(4 x 20 + 9)
90	quatre-vingt-dix	(4 x 20 + 10)
91	quatre-vingt-onze	(4 x 20 + 11)
95	quatre-vingt-quinze	(4 x 20 + 15)
99	quatre-vingt-dix-neuf	(4 x 20 + 19)

Count with the pupils from 80 to 99.

When "vingt" is multiplied it takes an "s", quatre-vingts (4 x 20 = 80). However, whenever there is a number after "vingt", the "vingt" does not require an "s" at the end. The "s" is used to indicate that the number ends there. For example, 87: quatre-vingt-sept; 95: quatre-vingt-quinze.

Write a series of numbers on the board and encourage the pupils to say them in French.

Play a "loto" (bingo) game with the pupils. Ask each pupil to write six numbers of their choice onto a piece of paper. Call out numbers at random. The winner is the first pupil to have all his/her numbers called out and to shout "loto" (bingo). Begin with numbers between 1 and 20, then 1 and 30, then 1 and 50.

Give the pupils a copy of Sheet 9a and ask them to write out the telephone numbers.

Vocabulaire

Quelle heure est-il?	What time is it?
il est dix heures	it is ten o'clock
il est minuit	it is midnight
il est midi	it is noon
il est six heures et demie	it is half past six
il est sept heures et quart	it is a quarter past seven
il est huit heures moins le quart	it is a quarter to eight
une montre	a watch
une heure	an hour

Materials

★ A large toy clock
★ Sheets 9b–9c (pages 184–185)
★ Je suis désolé(e)… (page 315)
★ CD, Track 32

Quelle heure est-il?

What time is it?

Point at your watch and ask a pupil the following question, "Quelle heure est-il?" The pupil may say, "Je suis désolé(e) (your name), je ne sais pas". You may need to hold up the flashcard with this sentence on to remind the pupil.

Position the hands on the toy clock so that it says 10 o'clock. Say "Quelle heure est-il?", then answer the question by saying "Il est dix heures". Move the hour hand on the clock to read 4 o'clock. Ask, "Quelle heure est-il?" and answer your own question by saying, "Il est quatre heures."

Then move the hour hand on the clock to 5 o'clock. Ask the class, "Quelle heure est-il?" This time wait for the class to respond, "Il est cinq heures." Move the hands on the clock and ask the class "Quelle heure est-il?" and wait for their reply. You could then ask individual pupils what the time is.

Move the hour on the clock to 12 o'clock. Say, "Il est douze heures. Il est midi."

Tell the pupils that the French write the time with an "h" (short for "heure") between the hour and the minutes.

 Write examples of times on the board and encourage the pupils to tell you the time:

10h00   Il est dix heures.
7h00   Il est sept heures.

Now move the hands of the clock to point at ten minutes past 5 o'clock on your toy clock and repeat twice, "Il est cinq heures dix". Tell the pupils that in French we always say the hour first, before the minutes. You could tell them that it is because the hours are more important than the minutes. Then move the hands of the clock to point at twenty past 5 o'clock and repeat twice, "Il est cinq heures vingt". Then move the hands of the cardboard clock and ask individual pupils, "Quelle heure est-il?" encouraging them to answer.

Examples:
7h20   Il est sept heures vingt.
12h25   Il est douze heures vingt-cinq ou
Il est midi vingt-cinq.
10h05   Il est dix heures cinq.
5h10   Il est cinq heures dix.
4h05   Il est quatre heures cinq.

Now move the hands of the cardboard clock to point at ten minutes to 5 o'clock. Say, "Il est cinq heures moins dix". Move the hands to twenty-five minutes to 2 o'clock and say, "Il est deux heures moins vingt-cinq".

Then move the hands on the clock and ask individual pupils, "Quelle heure est-il?"

Examples:

8h35	Il est neuf heures moins vingt-cinq.
10h55	Il est onze heures moins cinq.
7h35	Il est huit heures moins vingt-cinq.
12h40	Il est une heure moins vingt.

Now, move the hands of the clock to quarter past 5. Say, "Il est cinq heures et quart." Then move the hands to a quarter to 5 and say, "Il est cinq heures moins le quart".

Practise these times with the pupils:

5h15	Il est cinq heures et quart.
6h15	Il est six heures et quart.
5h45	Il est six heures moins le quart.
6h45	Il est sept heures moins le quart.
7h45	Il est huit heures moins le quart.

Then move the hands on the clock to half past 5 and say, "Il est cinq heures et demie." Move the hands again to half past 8 and say, "Il est huit heures et demie."

Practise these times with the pupils:

5h30	Il est cinq heures et demie.
6h30	Il est six heures et demie.
9h30	Il est neuf heures et demie.
12h30	Il est midi et demi.

Note:
"Demi" in "il est midi et demi" doesn't have a final "e" as "midi" is considered masculine.

Give the pupils a copy of Sheet 9b and ask them to draw the hands showing the correct time on the clock.

Give the pupils a copy of Sheet 9c. Listen to Track 32 on the CD and ask the pupils to draw the hands on the clock to show the times announced on the CD.

Hexagonie story

Give the pupils a copy of Sheet 9d and read the story with them. Discuss it to reinforce the issues raised in the story.

Materials

★ Sheet 9d (page 186)

Vocabulaire

du matin	in the morning
de l'après midi	in the afternon
du soir	in the evening

Materials

★ Large toy clock
★ Sheet 9e (page 187)

The 24-hour clock

Tell the pupils that the 24-hour clock is widely used in France. The French write times with an "h" (short for heure) between the hour and the minutes.

When using the 24-hour clock, if you are talking about a time in the afternoon, then you can only use numbers (not "et quart", "et demie" or "moins le quart").

Examples:

13h15	Il est treize heures quinze. (Do not say treize heures et quart.)
19h30	Il est dix-neuf heures trente. (Do not say dix-neuf heures et demi.)
21h45	Il est vingt et une heure quarante-cinq. (Do not say vingt-deux heures moins le quart.)

Write on the board various times for the pupils to practise saying the time using the 24-hour clock.

Tell the pupils that if they do not want to use the 24-hour clock, they must say "du matin" for "in the morning" (for example, 7:00 am would be "Il est sept heures du matin"). To say "in the afternoon", they should say "de l'après-midi" (for example, 5:00 pm would be "Il est cinq heures de l'après-midi"). For "in the evening" they need to say, "du soir" (for example, 8:00 pm would be "Il est huit heures du soir".)

 Pass the clock to one of the pupils and ask him/her to move the hands to a time of his/her choice. The pupil then asks another, "Marianne, quelle heure est-il?" The pupil replies and then the clock is passed to the responder. The second pupil sets a time and then asks "Mark, quelle heure est-il?" etc.

 Give Sheet 9e to the pupils and ask them to write out the times in numerals.

Commencer et terminer

To start and to finish

Say to the class, "Pendant la semaine, je commence mon travail à 8 heures et demie et je termine mon travail à 15 heures trente". "Je commence la leçon de français avec vous à (time) et je termine la leçon de français avec vous à (time)."

Ask individual pupils questions such as:

Teacher: À quelle heure est-ce que tu commences tes leçons?
À quelle heure est-ce que tu termines tes leçons?
À quelle heure est-ce que ton père commence son travail?

Give Sheet 9f to the pupils. Ask them to write down five questions about the time they would like to ask the class. Once they have worked out their questions, get one pupil to ask a question in front of the class. Then choose another pupil to answer it. Go around the class giving everyone a chance to ask at least one of their questions.

Point out the presence of a cedilla (ç) in "nous commençons" to create the sound "s" (as in "français").

Vocabulaire	
commencer	to start
terminer	to finish

Materials

★ Sheet 9f (page 188)

Le petit déjeuner

Breakfast

Tell the pupils that in French for every meal we use different expressions. For breakfast, the French say that they "take breakfast": "Je prends mon petit déjeuner" ("I take my breakfast)". Insist on the fact that pupils cannot say: "J'ai mon petit déjeuner" ("I have my breakfast").

Say that shortly they will listen to some sentences in French about a teacher having breakfast. She will say a new phrase, "la plupart du temps", which means "most of the time". She will also say a new word "vers", which means "about". Write "la plupart du temps" and "vers" on the board to help the pupils remember.

Tell the pupils that they are going to listen twice (or as many times as necessary) to the passage. Pupils may want to make some notes. Say that you will ask them questions about it afterwards.

Le matin à 7 heures 15, je mange. Je prends mon petit déjeuner. Pendant la semaine, je prends mon petit déjeuner seule car je mange rapidement. Pendant le week-end, je prends mon petit déjeuner avec ma

Vocabulaire	
je prends	I take
elle prend	she takes
elle mange	she eats
le petit déjeuner	breakfast
la plupart du temps	most of the time
vers	about
vers 2 heures	at about 2 o'clock
je prépare	I prepare
seul(e)	alone
rapidement	quickly
un élève	a pupil

Materials

★ CD, Track 33

famille. La plupart du temps, je prépare le petit déjeuner vers 7 heures. Je ne prends pas le petit déjeuner avec mes élèves car je ne prends pas le petit déjeuner à l'école.

Questions you could ask:

Teacher:	À quelle heure est-ce qu'elle prend le petit déjeuner?
Pupil:	Elle prend le petit déjeuner à sept heures et quart.
Teacher:	Pendant la semaine, est-ce qu'elle prend le petit déjeuner avec ses élèves?
Pupil:	Non, elle ne prend pas le petit déjeuner avec ses élèves car elle prend son petit déjeuner seule.
Teacher:	Pourquoi est-ce qu'elle prend le petit déjeuner seule pendant la semaine?
Pupil:	Parce qu'elle mange rapidement.
Teacher:	Quand est-ce qu'elle prend le petit déjeuner avec sa famille?
Pupil:	Elle prend le petit déjeuner avec sa famille pendant le week-end.

Vocabulaire

je prends	I take
tu prends	you take
il/elle prend	he/she takes

Materials

★ Sheet 9g (page 189)

Prendre

To take

Write on the board the verb "prendre" with je, tu and il/elle:

Je prends
Tu prends
Il/elle prend

Say that "prends" and "prend" are pronounced the same.

9g

Give pupils a copy of Sheet 9g and ask them to answer the questions.

Le déjeuner et le dîner

Lunch and dinner

Tell the pupils that for lunch, the French do not say "I have lunch" but "I lunch". "Déjeuner" is an "er" verb.

Ask the pupils to say the verb "déjeuner" in all its forms: je déjeune, tu déjeunes, il/elle déjeune, nous déjeunons, vous déjeunez, ils/elles déjeunent.

Tell the pupils that they are going to listen twice to some sentences in French. Ask them questions afterwards to check that they understand what it means.

À midi, je mange. Je déjeune. Pendant la semaine, je travaille à l'école, je déjeune avec mes collègues à la cantine. Pendant le week-end je ne travaille pas, et je déjeune chez moi. En général, je ne déjeune pas avec mes élèves car je n'ai pas le temps.

Questions you could ask:

Teacher: Quand est-ce qu'elle déjeune?
Quand est-ce qu'elle travaille?
Pendant la semaine, où est-ce qu'elle déjeune?
Est-ce qu'elle travaille pendant le week-end?
Où est-ce qu'elle déjeune pendant le week-end?

Divide the pupils in pairs. Give pupils a copy of Sheet 9h and ask them to think of five questions to ask their partner using the verb "déjeuner". The first pupil asks his/her questions and the second pupil answers them. Then they swap roles.

Tell the pupils that for dinner, the French do not say "I have dinner" but "I dine". Say that "dîner" is an "er" verb. Ask the pupils to say all the forms of the verb "dîner": je dîne, tu dînes, il/elle dîne, nous dînons, vous dînez, ils/elles dînent.

Tell the pupils that they are going to listen to what a French person says about meals. Say that the speaker will use the new expressions, "d'habitude", which means "usually", and "souvent", which means "often".

Le soir, je mange. Le soir, je dîne. D'habitude, je dîne chez moi avec ma famille. Nous dînons vers 19 heures car avant nous sommes occupés. Pendant le week-end, nous dînons souvent avec nos amis, chez nous ou chez eux.

Vocabulaire

déjeuner	to lunch
dîner	to dine
d'habitude	usually
souvent	often
avant	before
un/une collègue	a colleague
une cantine	a canteen
le temps	the time

Materials

★ Sheet 9h (page 190)
★ Sheet 9i (page 191)
★ CD, Tracks 34–35

"D'habitude" means "usually". If it is usual, it is a habit.

"Souvent" means "often". When you write the letter "f" by hand, it can look like an "s" and "s" is the first letter of "souvent". Both words have the letters o, e, n and t in common.

Play the track twice, then ask pupils to translate what has been said, one sentence at a time. Afterwards, ask the pupils questions to ensure that they have understood. For example:

Teacher: Quand est-ce qu'elle dîne?
            Où est-ce qu'elle dîne?
            D'habitude, avec qui est-ce qu'elle dîne?
            Pendant le week-end, avec qui est-ce qu'elle dîne?
            Pourquoi est-ce qu'elle ne dîne pas avant (before) 19 heures?

9i

You will need to have several Cootie Catchers (sometimes called a "fortune teller" or a "Chinese counter") made from sheet 9i. You could give the pupils a copy of the sheet and ask them to bring it to the next class.

Divide the pupils into pairs. Pupils take turns at being the Cootie Master. The Cootie Master holds the cootie-catcher and starts the game by asking "Quel numéro?" The Cootie Master then opens and closes the cootie catcher that number of times while counting out loud, "un, deux, trois" etc. When the Cootie Master has stopped counting, the other player must look inside and choose "(le) matin", "(l')après-midi", "(la) nuit" or "(le) soir". Then the Cootie Master must count how many letters that word contains and open and close the cootie catcher that number of times (so they would open and close it five times for "(le) matin"). Once the Cootie Master has stopped counting in French, the player must look inside the cootie catcher and choose again from "(le) matin", "(l')après-midi", "(la) nuit" or "(le) soir". The Cootie Master then flips up the panel with the chosen word on it and reads out the question to their partner who has to answer it in French.

De quelle heure à quelle heure...?

From what time until what time...?

Vocabulaire

de quelle heure à quelle heure...?	from what time until what time...?

Tell the pupils that you are going to say some sentences in French. To ensure that the pupils understand, you may need to mime.

Je travaille de 8 heures 30 à 15 heures 30.	I work from 8.30 am to 3.30 pm.
Je prends mon petit déjeuner de 7 heures 15 à 7 heures 30.	I have breakfast from 7.15 am to 7.30 am.
Pendant la semaine, je déjeune de midi à midi trente.	During the week, I have lunch from twelve to twelve thirty.
Pendant le week-end, je regarde la télé de 20 heures à 23 heures.	During the weekend, I watch television from 8.00 pm to 11.00 pm.

Then ask the pupils individual questions, such as:

De quelle heure à quelle heure est-ce que tu as une leçon de français avec moi aujourd'hui?
(From what time to what time do you have a French lesson with me today?)

De quelle heure à quelle heure est-ce que tu es à l'école?
(From what time to what time are you at school?)

De quelle heure à quelle heure est-ce que tu déjeunes à la cantine?
(From what time to what time do you lunch in the canteen?)

Durer

To last

Say the following sentences to the class and ask them to guess what the verb "durer" means:

Ma leçon de français avec vous commence à 10 heures et se termine à 11 heures. En conséquence, ma leçon avec vous **dure** une heure.

Je prends mon petit déjeuner de 7 heures 15 à 7 heures 30. En conséquence, mon petit déjeuner **dure** 15 minutes.

Tell them that "durer" means "to last".

 Something which lasts, has a "duration".

Vocabulaire

durer	to last
en conséquence	therefore
un film	a film

Materials

★ Sheet 9j (page 192)

Ask individual pupils the following questions:

Teacher: Le film commence à 8 heures et se termine à 10 heures. Combien de temps dure le film? Une heure, deux heures, ou trois heures?

Monsieur Villeray commence son travail à 9 heures et termine son travail à 18 heures. Combien de temps dure son travail?

Est-ce que la leçon de français dure une heure ou deux heures?

Tell the pupils that if you want to say "an hour and a half" in French, you say, "une heure et demie". But if you want to say half an hour, you say "une demi-heure". To remember whether or not to put an "e" on the end of "demie" you might find that the following memory trick helps.

Une demi-heure

Because the feminine noun "heure" is not mentioned before "demi", the word "demi" can not agree with a noun that has not appeared yet.

Une heure et demie

Because the feminine noun "heure" is already mentioned before "demi", the word "demi" has to agree with it and becomes "demie".

Give each pupil a copy of Sheet 9j. Ask them to answer the questions, which will help them to recap on all the time-related phrases they have learned in this unit.

Resources

★ Sheet 9k (page 193)

Essential words and phrases

At the end of this unit, give the pupils Sheet 9k, which will help them to remember essential words and phrases.

Au revoir! Bonne semaine! Bon week-end!

Remember always to wish the pupils a good week or weekend. Wait for them to reply "Merci Madame/Monsieur, vous aussi."

Nom:_____ **La date:**_____

Lis et écris

A French person has listed some phone numbers in French. Write out the numbers in figures.

Le téléphone

When the French say a phone number, they say a pair of numbers at a time. The number for the French Tourist Office in London is: 09068 244123, but a French person would say it as:

0	90	68	24	41	23
zéro	quatre-vingt-dix	soixante-huit	vingt-quatre	quarante et un	vingt-trois

Exemple:

> zéro un, trente, soixante-dix-neuf, zéro six, quarante-quatre

01 30 79 06 44

1.
> zéro deux, soixante-dix-huit, cinquante-six, douze, trente-quatre

_____

2.
> zéro cinq, quarante-six, quatre-vingt-huit, quatre-vingt-douze, vingt

_____

3.
> zéro un, soixante-cinq, trente-trois, vingt et un, cinquante-cinq

_____

4.
> zéro deux, quatre-vingt-huit, quatre-vingt-dix, cinquante-trois, vingt-deux

_____

5.
> zéro huit, quarante-cinq, trente-trois, vingt-six, onze

_____

6.
> zéro cinq, vingt-trois, quatorze, vingt-cinq, trente-six

_____

Nom:_____   **La date:**_____

Lis et dessine

Put hands on the clock face to show the times written below.

Il est une heure.

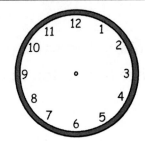

Il est une heure dix.

Il est une heure et quart.

Il est une heure vingt.

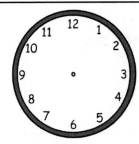

Il est une heure et demie.

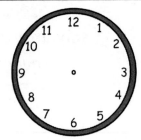

Il est deux heures moins vingt.

Il est deux heures moins le quart.

Il est deux heures moins dix.

Il est deux heures.

Il est midi.

Il est minuit.

Il est midi et demi.

Nom:_____ **La date:**_____

Écoute et dessine

Track
●
32

*Listen to Track 32 on the CD. Twelve different times will be read
out twice. Draw the hands on the clock to show the times.*

Nom:_____   **La date:**_____

Take time!

During my stay in Hexagonie I always felt that time was passing by slowly, since nobody was rushing anywhere. In fact, surprisingly, the Hexagonians always took their time.

It all started when King Être and Queen Avoir did not want the Hexagonians to rush around all the time. Therefore, they decided to have a bell in each town which would ring at different times during the day, to remind the inhabitants of special things to do.

"À 7 heures" (at 7.00 am), the bells would ring happily to welcome the new day and a voice would sing "il est 7 heures, c'est la bonne heure" (it is 7 o'clock, it is the great hour). Then the Hexagonians would get ready and go to their usual activities.

Then, "à 8 heures et quart" (at 8.15 am), "ding, dang, dong" – the bell would ring again to remind the inhabitants to walk, rather than take their car, if possible.

Then, "à midi et demi" (at 12.30 am), the bells would ring joyfully to remind the inhabitants to eat a healthy lunch so they can be strong for the afternoon ahead.

"À 6 heures moins le quart" (at 5.45 pm), there would be a nice music to remind the inhabitants to relax as the work hours were over, to get out of their car and to look out at shining stars.

"À huit heures" (at 8.00 pm), the bells would ring for the last time in the day and a voice would sing "Il est 8 heures, c'est le bonheur" (it is 8 o'clock, it is happiness) to remind the Hexagonians to be thankful for the day they have had.

I really thought this idea was great and not boring at all as every week the times and the recommendations would change.

Nom:_____ **La date:**_____

Lis et écris

Read the times and write them in figures in the French way using "h" between the hour and the minutes:

Exemple:

Vingt-deux heures trente-cinq   22h35

1. Huit heures quarante   _____

2. Dix-sept heures quinze   _____

3. Onze heures quarante-cinq   _____

4. Minuit dix   _____

5. Treize heures dix-huit   _____

6. Quatorze heures cinquante   _____

7. Douze heures cinq   _____

8. Neuf heures cinquante-cinq   _____

9. Six heures trente   _____

Lis et écris

Nom:_____ **La date:**_____

Lis 📖 et écris ✏️

Think of five questions using either "commencer" ("to start") or "terminer" ("to finish") to ask other pupils in the class.

	Commencer			**Terminer**	
Je	commenc	**e**	Je	termin	**e**
Tu	commenc	**es**	Tu	termin	**es**
Il/elle	commenc	**e**	Il/elle	termin	**e**
Nous	commenç	**ons**	Nous	termin	**ons**
Vous	commenc	**ez**	Vous	termin	**ez**
Ils/elles	commenc	**ent**	Ils/elles	termin	**ent**

Exemples:

À quelle heure est-ce que ton père commence son travail?

À quelle heure est-ce que tu commences l'école?

Questions:

1. À quelle heure est-ce que _____

2. _____

3. _____

4. _____

5. _____

Nom:_____   **La date:**_____

Lis et écris

Read through the questions and then write down the answers.

| **Prendre** |
| Je prends |
| Tu prends |
| Il/elle prend |

Exemple:
À quelle heure est-ce
que tu prends ton petit
déjeuner?
Je prends mon petit
déjeuner à 8 heures.

1. En général, à quelle heure est-ce que tu prends le petit déjeuner?

_____

2. Où est-ce que tu prends le petit déjeuner?

_____

3. Avec qui est-ce que tu prends le petit déjeuner?

_____

4. Est-ce que tu prends le petit déjeuner à l'école?

_____

5. Pendant le week-end, à quelle heure est-ce que tu prends le petit déjeuner?

_____

6. Quand est-ce que ton père prend le petit déjeuner avec toi?

_____

7. Est-ce que ta mère prend le petit déjeuner avec toi pendant le week-end?

_____

8. Est-ce que tu prends le petit déjeuner maintenant?

_____

9. Où est-ce que tu prends le petit déjeuner?

_____

10. Est-ce que tu regardes la télévision quand tu prends le petit déjeuner?

_____

Nom:_____   **La date:**_____

Lis  et écris

Read the examples, then think of five questions to ask your partner using the verb "déjeuner". Ask your partner these questions and listen to his/her answer. Then swap with your partner and answer his/her questions.

Déjeuner
Je déjeun**e**
Tu déjeun**es**
Il/elle déjeun**e**
Nous déjeun**ons**
Vous déjeun**ez**
Ils/elles déjeun**ent**

Exemples:

Pendant la semaine, où est-ce que tu déjeunes?

Est-ce que tu dejeunes au restaurant?

Questions:

1. _____

2. _____

3. _____

4. _____

5. _____

Nom:_____ **La date:**_____

Cootie catcher

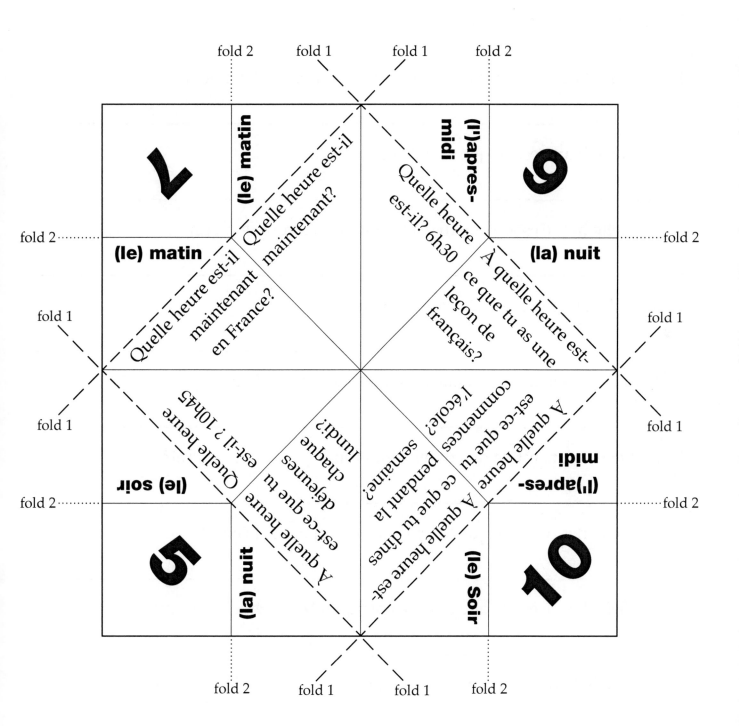

1. Fold corners **back** behind face of paper along fold 1: — — — —
2. Fold corners **inward** to centre along fold 2: ·················
3. Put the thumb and forefinger of both hands into the back of the resulting square and pinch up into a point.

Nom:_____ **La date:**_____

Lis 📖 et écris ✏️

Réponds aux questions suivantes.

1. Pendant la semaine est-ce que tu prends ton petit déjeuner à l'école?

   _____

2. À quelle heure est-ce que tu arrives à l'école?

   _____

3. À quelle heure est-ce que tu commences tes leçons le matin?

   _____

4. Tu as le français quand? À quelle heure?

   _____

5. Pendant la semaine, à quelle heure est-ce que tu déjeunes?

   _____

6. À quelle heure est-ce que tu termines ton déjeuner en général?

   _____

7. À quelle heure est-ce que tu arrives chez toi après l'école?

   _____

8. À quelle heure est-ce que tu dînes pendant la semaine? Avec qui?

   _____

9. De quelle heure à quelle heure est-ce que tu regardes la télévision?

   _____

10. En général, combien de temps dure un film à la télévision?

   _____

Nom:_____ **La date:**_____

Essential words and phrases

How to say numbers up to 99

1 un	11 onze	21 vingt et un	31 trente et un
2 deux	12 douze	22 vingt-deux	32 trente-deux
3 trois	13 treize	23 vingt-trois	33 trente-trois
4 quatre	14 quatorze	24 vingt-quatre	etc
5 cinq	15 quinze	25 vingt-cinq	40 quarante
6 six	16 seize	26 vingt-six	50 cinquante
7 sept	17 dix-sept	27 vingt-sept	60 soixante
8 huit	18 dix-huit	28 vingt-huit	70 soixante-dix
9 neuf	19 dix-neuf	29 vingt-neuf	80 quatre-vingts
10 dix	20 vingt	30 trente	90 quatre-vingt-dix

How to ask for the time

Quelle heure est-il ?

How to say the time

10h00	Il est dix heures
10h20	Il est dix heures vingt
10h40	Il est dix heures quarante ou il est onze heures moins vingt
10h15	Il est dix heures quinze ou il est dix heures et quart
10h30	Il est dix heures trente ou il est dix heures et demie
10h45	Il est dix heures quarante-cinq ou il est onze heures moins le quart
12h00	Il est douze heures ou il est midi
24h00	Il est minuit

How to say something is from one time until another

Le petit déjeuner est de 8h à 8h15   Breakfast is from 8 am to 8.15 am.

Names for the main meals   How to say you are eating a meal

le petit déjeuner	breakfast	Je prends mon petit déjeuner	I have my breakfast
le déjeuner	lunch	Je déjeune	I lunch
le dîner	dinner	Je dîne	I dine

How to ask questions about meals

À quelle heure est-ce que tu dînes?   At what time do you eat dinner?

À quelle heure est-ce que tu déjeunes?   At what time do you eat lunch?

Let's go!

Key teaching points

"Aller à" ("to go to")
Modes of transport
Days of the week

Bonjour

Say "Bonjour" to the whole class, waiting for the pupils to reply "Bonjour Madame/Monsieur." Call the register in French and expect every pupil to respond "présent(e)" when their name is called out. When you have no answer say "absent(e)". Call out the name of a pupil and ask him/her, "Comment vas-tu?" waiting for his/her answer "Je vais bien, merci." Ask other pupils how they are. Encourage the pupil to ask you "et vous?" then answer with "Je vais bien merci." Encourage pupils to use adjectives in their replies.

Materials

★ Large toy clock

Recap on the time

Indicate a time on the clock and ask the pupils, "Quelle heure est-il?" Continue with more times.

Ask the pupils to perform a Mexican wave, asking each other the time. Pass the clock to the first pupil, who moves the hands of the clock and then asks another pupil of his/her choice, '"Quelle heure est-il?" When the second pupil answers correctly, the first pupil passes them the clock for them to set a time. The second pupil then asks someone else the same question.

Quelle heure est-il?

Il est dix heures quarante.

Je vais à

I go to

Je vais à la (+ noun)

Say that "je vais" means "I go" or "I am going". If you are going to a place whose name is feminine and does not start with a vowel you say "Je vais à la...." For example:

Teacher: <u>Je vais</u> **à la** cantine,
<u>Je vais</u> **à la** boulangerie chaque jour.
<u>Je ne vais pas</u> **à la** piscine.

Other examples you could use are "la bibliothèque", "la boulangerie", "la boucherie" and "la pharmacie".

Ask the pupils to think of a sentence with "je vais" and feminine nouns in the singular starting with a consonant, then ask individual pupils to say their sentence out loud to the rest of the class. Congratulate a correct sentence with an enthusiastic "Très bien", "Excellent", "Bravo" or "Parfait".

Alternatively, ask one pupil at a time to say a sentence using a word suggested by you. For example:

Teacher: Laura, cantine
Laura: Je vais à la cantine chaque jour.

Teacher: Chris, boulangerie
Chris: Je ne vais pas à la boulangerie car ce n'est pas nécessaire.

Teacher: Victoria, piscine
Victoria: Moi, je vais à la piscine car j'aime ça.

Je vais à l' (+ noun)

Next, say that if you are going to a place whose name starts with a vowel or a silent "h" then you say "je vais à l'...". For example:

Teacher: <u>Je vais</u> **à l'**opéra très rarement.
<u>Je vais</u> **à l'**église chaque dimanche.
<u>Je ne vais pas</u> **à l'**hôpital avec plaisir.

Write suggestions for places they may want to say on the board: l'université, l'église, l'hôtel, l'aéroport or l'école. Ask the pupils to think of a sentence using "Je vais à l'...." Encourage some pupils to say their sentences out loud. Congratulate a correct sentence with an enthusiastic "Très bien" or "Excellent".

Vocabulaire

je vais à	I go to
la bibliothèque	the library
la boulangerie	the bakery
la boucherie	the butcher's
la pharmacie	the pharmacy
parfait	perfect
rarement	rarely
l'opéra (m)	the opera
plaisir	pleasure
l'université (f)	the university
l'aéroport (m)	the airport
un supermarché	a supermarket
un cinéma	a cinema
un théâtre	a theater

Materials

★ Sheet 10a (page 205)

Je vais au (+ noun)

Then say that if you are going to a place whose name is masculine and does not start with a vowel, you use "je vais au". For example:

Teacher: <u>Je vais</u> **au** restaurant très souvent.
<u>Je vais</u> **au** supermarché chaque samedi matin.
<u>Je vais</u> **au** cinéma pendant les vacances.
<u>Je ne vais jamais</u> **au** théâtre car je n'aime pas le théâtre.

Write on the board sentences with "à la", "à l'"and "au" such as:

Je vais **à la** banque.
Je vais **à l'**école.
Je vais **au** théâtre.

Ask the pupils to find a way to remember that we say "au" instead of "le". Listen to their suggestions and give them the following memory trick.

"Le" is used for singular masculine nouns, so we can think of it as being male or manly. Now let's imagine a French woman complaining about how men are untidy and never help around the house. Imagine the woman saying she wishes that she could change men. Well, in French grammar at least, the male word gets changed since "à + le" becomes "au"!

Then ask one pupil at a time to say a sentence using a word suggested by the teacher. For example:

Teacher: Emma, restaurant
Emma: Je ne vais pas souvent au restaurant.

Teacher: Alice, supermarché.
Alice: Je vais au supermarché.

Teacher: Ava, cinéma.
Ava: Je vais au cinéma pendant le weekend.

Je vais aux (+ noun)

Tell the pupils that very few places are plural but the most common one is the "États-Unis" (United States). "You go/are going to the United States" is "**Je vais aux** États-Unis".

Give Sheet 10a to the pupils and ask them to fill in the gaps with "à", "au", "à l'", "à la" or "aux".

Aller

To go

Write on the board the verb "aller" and the verb "avoir" in the present tense and show their similarities.

Vocabulaire

je vais	I go
tu vas	you go
il/elle va	he/she goes
nous allons	we go
vous allez	you go
ils/elles vont	they go

avoir		**aller**	
j'	**ai**	je	v**ai**s
tu	**as**	tu	v**a**s
il/elle	**a**	il/elle	v**a**
nous	av**ons**	nous	all**ons**
vous	av**ez**	vous	all**ez**
ils/elles	**ont**	ils/elles	v**ont**

Materials

★ Pieces of paper with countries written on them in French (see vocabulaire list on page 112)
★ Pieces of paper with places written on them (e.g. le supermarché, la boulangerie, la piscine, etc)
★ Sheet 10b (page 206)
★ Sheet 10c (page 207)

To practise the verb "aller", ask the pupils questions about where they are going and encourage them to ask questions of other pupils.

Teacher:	Louise, est-ce que tu vas à la piscine?
Louise:	Oui, je vais à la piscine car j'aime ça.
Louise:	Freddie, est-ce que tu vas au cinéma ce soir?
Freddie:	Non, je ne vais pas au cinéma ce soir car je suis occupé.
Freddie:	Simon, est-ce que tu vas à l'école avec ta mère?
Simon:	Oui, je vais à l'école avec ma mère.
Simon:	Katie, est-ce que tu vas aux États-Unis pendant les vacances?
Katie:	Non, je ne vais pas aux États-Unis pendant les vacances.

Mention that when you are going to somebody's house then they must use the expression "chez". For example:

Je vais chez Thomas.	(I go to Thomas' house.)
Je vais chez le docteur.	(I go to the doctor.)
Je vais chez mes amis.	(I go to my friends' house.)

Then to make sure the pupils listened carefully to all the answers (and to practise "il/elle va"), ask them to answer in chorus to some questions you will ask them with "il va" and "elle va":

Teacher:	Où va Louise?
Pupils:	Elle va à la piscine.
Teacher:	Est-ce que Freddie va au cinéma ce soir?
Pupils:	Non, il ne va pas au cinéma car il est occupé.

Play pass the bag. Write the names of some countries on some pieces of paper and put them in a bag e.g: Belgique, France, Japon, Allemagne, Inde, etc. Ask pupils to pass the bag around the room until you say "stop". The pupil holding the bag takes out a word card, for example "Irlande". The class chant "Où vas-tu? " and the pupil replies "Je vais en Irlande." Continue to play "pass the bag" in the same way.

Tell the pupils that now you will practise the verb "aller" with "nous", "vous" and "ils/elles". Put the pupils in pairs and give each pair a piece of paper with a place indicated on it, e.g: to Emma and Sunil give the word "supermarché" . Tell them to imagine a long sentence starting with "nous allons" or "nous n'allons pas" and the place indicated, e.g: "Nous n'allons pas au supermarché car nous allons à l'école". Then ask:

Teacher:	Emma et Sunil, est-ce que vous allez au supermarché?
Emma or Sunil (or both together):	Non, nous n'allons pas au supermarché car nous allons à l'école.

Continue doing the same activity with at least six pairs asking the rest of the class to pay attention to their answers because later you will ask questions about them.

Remember to always congratulate a good sentence by saying: "C'est très bien", "Bravo", "Excellent".

Now, ask the class to answer in chorus to questions with "ils vont" and "elles vont". Refer to the answers pairs of pupils gave earlier:

Teacher:	Où est-ce qu'Emma et Sunil ne vont pas? Pourquoi?
Pupils :	Ils ne vont pas au supermarché car ils vont à l'école.

Remember to always congratulate a good sentence by saying: "C'est très bien", "Bravo", "Excellent."

Give Sheet 10b to the pupils and ask them to answer the questions with the verb "aller" in the present tense. We have not included the conjugated forms on the sheet, but if you feel your pupils need them, you could add them prior to photocopying the sheet.

Give Sheet 10c to the pupils and ask them to fill in the correct form of "aller".

Hexagonie story

Give each pupil sheet 10d with the Hexagonie story on it. Read it and discuss with the pupils the points covered.

Materials

★ Sheet 10d (page 208)

En voiture, en avion, à pied, à vélo, etc

By car, by plane, on foot, by bike

Hold up a flashcard of a mode of transport, for example a car, and say "une voiture". Encourage the class to repeat it after you. Then hold up another card and say, for example, "une bicyclette" ("a bicycle"). When you have introduced all the modes of transport, you can practise them with the class by holding up a card at random and asking, "Qu'est-ce que c'est?", expecting them to answer, "C'est une voiture" etc.

Listen to Track 34 on the CD where some French people talk about how they get to various places. After each sentence, ask the pupils what mode of transport is used by the person talking.

En général, je vais à l'école en voiture parce que je n'habite pas près de l'école.

In general, I go to school by car because I don't live near the school.

Je vais au centre ville en métro parce que ce n'est pas pratique en voiture.

I go to the city centre by tube because it isn't convenient to go by car.

Je vais à pied à la boulangerie car elle est près de chez moi.

I go to the bakery on foot because it is near my house.

Je vais aux États-Unis en avion.

I go to the United States by aeroplane.

Je vais à l'aéroport en taxi.

I go to the airport by taxi.

Vocabulaire

en voiture	by car
en métro	by tube
à pied	on foot
en avion	by aeroplane
en taxi	by taxi
en autobus	by bus
en train	by train
en bateau	by boat
à cheval	on horse
à vélo/à bicyclette	on a bike
à moto	on a motorbike
Comment vas tu?	How do you go?
Je vais en taxi	I go by taxi
pratique	practical/convenient
une tante	an aunt

Materials

★ Pictures of different types of transport
★ CD, Track 36
★ Tableau d'honneur (page 314)
★ Sheet 10e–10f (pages 209–210)

Draw two columns on the board, then write the French phrases in each column, as in the table below. Only include the English phrases if you think they are absolutely necessary.

en	à
en voiture (by car)	à pied (on foot)
en autobus (by bus)	à cheval (on a horse)
en train (by train)	à vélo (on a bike)
en bateau (by boat)	à bicyclette (on a bike)
en métro (by underground)	
en taxi (by taxi)	
en avion (by plane)	

Ask the pupils if they can think of a way to remember whether to use "en" or "à". The pupils might come up with a good memory trick. Otherwise tell them this one.

If the means of transport used has an engine, you say "en" before it, because "en" is the start of "engine". For example, "en train", "en avion", en "autobus" etc. But if the mode of transport doesn't have an engine you say "à", for example, "à pied", "à bicyclette", "à cheval" and "à velo". The exception is a motorcycle, for which we say "à moto". This is because when motocycles were invented they were thought of as a type of bike.

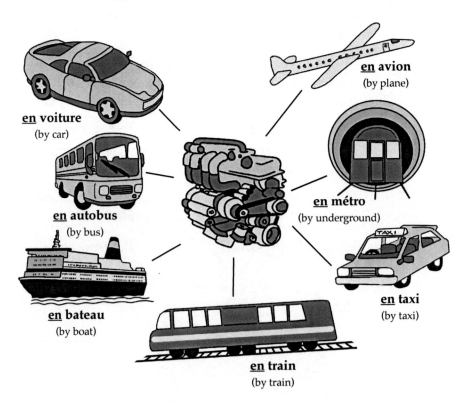

Practise using these expressions by asking everyone in the class, one by one, how they get to school, "Henry, comment vas-tu à l'école?" and wait for a reply, "Je vais à l'école en voiture."

Ask the pupils to ask at least six other pupils where they go on holiday. They could ask:

Où est-ce que toi et ta famille vous allez en vacances? Comment?   or
Où est-ce que tu vas en vacances? Comment?

When the pupil has the six answers he/she can go back to his/her place and write all the answers he got from his friends, for example:

Peter va en France avec sa famille en train car ils aiment le train.

Go around the class and encourage the pupils to do well. At the end of this activity ask the pupils to give you their work. Tell them that you will correct their work for the following lesson. When you mark their work and correct mistakes, make sure you remind them of some memory tricks for remembering what to say before countries, places or modes of transport. Reward the pupils who have done well with a "Tableau d'honneur".

Give the pupils Sheet 10e and ask the pupils to fill in the blanks. Can they remember a memory trick to help with this sheet?

Give the pupils Sheet 10f and ask them to complete the sentences with the correct form of the verb "aller" and fill in the gaps with "à", "à l' ", "à la", "aux" or "en".

Les jours de la semaine

Days of the week

Say the days of the week asking the pupils to repeat after you: "lundi, mardi, mercredi, jeudi, vendredi, samedi, dimanche". Then ask individual pupils to say the days of the week. You could write the days of the week on the board, missing out some letters. Are the pupils able to complete the words?

Remind the pupils that "chaque" means "each", then write on the board:

chaque lundi	= le lundi	= each Monday	= on Mondays
chaque mardi	= le mardi	= each Tuesday	= on Tuesdays
chaque mercredi	= le mercredi	= each Wednesday	= on Wednesdays

etc

Vocabulaire

lundi	Monday
mardi	Tuesday
mercredi	Wednesday
jeudi	Thursday
vendredi	Friday
samedi	Saturday
dimanche	Sunday
un jour	a day
une semaine	a week
un mois	a month
un an	a year
une fois	one time
quatre fois	four times
je mange	I eat
la maternelle	nursery school
l'école primaire (f)	primary school
par	per

Materials

★ CD, Tracks 37–40
★ Sheets 10g–10h (pages 211–212)

Check that the pupils understand this point, then ask individual pupils questions about their weekly routine such as:

Est-ce que tu vas à l'école le samedi?	Do you go to school on Saturdays?
Quels jours est-ce que tu vas à l'école?	Which days do you go to school?
Quels jours est-ce que tu vas à la piscine?	Which days do you go to the swimming pool?
Où vas-tu le dimanche?	Where do you go on Sundays?

Write the following on the board:

24 heures	=	un jour
7 jours	=	une semaine
4 semaines	=	un mois
12 mois	=	un an

Check that your pupils understand the meaning of the words above.

In a week there are "sept" days. The word "semaine" starts with "se" like "sept". The pronunciation of "maine" is "men", because "men" (and, of course, women) work during the week.

Listen to Track 37 on the CD, which is of French people talking about their day. You will need to explain that "une fois" means once and "deux fois" means twice and "trois fois" means three times, etc.

Je m'appelle Philippe. Je mange le matin, le midi et le soir. Je mange trois fois par jour.
Je m'appelle Emma. Je vais à l'école cinq jours par semaine.
Je m'appelle Matt. J'ai une leçon de français trois fois par semaine.
Je m'appelle Charlotte. Je vais en vacances quatre fois par an.

Afterwards ask the pupils some questions to check that they have understood, for example:

Combien de fois par jour est-ce que Philippe mange?
Combien de jours par semaine est-ce qu'Emma va à l'école?
Combien de leçons de français est-ce que Matt a pendant la semaine?
Combien de fois par an est-ce que Charlotte va en vacances?

Write "par" on the board and write some sentences using "par", for example:

Je joue au hockey deux fois **par** semaine.
Je vais au supermarché une fois **par** semaine.
Je vais au cinéma deux fois **par** mois.

Ask the pupils if they can think of a way to remember "par". The pupils might come up with a good memory trick. Otherwise, tell them this one.

Say to the pupils that "une fois par semaine" means "once per week". The word "par" in French reminds us of "per" in English:

une fois **par** semaine   once **per** week
deux fois **par** mois   twice **per** month
trois fois **par** an   three times **per** year

Sort pupils into pairs. Ask them to ask each other questions about the sports or games that they play in a week or the places where they go. For example, "John, combien de fois par semaine est-ce que tu joues au rugby?" and John could reply, "Je joue au rugby trois fois par semaine." Walk around the room listening to the pairs and congratulate good work with an enthusiastic "Très bien" or "Parfait".

Give the pupils Sheet 10g and read with the pupils the text about school in France. On CD Track 38 you can listen to the text being read by a French person. Ask them to answer the questions in class or at home.

L'école en France

De 3 ans à 6 ans, les petits enfants vont à la maternelle. Les enfants commencent l'école primaire à 6 ans. De 6 ans à 10 ans, ils vont à l'école primaire. Les élèves vont à l'école sans uniforme.
En général, il y a des cours le matin de 8h30 à 11h30 et l'après-midi, il y a des cours de 13h30 à 16h30. Le matin, il y a toujours une récréation de 15 minutes, de 10h15 à 10h30. À midi, les élèves déjeunent à la cantine de l'école ou déjeunent à la maison avec leurs parents.
Les élèves ne vont pas à l'école le mercredi mais ils vont à l'école le samedi matin. Le mercredi, beaucoup d'enfants ont des cours de musique ou de sport.

Give each pupil a copy of Sheet 10h. Listen to the French national anthem, "La Marseillaise" which is on Track 39 on the CD. Listen out for the verb "aller" in "Allons enfants de la Patrie". An instrumental version is on Track 40.

The French national anthem was composed during the French Revolution by Claude Joseph Rouget de Lisle, a captain in the army and an amateur musician stationed in Strasbourg in 1792. The anthem became known as "La Marseillaise" because it was popular with volunteer army units from the town of Marseille. It became the French national anthem in 1795. It has been banned and reinstated several times because of its revolutionary associations. It has been the national anthem of France since it was last reinstated in 1879.

You could ask questions, e.g:
Have you ever heard it before? When?
Do you like it?
How does it compare to our national anthem?

Essential words and phrases

10i

At the end of this unit, give the pupils Sheet 10i, which will help them to remember essential words and phrases.

Materials

★ Sheet 10i (page 213)

Au revoir! Bonne semaine! Bon week-end!

Remember always to wish the pupils a good week or weekend. Wait for them to reply "Merci Madame/Monsieur, vous aussi."

Nom:_____ **La date:**_____

Regarde 👁👁 et écris

Fill in the gaps with the words in the box below:

à	au	à l'	à la	aux

1. Je vais _____ banque.

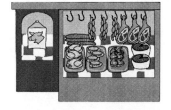

2. Je vais _____ boucherie.

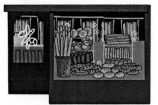

3. Je vais ____ boulangerie.

4. Je vais _____ aéroport.

5. Je vais _____ supermarché.

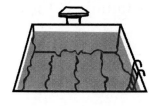

6. Je vais _____ piscine.

7. Je vais _____ école.

8. Je vais _____ Paris.

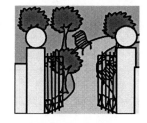

9. Je vais _____ parc.

10. Je vais _____ gare.

11. Je vais _____ église.

12. Je vais _____ librairie.

13. Je vais _____ bibliothèque.

14. Je vais _____ café.

15. Je vais _____ restaurant.

© Maria Rice-Jones and Brilliant Publications

Nom:_____   **La date:**_____

Réponds ✎ aux questions suivantes:

Answer the following questions about yourself and your family.

1. Quand est-ce que tu vas à l'école?

   _____

2. Vas-tu au cinéma avec tes parents?

   _____

3. Ta famille et toi, où allez-vous pendant le week-end?

   _____

4. Est-ce que tes parents vont souvent en vacances sans toi?

   _____

5. Est-ce que tes parents vont à l'église?

   _____

6. Est-ce que tes parents vont souvent au cinéma?

   _____

7. Qui va au supermarché dans ta famille?

   _____

8. Quand vas-tu à la gare?

   _____

9. Quand vas-tu chez le docteur?

   _____

10. Quand vas-tu chez tes amis? Pourquoi?

   _____

Nom:_____   **La date:**_____

Lis et écris

Read the sentences and fill in the gaps with the correct form of "aller".

1. Les enfants _____ à l'école.

2. Il _____ au bureau.

3. Elle _____ à la bibliothèque.

4. L'ambulance _____ _____ à l'hôpital.

5. Nous _____ au cinéma.

6. Vous _____ au restaurant.

7. Il _____ à la piscine.

8. Ils _____ à l'aéroport.

© Maria Rice-Jones and Brilliant Publications

Nom:_____   **La date:**_____

Aller is always on the go

Throughout the year Queen Avoir and King Être receive many invitations to go and visit other countries. It is a great opportunity for them to be known in the world and also to learn from other countries. However, when King Être is unable to go, he asks the verb Aller (to go) to accompany the Queen instead.

Queen Avoir is always very excited to travel with Aller because he is always on the go and tells her lots of stories about his wonderful trips. He calls his trips his "voyages" to make them seem even more special. She could listen to him for hours.

She feels he understands her since they are quite similar: their names start with the same letter and contain the same amount of letters. Like the Queen, Aller likes almost the same outfits because when she talks about herself she says "j'ai"and he says "je vais" keeping the same letters, but adding "v" and "s", the first and last letters of "voyages", of course. They have fun together during those long hours when they decide which outfits to take. And of course, they always end up taking too many suitcases.

What Queen Avoir likes most is when they decide where to go on a trip. They sit down together and look at a list of countries. In front of countries ending in "e", which Aller likes enormously, he puts the abbreviation "en" (en Chine, en Irlande, etc) and in front of those he does not like very much because they don't end in "e" he writes the abbreviation "au" which is short for "aunt", as he says those countries would please his old aunty (au Canada, au Portugal, etc). This always makes Queen Avoir laugh.

They really have a good time together. What fun it would be for me to travel with someone like Aller instead of always travelling on my own. However, I am so used to it now that I am sure it is better as it is.

Nom:_____ **La date:**_____

Regarde et écris

In front of each means of transport, write "en" or "à".

_____ bateau	_____ pied	_____ voiture

_____ avion	_____ moto	_____ cheval

_____ vélo	_____ autobus	_____ métro

Nom:_____   **La date:**_____

Regarde 👁👁 et écris

Complete the sentences below with the correct form of the verb "aller" and fill in the gaps with "à", "au", "à l' ", "à la", "aux" or "en":

1. Chaque jour, je _____ _____ école.

2. Chaque week-end, nous _____ _____ cinéma.

3. Tu _____ _____ France _____ avion.

4. Il _____ _____ Paris _____ autobus.

5. Ma mère_____ _____ supermarché _____ voiture.

6. Ils _____ _____ parc _____ pied.

7. Elle _____ _____ bureau _____ métro.

8. Vous _____ _____ église _____ cheval.

9. Je _____ _____ États-Unis _____ avion.

10. Je _____ _____ école _____ vélo.

Nom:_____ **La date:**_____

L'école primaire en France

De 3 ans à 6 ans, les petits enfants vont à la maternelle. Les enfants commencent l'école primaire à 6 ans. De 6 ans à 10 ans, ils vont à l'école primaire. Les élèves vont à l'école sans uniforme.

En général, il y a des cours le matin de 8h30 à 11h30 et l'après-midi, il y a des cours de 13h30 à 16h30. Le matin, il y a toujours une récréation de 15 minutes, de 10h15 à 10h30. À midi, les élèves déjeunent à la cantine de l'école ou déjeunent à la maison avec leurs parents.

Les élèves ne vont pas à l'école le mercredi mais ils vont à l'école le samedi matin. Le mercredi, beaucoup d'enfants ont des cours de musique ou de sport.

Vocabulaire					
la maternelle	nursery school	l'uniforme	the uniform	la récréation	the break time
l'école primaire	primary school	un cour	a lesson		

Réponds aux questions:

1. À quel âge est-ce que les enfants commencent l'école primaire en France et dans ton pays?

   _____

2. En France, est-ce que les enfants vont à l'école en uniforme?

   _____

3. Vas-tu à l'école en uniforme?

   _____

4. Est-ce que tu aimes ton uniforme?

   _____

5. Dans ton école, est-ce qu'il y a une récréation le matin?

   _____

6. Est-ce que tu vas à l'école tous les jours?

   _____

7. Et en France, est-ce que les élèves vont à l'école tous les jours?

   _____

8. Est-ce que tu manges à la cantine?

   _____

Nom:_____ **La date:**_____

"La Marseillaise"

Track 39-40

The French national anthem is "La Marseillaise". The full French national anthem is much longer but the first verse and chorus are shown here.

Allons enfants de la Patrie
Le jour de gloire est arrivé!
Contre nous de la tyrannie
L'étendard sanglant est levé
L'étendard sanglant est levé!
Entendez-vous dans nos campagnes
Mugir ces féroces soldats?
Ils viennent jusque dans vos bras
Égorger vos fils, vos compagnes!

Let's go children of the Fatherland
The day of glory has arrived!
Against us tyranny's
Bloody standard is raised.
Bloody standard is raised!
Do you hear, in the countryside
The roar of these wild soldiers?
They come right into your arms
To cut the throat of your sons, your partners!

Chorus
Aux armes citoyens
Formez vos bataillons
Marchons, marchons
Qu'un sang impur
Abreuve nos sillons.

To arms, citizens
Form your battalions
Let us march, let us march
May impure blood
Water our fields.

Nom:_____ **La date:**_____

Essential words and phrases

How to conjugate "aller" (to go) in the present tense

(the verb "avoir" in the present tense has similar endings.)

je	v**ai**s	j'	**ai**
tu	v**as**	tu	**as**
il/elle	v**a**	il/elle	**a**
nous	all**ons**	nous	av**ons**
vous	all**ez**	vous	av**ez**
ils/elles	v**ont**	ils/elles	**ont**

How to say "to go to" – "aller à"

aller au + singular masculine noun, starting with a consonant   Je vais **au** cinéma.

aller à la + singular feminine noun, starting with a consonant   Je vais **à la** piscine.

aller à l' + all singular nouns starting with a vowel   Je vais **à l'**église.

aller aux + all plural nouns   Je vais **aux** États-Unis.

How to say "by car" etc

If the mode of transport has an <u>engine</u>:

en voiture	(by car)
en train	(by train)
en autobus	(by bus)
en avion	(by plane)
en hélicoptère	(by helicopter)
en taxi	(by taxi)

If it doesn't have an engine:

à vélo	(by bike)
à cheval	(by horse)
à pied	(on foot)

The exception is: **à** moto (by motorbike) because a motorbike is a type of bike.

How to say "How are you?"

Comment vas-tu?	How are you?
Comment va-t-il?	How is he?
Comment va-t-elle?	How is she?
Comment allez-vous ?	How are you? (to be polite or to a group of people)
Comment vont-ils?	How are they? (to a group with at least one male in it)
Comment vont-elles?	How are they? (to an all female group)

How to say "once per week" etc

par = per

une fois par jour	once a/per day
une fois par semaine	once a/per week
deux fois par mois	twice a/per month
cinq fois par an	five times a/per year

Food and Drink: That's what life is all about!

Key teaching points/vocabulary

Food and drink
The verb "manger" ("to eat") in the present tense
The verb "boire" ("to drink") in the present tense
"Pas de" / "beaucoup de"

Bonjour

Say "Bonjour" to the whole class, waiting for the pupils to reply "Bonjour Madame/Monsieur." Call the register in French and expect every pupil to respond "présent(e)" when their name is called out. When you have no answer say "absent(e)". Call out the name of a pupil and ask him/her, "Comment vas-tu?" waiting for his/her answer "Je vais bien, merci." Ask other pupils how they are. Encourage the pupil to ask you "Et vous?" then answer with "Je vais bien merci." Encourage pupils to use adjectives in their replies.

Recap the verb "aller" in the present tense

Perform a Mexican wave where one pupil asks another pupil of his/her choice a question using the verb "aller" such as:

> Emma, avec qui est-ce que tu vas en vacances?

> Je vais en vacances avec mes parents.

> Jack, est-ce que tu vas souvent au cinéma?

> Non, je ne vais pas souvent au cinéma car je n'aime pas ça.

La nourriture

Food

To introduce the food that is commonly eaten for breakfast, collect together different food items or use pictures of food. Say to the class, "c'est le petit déjeuner" (it is breakfast). Hold up a box of cereals and say to the class, "les céréales". Encourage the class to repeat "les céréales" after you. Then hold up another food item, for example, yoghurt and say, "le yaourt". Repeat this for all the breakfast items.

Then say to the class "c'est le déjeuner" or "c'est le dîner". Then hold up items (or pictures of them) that are commonly eaten for dinner saying their name in French and encouraging the class to repeat the name after you. For example, if you held up a picture of a roast chicken, you would say, "le poulet" (the chicken). Repeat this for the commonly eaten food items listed on Sheets 11a-11b and in the "Vocabulaire" for this section.

French specialities

Ask the pupils if they know some French specialities. Here are a few suggestions:

Une salade niçoise

This salad is from the Nice area of France and is made of raw vegetables, hard-boiled eggs, anchovies, tuna and olive oil.

Un croque-monsieur ou un croque-madame

A croque-monsieur is a toasted cheese and ham sandwich. It is often served in cafés and bars in France. If a fried egg is placed on the top, then it is known as a croque-madame. "Croquer" means "to crunch".

Une omelette nature

An omelette nature is a plain omelette and is often served in cafés in France.

Manger

To eat

Ask the pupils if it is usual in English to say, "I eat one meat with four mushrooms and fifteen chips and I drink one litre of water". Of course the pupils will answer "no" because it sounds absurd to indicate the exact number of items of food that we eat and drink. Instead English people give an approximate quantity by using the word "some".

Say that "some" is said in four different ways in French ("du", "de la", "de l'" and "des") depending on whether you are talking about something that is masculine, feminine or plural etc.

Vocabulaire

Le petit déjeuner

la nourriture	food
un café	a coffee
un thé	a tea
un chocolat chaud	a hot chocolate
un yaourt	a yoghurt
un croissant	a croissant
le sucre	the sugar
la confiture	the jam
un jus d'orange	an orange juice
les céréales (f)	the cereals
le beurre	the butter
le lait	the milk
les fruits (m)	the fruit
le pain	the bread

Le déjeuner et le dîner

la viande	meat
le poulet	chicken
le bœuf	beef
le porc	pork
l'agneau (m)	lamb
les saucisses (f)	sausages
le jambon	ham
le poisson	fish
le saumon	salmon
la truite	trout
le cabillaud	cod
les crevettes (f)	prawns
les légumes (m)	vegetables
une aubergine	an aubergine
une courgette	a courgette
les petits pois (m)	peas
les haricots verts (m)	French beans
un poivron	a pepper
des pommes de terre (f)	potatoes
les fraises (f)	strawberries
un kiwi	a kiwi
une pomme	an apple
une poire	a pear
une mangue	a mango
un melon	a melon
des pâtes (f)	pasta
des spaghettis (m)	spaghetti
une lasagne/ des lasagnes	lasagne
le fromage	cheese
le brie	brie
le camembert	camembert

Vocabulaire (cont.)

le roquefort	Roquefort
le riz	rice
les frites (f)	chips
l'eau (f)	water
l'eau gazeuse (f)	sparkling water
une limonade	a lemonade
l'huile (f)	oil
l'ail (m)	garlic
croquer	to crunch

Materials

★ Plastic models of food or real food
★ Pictures of food

Vocabulaire

je mang**e**	I am eating/ I eat
tu mang**es**	you are eating/you eat
il/elle mang**e**	he is eating/ he/she eats
nous mang**eons**	we are eating/ we eat
vous mang**ez**	you are eating/you eat
ils/elles mang**ent**	they are eating/ they eat
du	some (+ masculine singular)
de la	some (+ feminine singular)
de l'	some (+ any singular noun beginning with a vowel)
des	some (+ plural)

Write this table on the board:
Some = du, de la, de l', des

Incorrect	Correct	
Je mange de le riz.	Je mange du riz.	I eat some rice.
	Je mange de la salade.	I eat some salad.
	Je mange de l'agneau.	I eat some lamb.
Je mange de les pâtes.	Je mange des pâtes.	I eat some pasta.

Ask if they have any idea why we cannot say "de le" or "de les" but instead have to say "du" and "des" before a quantity. The pupils might come up with a reason or a system to remember "du" and "des". If not, tell the pupils our memory trick.

de + le = **du**
In French it is incorrect to say "de le" - we say "du" instead. However, as pupils commonly make the mistake of saying and writing "de le", we have designed a memory trick to help.

"Le" is used for singular masculine nouns so we can think of it as being male or manly. Now let us imagine a French woman complaining about how men are untidy and never help around the home. She's always moaning about how men always create problems and that she wishes that she could change men. Well, in French grammar at least, the male word "le" does change since "de + le" becomes "du"!

Practise using "du", "de l' ", "de la" and "des" and the verb "manger" with the class by asking simple questions. For example:

Teacher: George, est-ce que tu manges du pain?
George: Oui, je mange du pain.

Teacher: Eddie, est-ce que tu manges de la confiture?
Eddie: Oui, je mange de la confiture.

Teacher: Victoria, est-ce que tu manges des pâtes?
Victoria: Oui, je mange des pâtes.

Teacher: Alice, est-ce que tu manges de l'ail?
Alice: Oui, je mange de l'ail.

Say that you are going to write the verb "manger" ("to eat") on the board. Point out that "manger" is an "er" verb and ask the pupils to help you with the endings. Write the endings in red to help them to stand out and underline the extra "e" in "mangeons".

je mang	**e**	I am eating/ I eat
tu mang	**es**	you are eating/ you eat
il/elle mang	**e**	he is eating/ he/she eats
nous mang<u>e</u>	**ons**	we are eating/ we eat
vous mang	**ez**	you are eating/ you eat
ils/elles mang	**ent**	they are eating/ they eat

Point out that an extra "e" has been added to "nous mangeons". Ask the pupils if they have any idea why. If they do not know, tell them that it has been added in order to keep the soft "g".

Manger means "to eat". When we eat we must open our mouth. If we look at the shape of the letter "e" we can imagine that the letter "e" is opening its mouth to eat. That is why the letter "e" always appears in the conjugation of "manger" for "je, tu, il/elle, nous, vous, ils/elles".

Boire

To drink

Stand in front of the class and take a sip of water from the glass and say, "Je bois de l'eau." Then pretend to pour yourself a glass of coca-cola and say, "Je bois du coca-cola." Pretend to pour other drinks to introduce the words "un thé, un café, un jus d'orange", etc.

Ask the pupils what they think "je bois" means, and they should say "I am drinking" or "I drink." Say that the verb "to drink" in French is "boire". Point out that this verb does not end in "er" and so doesn't follow the pattern of the "er" verbs.

Write the verb "boire" on the board and colour the endings in green.

Boire

je	boi	**s**	I am drinking/ I drink
tu	boi	**s**	you are drinking/ you drink
il/elle	boi	**t**	he/she is drinking/he/she drinks
nous	buv	**ons**	we are drinking/ we drink
vous	buv	**ez**	you are drinking/ you drink
ils/elles	boiv	**ent**	they are drinking/ they drink

Vocabulaire

je bois	I am drinking/ I drink
tu bois	you are drinking/ you drink
il/elle boit	he/she is drinking/ he/she drinks
nous buvons	we are drinking/ we drink
vous buvez	you are drinking/ you drink
ils/elles boivent	they are drinking/ they drink
un coca-cola	a cola
l'huile (f)	oil

Materials

★ A glass of water
★ A bottle of coca-cola
★ A bottle of lemonade
★ A kettle
★ A cup
★ Sheets 11a–11b (pages 226–227)

Ask pupils to create a memory trick to remember the endings for the verb "boire". If they cannot think of one, tell them the following ones.

Nous b**uv**ons
Vous b**uv**ez
How can you remember the "uv"? The verb "boire" means "to drink", so let us imagine that the verb "to drink" has become drunk and is behaving strangely for "nous" and "vous". When we look at the endings for "je, tu, il/elle" they are "S, S, T":

je boi**s**
tu boi**s**
il/elle boi**t**

If we continue in alphabetical order, the next letters are "U" and "V", and "uv" is in 'nous b**uv**ons" and "vous b**uv**ez". The memory trick is to remember that the verb "to drink" has become drunk and does not know what it is doing anymore.

"Ils/elles boivent" takes the "boi" from "il/elle boit", but because "ils/elles" is plural, it adds the "v" used in "nous buvons" and "vous buvez".

Practise using "manger" and "boire" with "du", "de l'", "de la" and "des" by suggesting a word and encouraging individual pupils to say that they eat or drink that food.

Practise with masculine singular nouns such as: le thé, le chocolat, le riz, le poisson, etc:

Teacher:	Rebecca, le café
Rebecca:	Je bois du café.

Teacher:	Alfie, le pain
Alfie:	Je mange du pain.

Practise with feminine singular nouns such as: la salade, la viande, la limonade, etc:

Teacher:	Eddie, la confiture
Eddie:	Je mange de la confiture.

Practise with plural nouns such as: les légumes, les carottes, les tomates, les fruits:

Teacher:	Victoria, les pâtes
Victoria:	Je mange des pâtes.

Practise with singular nouns starting with a vowel or a silent "h" such as: l'huile (oil), l'eau gazeuse (sparkling water), l'ail (garlic), etc.

Teacher:	Matthew, l'eau
Matthew:	Je bois de l'eau.

Give the pupils a copy of Sheet 11a and ask them to fill in "le", "la", "l' " or "les" in front of each word. Note that "le sucre" and "le beurre", despite both ending in "e", are masculine nouns. You could ask your class for their ideas for memory tricks for these words.

Our memory trick is that "le sucre" and "le beurre" are both bad for you, and they don't behave as they should.

Give the pupils a copy of Sheet 11b and ask them to fill in "le", "la", "l' " or "les" in front of each word.

Hexagonie story

Give the pupils Sheet 11c and read it with them. Discuss the story to reinforce the points covered.

Materials
★ Sheet 11c (page 228)

Pas de

Not any

Say a few sentences to the class using "pas de" with the verbs "manger" and "boire" (stressing "pas de"). For example:

En général, je ne bois **pas de** thé car je n'aime pas ça.
Je ne bois **pas de** vin.
Mes parents ne mangent **pas de** viande car ils sont végétariens.
À midi, je ne mange **pas de** fruits mais je mange un yaourt.

Ask the pupils if they can suggest a reason why negative sentences always use "pas de" instead of "pas du", "pas de la" etc. The pupils might come up with an interesting idea. If not, tell the pupils the memory trick below.

Vocabulaire	
pas de	not any (+ consonant)
pas d'	not any (+ vowel)
un kilo	a kilo
un/une végétarien(ne)	a vegetarian

Materials
★ Sheet 11d (page 229)

The French like eating and drinking so, when they eat or drink, they want to know exactly what is on their plate or in their glass and that includes knowing whether it is masculine, feminine or plural. That is why when French people want to say that they are eating something the gender of the noun is always indicated by saying "du", "de la", "de l' " or "des". For example, "Elle mange de la salade", "Elle mange de l'huile avec sa salade" or "Elle mange du pain".

However when a French person is not eating or drinking something, then they are not really all that bothered about it and can get by just fine without knowing if it is masculine, feminine or plural. That is why in negative sentences French people just use "pas de" instead.

Positive sentences	Negative sentences
Je mange **du** pain.	Je ne mange **pas de** pain.
I eat some bread.	*I don't eat any bread.*
Je bois **de la** limonade.	Je ne bois **pas de** limonade.
I drink some lemonade.	*I don't drink any lemonade.*
Je bois **de l'**eau.	Je ne bois **pas d'**eau.
I drink some water.	*I don't drink any water.*
Je mange **des** pâtes.	Je ne mange **pas de** pâtes.
I eat pasta.	*I don't eat any pasta.*

Tell the pupils that with specific nouns, they must use the definite article as shown below:

Je mange le pain qui est devant moi.	Je ne mange pas le pain qui est devant moi.
I eat the bread in front of me.	*I don't eat the bread in front of me.*
Je mange les fruits devant moi.	Je ne mange pas les fruits devant moi.
I eat the fruit in front of me.	*I don't eat the fruit in front of me.*

To practise using "pas de" (or "pas d'" if the food or drink begins with a vowel) ask pupils questions and encourage them to answer in the negative saying that they do not eat or drink that food or drink.

Teacher: Rebecca, est-ce que tu bois du café?
Rebecca: Non, je ne bois pas de café.

Teacher: George, est-ce que tu manges du pain?
George: Non, je ne mange pas de pain.

Teacher: Eddie, est-ce que tu manges de la confiture?
Eddie: Non, je ne mange pas de confiture.

Teacher: Victoria, est-ce que tu manges des pâtes?
Victoria: Non, je ne mange pas de pâtes.

Teacher: Amber, est-ce que tu manges de l'ail?
Amber: Non, je ne mange pas d'ail.

Sort pupils into pairs and say that you want one pupil to pretend to be a guest staying with the other pupil (the host). The host has to find out what the guest likes to eat so he can serve him food that he likes. For example:

Host: Qu'est-ce que tu manges le matin pour ton petit déjeuner?
Guest: Je mange de la baguette avec du beurre et de la confiture.
Host: Est-ce que tu manges des sandwichs pour le déjeuner?

Guest: Oui, je mange des sandwichs.
Host: Est-ce que tu manges des pâtes?
Guest: Non, je ne mange pas de pâtes.

Walk around the room listening to the pairs and correcting if necessary. Praise pupils with an enthusiastic "Très bien" or "Bravo".

Give the pupils a copy of Sheet 11d and ask them to answer the questions about the menu.

Beaucoup de

A lot of

Hold up a chocolate bar or a picture of a chocolate bar and pretend to eat lots of it, perhaps patting your stomach to indicate that you're full. Then say, "Je mange beaucoup de chocolat" (I eat a lot of chocolate). Then hold up a bottle of water and pretend to drink lots of water. Then say, "Je bois beaucoup d'eau" (I drink a lot of water). Ask the pupils if they can guess what "beaucoup de" means and say "Très bien" or "Excellent" if they say "a lot of".

Write on the board the following sentences in French:

Je mange **beaucoup de** chocolat.
Je mange **beaucoup de** salade.
Je mange **beaucoup de** légumes.
Je bois **beaucoup d'**eau.
Je mange **beaucoup d'**oranges.

Ask the pupils if they have any idea why we always say "de" before a noun with the expression "beaucoup de". The pupils might come up with an interesting idea, if not tell them the memory trick below.

Remind the pupils that "du", "de l' ", "de la" and "des" all mean "some". Tell them that you can't say "J'ai beaucoup des amis" because it would mean "I have a lot some friends" and that would be incorrect. In English they would say "I have a lot of friends". Therefore, we say in French "J'ai beaucoup d'amis."

A few more examples:

There are a lot of French people in London = Il y a beaucoup de Français à Londres.

I do not have a lot of time = Je n'ai pas beaucoup de temps.

Vocabulaire

beaucoup de   a lot of

Materials

★ Pictures of food or drink or miniature food and drink

Ask the pupils questions using "beaucoup de" such as:

Teacher: Ellie, est-ce que tu manges beaucoup de chocolat?
Ellie: Oui, je mange beaucoup de chocolat.

Teacher: Simon, est-ce que tu bois beaucoup de coca-cola?
Simon: Oui, je bois beaucoup de coca-cola.

Teacher: Sally, as-tu beaucoup d'amis français?
Sally: Non, je n'ai pas beaucoup d'amis français.

Vocabulaire

un verre	a glass
une tasse	a cup
une bouteille	a bottle
du vin (m)	some wine
un marché	a market
la liste des courses	a shopping list
marchand (e)	market stall holder

Materials

★ Shopping lists for the class
★ Sheets 11e–11f (pages 230–231)
★ Sheet 11g (page 232), cut into shopping lists – one list per pair of pupils
★ Sheet 11h (page 233)
★ CD, Tracks 41

Un verre de, une tasse de, un kilo de

A glass of, a cup of, a kilo of

Say to the pupils that "a glass" in French is "un verre". Now ask them how they would say "a glass of water" or "a glass of orange juice". They should say "un verre d'eau" and "un verre de jus d'orange".

Tell the pupils that "une tasse" means "a cup". Now ask them how they would say "a cup of tea", "a cup of coffee" or "a cup of hot chocolate". They should say, "une tasse de thé", "une tasse de café" and "une tasse de chocolat chaud".

Tell the pupils that "un kilo" means "a kilo". Now ask them how they would say "a kilo of potatoes" or "a kilo of carrots". They should say, "un kilo de pommes de terre" and "un kilo de carottes".

Tell the pupils that "une bouteille" means "a bottle". Now ask them how they would say "a bottle of coca-cola". They should say "une bouteille de coca-cola".

Ask them if they know why we say "de" after "un verre", "une tasse" and "un kilo". Tell them the memory trick below to help them remember.

Memory trick

Remind the pupils that "du", "de l' ", "de la" and "des" all mean "some".

Tell them that it isn't correct to say "un verre de l'eau" because it would mean "a glass some water". In correct English it is "a glass of water". Therefore, in French it is "un verre d'eau".

Few more examples:
A bottle of wine	= Une bouteille de vin
A bottle of water	= Une bouteille d'eau
A glass of orange juice	= Un verre de jus d'orange
A kilo of potatoes	= Un kilo de pommes de terre

Give each pupil a copy of Sheet 11e and ask them to fill in the blanks.

Give the pupils a copy of Sheet 11f and ask them to fill in the gaps with "du", "de l' ", "de la", "des" or "pas de". You can listen to this dialogue on Track 41 on the CD.

Organize the pupils into pairs. Hand each pair a shopping list (from Sheet 11g). One of them should play the part of a shopkeeper and the other the shopper. The shopper should ask for all the items on the shopping list, and the shopkeeper should pretend to pass all the items to the shopper and say how much the shopping costs. Once the shopper has finished, they should swap roles and swap shopping lists with another couple.

Give the pupils a copy of Sheet 11h and ask them to tick the correct sentences and put a cross by those that are wrong.

Aimer, préférer, détester

To love, to prefer, to hate

Remind pupils that "aimer" means "to like" or "to love". Say that if they want to indicate which foods they prefer then they need to use the verb "préférer" and if they want to say what they hate then they should use "détester".

Tell the pupils that after the verbs "aimer", "préférer" and "détester", we do not need to say "du", "de l' ", "de la" or "des".

Incorrect	Correct
J'aime de la France.	J'aime la France.
I love some France.	*I love France.*
Je préfère de la France.	Je préfère la France.
I prefer some France.	*I prefer France.*
Je déteste de la France.	Je déteste la France.
I hate some France.	*I hate France.*

That is why in French, after the verbs "aimer", "préférer" and "détester" you say:

J'aime la France.   *I like France.*
Je n'aime pas la France.   *I don't like France.*

Vocabulaire

un repas	a meal
aimer	to like/to love
préférer	to prefer
détester	to hate
la farine	flour
l'huile de tournesol	sunflower oil
le sel	salt
adorer	to adore
un saladier	a bowl
une crêpière	a crêpe pan
mélanger	to mix
casser	to break
verser	to pour
ajouter	to add
retourner	to turn over
poser	to put
cuit(e)	cooked
le chocolat liquide	chocolate sauce
une assiette	a plate

Materials

★ White paper plates (or circles made from white card)
★ Food magazines (for example those from supermarkets)
★ Scissors and glue
★ Sheets 11i–11n (pages 234–239)
★ CD, Tracks 42–44
★ Ingredients listed on Sheet 11e (optional)

J'aime beaucoup la France.	*I like France a lot.*
Je n'aime pas beaucoup la France.	*I do not like France very much.*
Je préfère le lundi.	*I prefer Mondays.*
Je ne préfère pas le lundi.	*I do not prefer Mondays.*
Je déteste les pâtes.	*I hate pasta.*
Je ne déteste pas les pâtes.	*I do not hate pasta.*

Ask the pupils questions using the verbs "aimer", "adorer", "préférer" and "détester" such as:

Teacher: Catherine, est-ce que tu aimes la France?
Teacher: Freddie, est-ce que tu préfères la viande ou le poisson?
Teacher: Anne, qu'est-ce que tu détestes?

Choice of activities

 Give everyone a copy of Sheet 11i. Ask them to draw (or cut out from magazines) their favourite lunch and label it in French.

Nos repas préférés (Our favourite meals)
Give each pupil a white paper plate (or a white circle of card) and say that you'd like them to draw or make a collage of their preferred meal ("un repas préféré"). Once they have completed their pictures or collages, ask them to write a description of their meal in French. Mount the plates with their descriptions on the wall to make a display of their favourite meals.

 Give each pupil a copy of Sheet 11j and read the information with them about typical French meals. You could listen to the text on Track 42 on the CD. Ask pupils questions about the text, for example:

En général, que mangent les Français au petit déjeuner?
Est-ce que le déjeuner est important pour les Français? Et pour toi?
Qu'est-ce que tu manges pour ton goûter?
Qu'est-ce que tu manges pour le dîner?

 Give each pupil a copy of Sheet 11k and ask them to answer the questions.

 Give each pupil a copy of Sheet 11l about making pancakes. If you have the time and the facilities you might like to try making pancakes with the class. (Use a flat bottomed frying pan if you don't have a proper "crêpière" (crêpe pan). Alternatively, you could read the recipe, and the pupils could mime making them.

Give each pupil a copy of Sheet 11m. Ask the pupils to draw the food and drinks described in the notes.

Listen to the words of the song "La capucine" on Track 43. There is an instrumental version on Track 44. Carry out the dance actions as described on Sheet 11n.

Essential words and phrases

At the end of this unit, give the pupils Sheet 11o, which will help them to remember essential words and phrases.

Materials
★ Sheet 11o (page 240)

Au revoir! Bonne semaine! Bon week-end!

Remember always to wish the pupils a good week or weekend. Wait for them to reply "Merci Madame/Monsieur, vous aussi."

Nom:_____   **La date:**_____

Le petit déjeuner

Breakfast

Fill in the blanks with "le", "l'", "la" or "les":

_____ café

_____ sucre (m)

_____ beurre (m)

_____ thé

_____ confiture

_____ lait

_____chocolat chaud

_____ jus d'orange

_____ fruits

_____ yaourt

_____ céréales

_____ pain

_____ croissant

Nom:_____   **La date:**_____

Le déjeuner et le dîner

Lunch and dinner

Fill in the blanks with "le", "l'", "la" or "les":

La viande (meat)

____ poulet (chicken)

____ bœuf (beef)

____ porc (pork)

____ agneau (lamb)

____ saucisses (sausages)

____ jambon (ham)

Les légumes (vegetables)

____ aubergines (aubergines)

____ courgettes (courgettes)

____ carottes (carrots)

____ tomates (tomatoes)

____ petits pois (peas)

____ haricots verts (green beans)

____ poivrons (peppers)

____ pommes de terre (potatoes)

____ salade (lettuce)

Les pâtes (pasta)

____ spaghettis (spaghetti)

____ lasagnes (lasagne)

Le riz (rice)

____ riz blanc (white rice)

____ riz brun (brown rice)

Le poisson (fish)

____ saumon (salmon)

____ truite (trout)

____ crevettes (prawns)

____ cabillaud (cod)

Les fruits (fruits)

____ fraises (strawberries)

____ bananes (bananas)

____ cerises (cherries)

____ oranges (oranges)

____ kiwis (kiwis)

____ pommes (apples)

____ poires (pears)

____ mangues (mangoes)

____ melon (melon)

Le fromage (cheese)

le brie (m)

____ camembert

____ Roquefort

Nom:_____   **La date:**_____

The good friends "Manger" and "Boire"

Everywhere I went in Hexagonie, I saw that the nouns were always eating and drinking or planning to eat and to drink. There were food shops, restaurants and bars everywhere, and the nouns always seemed to be talking about food and drinks with great passion. They thought they had the best food and the best wines in the world.

So, inevitably, one day I met Manger and Boire. They were never seen apart from each other and were the best of friends.

Both verbs were regularly seen with many nouns such as "je", "tu", "il/elle", "nous", "vous" and "ils/elles". Being an "er" verb, Manger behaved like them and wore the same outfits according to the nouns he was with: je mange, tu manges, il mange, nous mangeons, vous mangez, ils/elles mangent. He added an "e" to "nous mangeons" so that all his outfits would have an "e" in them, as he thought the letter "e" looked a bit like an open mouth, about to gobble up food.

However, Boire was different and more imaginative. He loved to keep changing his outfits and each one was more eccentric than the last. The first one he wore was the versatile letter "s" which he could wear in all sorts of ways. When next to "je" and "tu", he wore it instead of "re" (je bois, tu bois). He did not want to end the fun of changing outfits too early so he tried on other letters. Logically the next one was "t" and he wore it for "il" and "elle" (il/elle boit). Then with "nous" and "vous", Boire became even wilder, choosing letters he had never worn before. He chose "u" and "v" because they were the next letters after "t" (nous buvons, vous buvez). He looked at himself and thought he was stunning. As for "ils/elles" he changed again into an even more eccentric outfit: ils/elles boivent.

Manger thought that Boire was rather mad with his obsession about outfits, but they were good friends anyway.

Nom:_____ **La date:**_____

Au restaurant

At the restaurant

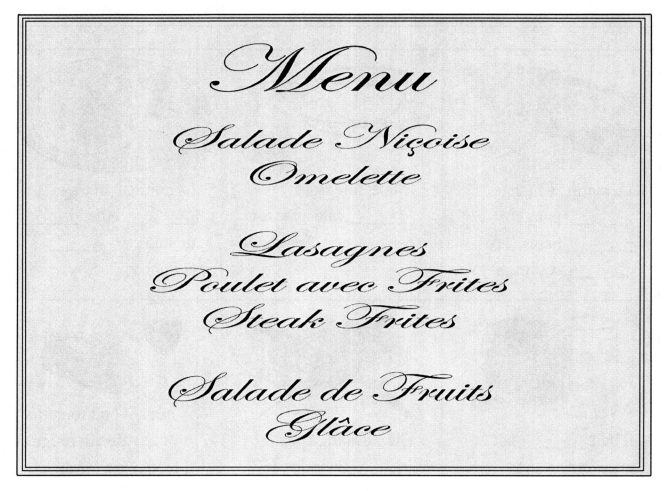

Menu
Salade Niçoise
Omelette

Lasagnes
Poulet avec Frites
Steak Frites

Salade de Fruits
Glâce

Coche ✓

Tick the types of food that are on the menu for today:

Des pâtes ☐　　　Des œufs ☐　　　De la viande ☐

Du riz ☐　　　Du poisson ☐　　　Des fruits ☐

Du fromage ☐　　　Des légumes ☐　　　Des gâteaux ☐

Lis et écris

Read the sentences below and fill in the gaps with the words from the box:

de	de la	de l'	des	du	d'

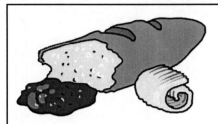

1. Le matin, je mange
   _____ pain avec
   _____ beurre et
   _____ confiture.

2. Je bois une tasse
   _____ café avec un
   peu _____ lait chaud.

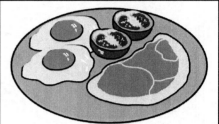

3. Le matin, il mange
   _____ œufs, _____
   tomates, et _____
   jambon.

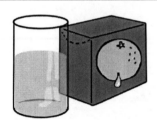

4. Il boit _____ lait et
   aussi un jus _____
   orange.

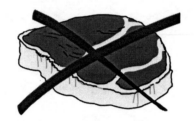

5. Elle ne mange pas
   _____ viande car
   elle est végétarienne.

6. À midi, il boit toujours
   un verre de vin rouge et
   il mange un sandwich
   avec _____ jambon
   et _____ fromage.

7. Il mange beaucoup
   _____ légumes car il
   aime ça.

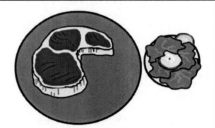

8. Le soir, nous mangeons
   toujours _____ salade
   avec _____ poisson
   ou _____ viande.

9. Nous mangeons
   beaucoup _____
   viande car nous aimons
   ça.

Nom:_____   **La date:**_____

Lis et complète

*Read the conversation below between the market stall holder
(le marchand) and Madame Neville at the market (au marché) then fill in the gaps
with the words in the box below.*

du	de la	de l'	des	de

Au marché

Marchande: Bonjour Madame! Qu'est-ce que vous désirez aujourd'hui?

Mme Neville: Je voudrais _____ lait et _____ œufs, une douzaine
d'œufs s'il vous plaît.

Marchand: Voilà Madame, autre chose?

Mme Neville: Oui, je voudrais _____ légumes: _____ carottes, un
kilo _____ carottes. _____ courgettes, seulement
quatre, puis deux kilos _____ pommes de terre et pour finir
_____ champignons, un kilo _____ champignons.

Marchand: Voilà, et avec ça?

Mme Neville: _____ moutarde, _____ ail et _____ oignons
s'il vous plaît.

Marchand: Voilà! Ça vous fait 9 euros 50, s'il vous plaît.

Mme Neville: Voilà.

Marchand: Merci beaucoup Madame! Bonne journée!

Mme Neville: Vous aussi!

Vocabulaire

Qu'est ce que vous désirez?	What would you like?
une douzaine	a dozen
Autre chose?	Anything else?
seulement	only
puis	then
et pour finir	and to finish
champignons (m)	mushrooms
oignons (m)	onions

Nom:_____   **La date:**_____

La liste des courses

Un kilo de pommes de terre

Une bouteille de limonade

Deux kilos d'oranges

Un kilo de tomates

Trois bouteilles de coca-cola

Une bouteille de lait

Une baguette

La liste des courses

Un kilo de carottes

Trois bouteilles de lait

Deux kilos d'haricots verts

Un kilo de champignons

Une bouteille de coca-cola

Une douzaine d'œufs

Deux aubergines

La liste des courses

Une bouteille d'eau gazeuse

Un kilo de pommes de terre

Trois kilos de bananes

Un kilo de tomates

Deux bouteilles de limonade

Une bouteille de lait

Une baguette

La liste des courses

Une bouteille de limonade

Deux kilos de cerises

Un kilo de tomates

Deux bouteilles de coca-cola

Une bouteille de lait

Six kiwis

Une mangue

Nom:_____ **La date:**_____

Lis 📖 et coche ✓

Read the sentences below and put a cross by any sentences that are incorrect and a tick by those that are correct:

Je voudrais un kilo des pommes de terre. ☐

Je voudrais un kilo de pommes de terre. ☐

Chaque matin, je bois une tasse du thé. ☐

Chaque matin, je bois une tasse de thé. ☐

Une fois par jour, il boit un verre de vin. ☐

Une fois par jour, il boit un verre du vin. ☐

Elle boit une bouteille d'eau chaque jour. ☐

Elle boit une bouteille de l'eau chaque jour. ☐

Je voudrais trois bouteilles du lait. ☐

Je voudrais trois bouteilles de lait. ☐

Je voudrais une bouteille de limonade. ☐

Je voudrais une bouteille de la limonade ☐

Nom:_____ **La date:**_____

Dessine et écris

Draw your favourite lunch and then label it in French.

Mon déjeuner préféré

Nom:_____   **La date:**_____

Lis et écoute

Read and listen to the text.

Le petit déjeuner

En général, les Français boivent du café noir, une tasse de thé ou un chocolat chaud. Ils mangent du pain beurré, avec de la confiture ou du miel. Les enfants mangent des céréales ou un yaourt. Puis, ils boivent un jus d'orange.

Le déjeuner

Le déjeuner est important pour les Français. Ils mangent de la viande ou du poisson avec du riz ou des pâtes ou de la salade. Après, ils mangent des fruits. Ils boivent de l'eau et, pour terminer, un café ou un thé. De temps en temps, il mangent un croque-monsieur ou un steak avec des pommes frites.

Le goûter des enfants

Quand les enfants rentrent de l'école, ils mangent un goûter (a snack): un pain au chocolat, une barre de céréales, du pain avec de la confiture, une pomme, une orange ou des biscuits.

Le dîner

Pour commencer, les Français mangent une salade ou du jambon ou de la soupe. Pour continuer, ils mangent de la viande ou du poisson avec des légumes ou des pommes de terre, ou de la salade. Pour terminer, ils mangent du fromage et un dessert.

Lis et écoute

Nom:_____   **La date:**_____

Réponds ✎ aux questions suivantes.

Answer the following questions.

1. Que manges-tu le matin?

   _____

2. En général, avec qui prends-tu ton petit déjeuner?

   _____

3. À quelle heure est-ce que tu prends ton petit déjeuner?

   _____

4. Pendant la semaine, où déjeunes-tu? Pourquoi?

   _____

5. Qu'est-ce que tu manges pour le déjeuner?

   _____

6. Le soir, avec qui est-ce que tu dînes?

   _____

7. Qui cuisine chez toi?

   _____

8. En général, qu'est-ce que tu manges le soir?

   _____

9. Est-ce que tu cuisines des gâteaux?

   _____

10. Manges-tu beaucoup de fruits?

    _____

Nom:_____   **La date:**_____

La recette des crêpes

Pancake recipe

Ingrédients

250 grammes de farine (flour)   3 œufs (eggs)

70 grammes de sucre (sugar)   Huile de tournesol (sunflower oil)

½ litre de lait (milk)   Sel (salt)

Pour 6 personnes

1. Mélange la farine et le sucre dans un saladier. 	2. Casse les œufs. Verse les œufs dans le saladier. 	3. Mélange pendant quelques minutes. 
4. Ajoute une cuillère à soupe d'huile puis une pincée de sel. Mélange. 	5. Verse lentement le lait et mélange. 	6. Prends une crêpière. Ajoute un peu de beurre dans la crêpière. 
7. Ajoute un peu de pâte dans la crêpière. 	8. Après une ou deux minutes, quand la pâte est cuite, retourne la pâte. 	9. Quand elle est cuite, pose la crêpe sur une assiette et ajoute du sucre sur toute la crêpe ou de la confiture ou du chocolat liquide. 

Bon appétit!

Vocabulaire

un saladier	a bowl	mélanger	to mix	casser	to break
verser	to pour	ajouter	to add	cuit(e)	cooked
poser	to put	retourner	to turn over	une crêpière	a crêpe pan

Nom:_____   **La date:**_____

Lis  et dessine

Read the note written by a mother and left on a refrigerator door. Then draw the food and drink described in it.

- -

Lis  et traduis [TRANSLATE]

You arrive at your holiday home in Normandy. You find a note on the table left by the landlord. Read and translate it.

Nom:_____   **La date:**_____

La capucine

Nasturtium dance

Listen to this old song from the 18th century. At that time, many people in France were very poor and did not have enough to eat. Une capucine is a kind of flower (a nasturtium).

The singers dance around in a circle "la capucine" because it makes them happy, even though they are hungry. There is bread in the house next door, but it is not for them. Despite having bread though, the people next door are crying.

1. While you sing this song, dance around in a circle.
2. Shout Piou! at the end of each verse and jump in the air.
3. When you land, crouch down.
4. When you begin the next verse, stand up straight again.

Dansons la capucine,

Y'a pas de pain chez nous,

Y'en a chez la voisine,

Mais ce n'est pas pour nous. Piou!

Dansons la capucine,

Y'a du plaisir chez nous

On pleure chez la voisine,

On rit toujours chez nous. Piou!

Nom:_____   **La date:**_____

Essential words and phrases

How to conjugate "manger" (to eat) in the present tense

je mange
tu manges
il/elle mange
nous mangeons
vous mangez
ils/elles mangent

How to conjugate "boire" (to drink) in the present tense

je bois
tu bois
il/elle boit
nous buvons
vous buvez
ils/elles boivent

How to say "some"

de + le	**du** café (some coffee)
de la	**de la** salade (some salad)
de l'	**de l'**eau (some water)
de + les	**des** tomates (some tomatoes)

How to say "a lot of" (of = de/d')

beaucoup **de**	a lot **of**
beaucoup **de** chocolat	a lot **of** chocolate
beaucoup **d'**eau	a lot **of** water
beaucoup **de** légumes	a lot **of** vegetables
beaucoup **de** tomates	a lot **of** tomatoes

How to say "not any" (not any = pas de/pas d')

Je ne mange **pas de** poisson.	I do not eat any fish.
Je ne mange **pas de** viande.	I do not eat any meat.
Je ne mange **pas d'**aubergines.	I do not eat any aubergines.
Je ne mange **pas de** tomates.	I do not eat any tomatoes.

How to say "a glass of, a bottle of, a cup of" etc (of = de/d')

un verre **de** vin	a glass **of** wine
un verre **d'**eau	a glass **of** water
une tasse **de** thé	a cup **of** tea
une bouteille **de** vin	a bottle **of** wine
une bouteille **d'**eau	a bottle **of** water
un kilo **de** tomates	a kilo **of** tomatoes

To do everything in life

Key teaching points/vocabulary
The verb "faire" ("to do") in the present tense

Bonjour...

Say "Bonjour" to the whole class, waiting for the pupils to reply "Bonjour Madame/Monsieur." Call the register in French and expect every pupil to respond "présent(e)" when their name is called out. When you have no answer say "absent(e)". Call out the name of a pupil and ask him/her, "Comment vas-tu?" waiting for his/her answer "Je vais bien, merci." Ask other pupils how they are. Encourage the pupil to ask you "et vous?" then answer with "Je vais bien merci." Encourage pupils to respond using adjectives.

Recap on the verbs "manger" and "boire" in the present tense

Ask the pupils to stand up ("levez-vous") and say that before they sit down they have to answer a question using "manger" or "boire". Once they have answered a question correctly, the pupil sits down.

© Maria Rice-Jones and Brilliant Publications

Vocabulaire

faire	to do/make
je fais	I do/make
tu fais	you do/make
il/elle fait	he/she does/makes
nous faisons	we do/make
vous faites	you do/make (plural and polite)
ils/elles font	they do/make
faire les courses	to do the shopping
ouvrir	to open
j'ouvre	I open
tu ouvres	you open
il/elle ouvre	he/she opens
nous ouvrons	we open
vous ouvrez	you open (plural and polite)
ils/elles ouvrent	they open
fermer	to close
un magasin	a shop
acheter (j'achète)	to buy (I buy)
la plupart du temps	most of the time
autre	other

Materials

★ Sheet 12a (page 246)
★ CD, Track 45

Vocabulaire

faire la vaisselle	to do the washing up
je fais la vaisselle	I am washing up
laver (je lave)	to wash (I wash)
une cuillère	a spoon
une assiette	a plate
un couteau	a knife
une fourchette	a fork
un lave-vaisselle	a dishwasher
par exemple	for example

Materials

★ Sheet 12b (page 247)
★ CD, Track 46

Faire les courses

To do the shopping

Tell the pupils that "je fais" means "I do" or "I make".

Give the pupils sheet 12a and read the text with the pupils, or listen to it on the CD, Track 45. Ask them to guess what "Je fais les courses" means.

"Je fais les courses" literally means "I do the shopping" and is used mostly when shopping for food. When shopping for things other than food, the French use the English word "shopping": "Je fais du shopping".

Ask them to think of a memory trick to remember the expression "faire les courses" and if they cannot think of one then tell them the one below:

When you do the shopping, you buy food for the first course of the meal, the second course and so on. That is why the word "courses" (food shopping) is plural.

Ask individual pupils questions with the expression "faire les courses" (with "je", "tu", "il", "elle") such as:

Est-ce que ta mère fait les courses avec toi?
Où est-ce que ta mère fait les courses? Pourquoi?
Est-ce que tu aimes faire les courses?
Quel est ton supermarché préféré?
À quelle heure est-ce que les magasins ouvrent dans ta ville?
À quelle heure est-ce que les magasins ferment dans ta ville?
Combien de supermarchés est-ce qu'il y a dans ta ville?
Est-ce qu'il y a un marché dans ta ville? Et une poissonnerie?

Faire la vaisselle

To do the washing up

Give the pupils Sheet 12b and read the text with the pupils, or listen to it on the CD, Track 46. Ask them to guess what "Je fais la vaisselle" means.

"Je fais la vaisselle" means "I am doing the washing up". Ask the pupils to find a memory trick to remember the expression "faire la vaisselle" and if they cannot think of any suggest the one below:

The word "vaisselle" is a bit like the English word "vessel". A vessel is a ship that floats on the water rather like dishes do in a washing-up bowl.

Ask individual pupils questions with "faire la vaisselle" such as:

Est-ce que tu fais la vaisselle de temps en temps?
Quand est-ce que tu fais la vaisselle?
Est-ce qu'il y a un lave-vaisselle chez toi?
Qui fait la vaisselle chez toi?
Est-ce que ton père fait la vaisselle?

Faire le ménage

To do the housework

Give the pupils Sheet 12c. Read the text together or listen to it on the CD, Track 47. Ask them to guess what "Je fais le ménage" means.

"Je fais le ménage" means "I do the housework". Ask the pupils to think of a memory trick to remember the expression "faire le ménage" and, if they do not think of one, tell them the one below:

"Men" and "age" are both found in "ménage". We could say that "men" of any "age" can do the housework if they put their mind to it. To help them remember that "ménage" is masculine remember that it starts with "men".

Ask the class questions to practise "Je fais le ménage" such as:

Qui fait le ménage chez toi?
Est-ce que ton père fait souvent le ménage?
Est-ce que tu as une femme de ménage?
Est-ce que tu fais le ménage dans ta chambre? Quand?

Say that there are two other phrases using "faire" for jobs around the house. Tell them that "Je fais la lessive" means "I do the (clothes) washing" and "Je fais le repassage" means "I do the ironing."

Ask the pupils if they can think of a way of remembering these phrases. If they don't have any suggestions, tell them the ones below:

Je fais la lessive: when you wash your clothes, you want them to be "less" stained. The word "lessive" starts with "less".

Je fais le repassage: when you iron, you "pass" and "re-pass" the iron over the clothes. Note that the word "repassage" is masculine.

Ask the pupils some questions with the expressions "faire la lessive" and "faire le repassage" such as:

Qui fait la lessive chez toi?
Qui fait le repassage chez toi?
Est-ce que tu fais le repassage?

Vocabulaire

faire le ménage	to do the housework
je fais le ménage	I do the housework
un aspirateur	a vacuum cleaner
passer l'aspirateur	to vacuum
paresseux/ paresseuse	lazy
quelquefois	sometimes
faire la lessive	to do the washing (of clothes)
faire le repassage	to do the ironing
une femme de ménage	a cleaning lady

Materials
★ Sheet 12c (page 248)
★ CD, Track 47

Vocabulaire

faire une promenade	to go for a walk
je fais une promenade	I go for a walk
à côté de	next to
marcher (je marche)	to walk (I walk)
longtemps	a long time
une chose	a thing

Materials

★ Sheet 12d–12g (pages 249–252)

★ CD, Track 48

Faire une promenade

To go for a walk

Give the pupils Sheet 12d and read the text with them or listen to it on the CD, Track 48. Ask them to guess what "Je fais une promenade" means.

"Je fais une promenade" means "I go for a walk". Ask the pupils some questions that use this expression. For example:

Quand est-ce que tu fais une promenade?
Sally, est-ce que tu fais une promenade maintenant?

Write the verb "faire" on the board, with "aller" to show some similarities:

Faire		Aller	
je	**fais**	je	**vais**
tu	**fais**	tu	**vas**
il/elle	**fait**	il/elle	**va**
nous	fais**ons**	nous	all**ons**
vous	**FAITES**	vous	all**ez**
ils/elles	**font**	ils/elles	**vont**

Your pupils might be interested to know that even French toddlers get "vous faites" wrong and need to be corrected.

Choice of activities

Give the pupils Sheet 12e and ask them to write memory tricks for the expressions.

Give the Sheet 12f to the pupils and ask them to answer the questions.

Give Sheet 12g to the pupils and ask them to write about their daily routine for every day of the week.

Materials

★ Sheet 12h (page 253)

Hexagonie story

Give the pupils Sheet 12h and read the story with them. Afterwards, discuss it to reinforce the points covered.

Essential words and phrases

At the end of this unit, give the pupils Sheet 12i, which will help them to remember essential words and phrases.

Resources

★ Sheet 12i (page 254)

Au revoir! Bonne semaine! Bon week-end!

Remember always to wish the pupils a good week or weekend. Wait for them to reply "Merci Madame/Monsieur, vous aussi."

Nom:_____   **La date:**_____

Lis 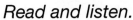 et écoute

Read and listen.

Je fais les courses

En général, je ne fais pas les courses pendant la semaine car je suis très occupé avec mon travail. Je fais les courses au supermarché pendant le week-end. D'habitude, je vais dans un petit supermarché près de chez moi car c'est rapide. La plupart du temps, je fais les courses pour toute la semaine. J'achète de la viande, du poisson, des légumes, des œufs et beaucoup d'autres choses.

Nom:_____ **La date:**_____

Lis et écoute

Read and listen.

Je fais la vaisselle

Chaque jour à la maison, après le petit déjeuner, le déjeuner et le dîner, ma mère lave les assiettes, les verres, les fourchettes, les couteaux et les cuillères. Elle fait la vaisselle car nous n'avons pas de machine pour faire la vaisselle. Nous n'avons pas de lave-vaisselle. Moi, je suis encore petit, alors je ne fais pas la vaisselle mais quelquefois j'aide ma mère. Par exemple, si j'ai le temps après le petit déjeuner, je lave mon bol, mon verre, ma cuillère, et mon assiette. Ma mère est très contente quand je fais ça.

Vocabulaire					
une assiette	a plate	une cuillère	a spoon	laver	to wash
une fourchette	a fork	une machine	a machine	un bol	a bowl
un couteau	a knife	un lave-vaisselle	a dishwasher	aider	to help

Lis et écoute

© Maria Rice-Jones and Brilliant Publications

Nom:_____   **La date:**_____

Lis et écoute

Read and listen.

Je fais le ménage

Non, non, non, non, je déteste le ménage! Je ne fais pas le ménage dans ma chambre car je n'ai pas le temps. Je préfère quand ma mère fait le ménage mais elle n'est pas contente de moi. Elle pense que je suis paresseuse. Mais quelquefois, je fais des actions gentilles et j'aide ma mère car je passe l'aspirateur dans toute la maison.

Vocabulaire

un aspirateur	a vacuum cleaner (reminds us of the English verb "to aspirate" which means "to suck up" or "to breathe in")
paresseux/ paresseuse	lazy (remember "To be lazy like a parasite")
quelquefois	sometimes

Nom:_____ **La date:**_____

Lis et écoute

Read and listen.

Je fais une promenade

Pendant le week-end, je fais souvent une promenade dans le parc à côté de chez moi. Je marche longtemps et je pense à beaucoup de choses. J'adore faire des promenades. Quand je suis en vacances, je fais beaucoup de promenades car j'aime marcher.

Vocabulaire	
à côté de	next to
longtemps	a long time
une chose	a thing
marcher	to walk
je marche	I walk

© Maria Rice-Jones and Brilliant Publications

Nom:_____   **La date:**_____

Écris

Write a memory trick for each of the following expressions.

Faire le ménage

Faire la lessive

Faire la vaisselle

Faire le repassage

Faire les courses

Nom:_____ **La date:**_____

Lis et écris

Answer the following questions.

1. Est-ce que tu fais les courses?	2. Où est-ce que tes parents font les courses?	3. Est-ce qu'il y a un marché dans ta ville?
4. Est-ce que tu fais la vaisselle de temps en temps?	5. Est-ce que ton père fait souvent la vaisselle?	6. Est-ce qu'il y a un lave-vaisselle chez toi?
7. Qui fait le ménage chez toi?	8. Fais-tu le ménage dans ta chambre?	9. Est-ce que tu fais souvent une promenade? Avec qui?

Lis et écris

© Maria Rice-Jones and Brilliant Publications

Nom:_____   **La date:**_____

Ta routine pendant la semaine

Write your daily routine for every day of the week using the verbs "aller", "faire" and any other "er" verbs you'd like to use.

lundi	*Exemple: Le lundi, je vais à l'école à pied car j'habite près de l'école.*
mardi	
mercredi	
jeudi	
vendredi	
samedi	
dimanche	

Nom:_____   **La date:**_____

The fairy "faire"

One day, Guide introduced me to the fairy called "Faire" who was helping him in his house.

The fairy "Faire" had beautiful, elegant wings and flew from one job to the next. With her magical wand she could change things in a few seconds. She would daintily wave her wand and the dirtiest place would become spotless.

When she saw a pile of washing up, she would let the dishes float like a vessel floating on the sea while she repeated the magical sentence three times "je fais la vaisselle, je fais la vaisselle, je fais la vaisselle."

As for piles of dirty clothes she would say "je fais la lessive, je fais la lessive, je fais la lessive," and straight away the clothes would have less dirt in them ready to be ironed. Then she would say in the same way "je fais le repassage" and the iron would "pass" and "repass" over the clothes, leaving them ironed.

As for the housework, Faire believed that "men of any age" could do it. Therefore she repeated three times "je fais le ménage" and the entire house would be spick and span.

Before leaving Guide's house she would fill the fridge with the food needed to make all the courses for every meal of the week. So again, she repeated three times "je fais les courses" and then the fridge would be full of delicious food.

I thought Guide was so lucky to have such a useful and pretty fairy.

Hexagonie, Part 2
© Maria Rice-Jones and Brilliant Publications

Nom:_____ **La date:**_____

Essential words and phrases

How to say "I do the washing up"

Je fais la vaisselle.

The word "vaisselle" is similar to the English word "vessel". A vessel is a ship which floats on water, rather like the dishes in a washing up bowl.

How to say "I do the housework"

Je fais le ménage.

"Men" and "age" are both found in "ménage". We can say that "men of any age" could do the housework if they wanted to. Note that the "ménage" is masculine as it starts with "men".

How to say "I do the shopping"

Je fais les courses.

When you do the shopping, you buy food for the first course, the second course, and so on. That is why the word "courses" is in the plural.

How to say "I do the washing"

Je fais la lessive.

When you wash your clothes, you want them to have "less" stains. The word "lessive" starts with "less".

How to say "I do the ironing"

Je fais le repassage.

When you iron, you "pass" and "re-pass" the iron over the clothes. Note the word "repassage" is masculine.

How to say "I go for a walk"

Je fais une promenade.

"A promenade" in English is a paved public walk, often found along a seaside.

The verb "faire" in the present tense

Je fais

Tu fais

Il/elle fait

Nous faisons

Vous faites

Ils/elles font

What is the weather doing?

Key teaching points
Months of the year
Seasons
Weather

Bonjour...

Say "Bonjour" to the whole class, waiting for the pupils to reply "Bonjour Madame/Monsieur." Call the register in French and expect every pupil to respond "présent(e)" when their name is called out. When you receive no answer say "absent(e)". Call out the name of a pupil and ask him/her, "Comment vas-tu?" waiting for his/her answer "Je vais bien, merci." Ask other pupils how they are. Encourage the pupil to ask you "Et vous?" then answer with "Je vais bien, merci." Always try to use some adjectives that the pupils already know and encourage them to do the same.

Recap on the verb "faire" in the present tense

Ask the pupils to tell you the verb "faire" in the present tense. Then ask them questions that use expressions with "faire" learned in the previous unit. For example, "Charlie, est-ce que tu fais le ménage?", "John, est-ce que tu fais une promenade pendant le week-end?"

Recap the days of the week

Ask for volunteers to say the days of the week in order in French (lundi, mardi, mercredi, jeudi, vendredi, samedi, dimanche).

Ask if pupils can remember how the days from Monday to Friday got their names. They take their names from planets and other heavenly bodies.

English	French	Reason for name
Monday	lundi	from the French word "lune" (moon)
Tuesday	mardi	from "Mars" (Mars)
Wednesday	mercredi	from "Mercure" (Mercury)
Thursday	jeudi	from "Jupiter" (Jupiter)
Friday	vendredi	from "Vénus" (Venus)
Saturday	samedi	
Sunday	dimanche	

© Maria Rice-Jones and Brilliant Publications

Remind pupils that when "le" is in front of "lundi", it means "every Monday" or "on Mondays":

le lundi	on Mondays
le mardi	on Tuesdays
le mercredi	on Wednesdays
le jeudi	on Thursdays
le vendredi	on Fridays
le samedi	on Saturdays
le dimanche	on Sundays

Les mois de l'année

Months of the year

Say that you are going to introduce the months of the year. Say one month at a time in French encouraging the class to repeat each month after you: "janvier, février, mars, avril, mai, juin, juillet, août, septembre, octobre, novembre, décembre". Focus on the months which sound the most different from the English version and which therefore are harder to learn: janvier, février, juin, juillet, and août.

Note:
Point out that the initial letters of days and months are written in lower case in French because there are many Mondays etc and many Aprils etc in a lifetime.

Before asking some questions about the months, introduce the following vocabulary:

Célébrer:	As this word is very similar to the English word, ask pupils to guess what the verb "célébrer" means.
Saint:	As this word is very similar to the English word, ask pupils to guess what the word "saint" means.
Le début de l'année:	Ask the pupils if they know the English word "debut" which means a person's first appearance in a capacity or role. They may have heard of actors having their film or stage debut. Discuss the meaning with them and explain that in French "le début" means "the beginning".
La fin de l'année:	Talk about what the word "**fin**al" means in English. Then explain that "la **fin**" means "the end" and point out that "**fin**" appears in "**fin**al". Make them notice that we say "la fin" and not "le fin".
Un jour de congé:	Tell the pupils that "un jour de **congé**" is "a day off". Ask them to think of the English word "**conge**stion" and to see if they can find a memory trick such as: "When

Vocabulaire

janvier	January
février	February
mars	March
avril	April
mai	May
juin	June
juillet	July
août	August
septembre	September
octobre	October
novembre	November
décembre	December
le début de l'année	the beginning of the year
saint	saint
célébrer	to celebrate
la fin de l'année	the end of the year
Pâques	Easter
un jour de congé	a day off
la fête	the festival
Noël	Christmas

Materials

★ Envelopes
★ Sheet 13a (page 265), photocopied on to card
★ Scissors

people have a day off they all take their car to go somewhere nice and the roads are **conge**sted."

Une fête: Tell them that this word means "festival" or "party". Ask them what the English word "fête" means. Does your school or village/ town have a summer fête?

Pâques: Ask pupils to find a memory trick for "Pâques" which means Easter. Our memory trick is: people **pack** to go away at **Easter** as it is a Bank Holiday weekend.

Noël: Pupils may know this word from Christmas cards or the carol, "The First Noel". Point out that it starts with the same letter as "nativity".

13a
Give each pupil a copy of Sheet 13a photocopied on to card and ask each pupil to cut out the months of the year. Then you can ask the class questions for them to answer by holding up these cards or arranging them on their desks. After the activities, keep the cards so that they can be used with Sheet 13c later in the unit. The pupils could put them in an envelope with their name on it to keep them safe.

Activity 1
Say that you will call out the name of a month in French and that pupils have to hold up the card with that month written on it. For example, if you say "août" then they need to hold up the card with "août" on it.

Activity 2
Ask the pupils to put the months of the year in order in front of them on the desk.

Activity 3
Ask the pupils to find all the months that begin with the letter "j" and place them in front of them on the desk.

Activity 4
Say that you are going to ask a question about an event during the year and that the pupils should hold up a card showing the month in which the event is celebrated or occurs.

Examples:
Teacher: Quand est-ce que l'école commence?
Pupils septembre

Teacher:	C'est quand la fête d'Halloween?
Pupils:	octobre

Teacher:	C'est quand la fête de Noël?
Pupils:	décembre

Teacher:	C'est quand le début de l'année?
Pupils:	janvier

Teacher:	C'est quand la fin de l'année?
Pupils:	décembre

Teacher:	C'est quand la Saint Valentin?
Pupils:	février

Teacher:	Quand est-ce que nous célébrons Pâques?
Pupils:	mars ou avril

Ask pupils questions about events during the year, and listen to their answers. For example:

Teacher:	C'est quand Noël, en décembre ou en mars?
Pupil:	Noël est en décembre.

Teacher:	Est-ce que le 31 octobre les enfants célébrent la fête d'Halloween ou Pâques?
Pupil:	Les enfants célébrent la fête d'Halloween.

Teacher:	En janvier, est-ce que nous célébrons le début de l'année ou la fin de l'année?
Pupil:	En janvier, nous célébrons le début de l'année.

Teacher:	Noël, c'est le 20 ou le 25 décembre?
Pupil:	Noël, c'est le 25 décembre.

Vocabulaire

le premier janvier	the first of January
le deux mars	the second (literally, the two) of March
le trois septembre	the third (literally, the three) of September
la date	the date
un anniversaire	a birthday
mon anniversaire	my birthday

Materials

★ Sheet 13b (page 266)

Les dates

The dates

Tell the pupils that in French it is simpler than in English to say dates because after "the first" of the month, "le premier", for the rest of the days of the months, the French use the numbers from 2 to 31 and say "le deux mai" or "le trois avril" rather than the "second of May" or the "third of April".

Say, "La date de mon anniversaire est le 11 juillet" (The date of my birthday is the 11th of July). Ask every pupil the date of their birthday, "Quelle est la date de ton anniversaire?" expecting them to reply, "Le premier mai" or "Le vingt-cinq juillet", etc.

Continue by asking questions such as: "Quelle est la date d'aujourd'hui?" or "Quel jour est la fête de Noël?"

Give the pupils a copy of Sheet 13b and ask them to answer the questions.

Les quatre saisons

The four seasons

Hold up the picture showing the scene for autumn (use Sheets c(i)–c(ii)). Introduce "l'automne" (autumn) by saying "C'est l'automne". Then hold up the picture for winter and say, "C'est l'hiver" (It is winter). Then hold up the picture for spring and say, "C'est le printemps" (It is spring). Finally, hold up the picture for summer and say "C'est l'été" (It is summer).

Then hold up one of the pictures, for example, autumn, and ask "C'est quelle saison?" ("What season is it?) and wait for the class to reply, "C'est l'automne". Repeat the question with the other pictures and ask individual pupils.

Put the pupils into pairs and give each pair copies of Sheets 13c(i)–13c(ii). Tell them to point to one of their pictures of a season and ask which one it is by saying, "C'est quelle saison?" The other pupil should answer the question by saying "C'est l'automne" or "C'est l'hiver" etc.

Use the months of the year cut out from Sheet 13a earlier in this Unit. Ask the pupils to sort the months according to season. Walk around the class looking at the pupils' work to ensure that they have arranged the seasons and the months correctly. Once you have checked them, they could stick the words down or write them on another sheet of paper.

L'été	L'automne
juin	septembre
juillet	octobre
août	novembre

L'hiver	Le printemps
décembre	mars
janvier	avril
février	mai

To help the pupils remember the seasons in French ask them to come up with a memory trick. If they can't think of anything you could suggest the ones below.

Vocabulaire

une saison	a season
l'automne (m)	the autumn
le printemps	the spring
l'été (m)	the summer
l'hiver (m)	the winter

Materials

★ Pictures of the four seasons
★ Sheets 13c(i)–13c(ii) (pages 267–268), photocopied onto card and cut up. Additional copies photocopied so each pair has a copy of each sheet
★ Month cards from Sheet 13a (page 265)

In winter, "**hiver**", you **sh**iver.
In summer, "**été**", you **eat** outside.
The word "automne" is similar to the English word autumn.
"**Prin**temps" has letters in common with **spr**ing.

Say to the pupils that all the months of the year take "en" for "in" the month, for example "en janvier" (in January). Then say that three of the seasons "été", "hiver" and "automne" take "en" but "au" is used before "printemps", "au printemps". Write this table on the board to show the pupils.

en	au	le
en janvier	au printemps	le premier janvier
en février		le premier mai
en mars		le deux février
en avril		le trois mars
en mai		le quatre juin
en juin		le vingt avril
en juillet		etc...
en août		
en septembre		
en octobre		
en novembre		
en décembre		
en été		
en hiver		
en automne		

We use "en" before a vowel or silent "h" because "en" ends in an "n" which makes it easier to pronounce in front of a vowel. Because "printemps" starts with a consonant, there's no need to put "en" and we put "au".

Quel temps fait-il?

What is the weather like?

13c (ii)

Hold up the picture for the summer (on Sheet 13c(ii)) and say to the pupils:

En général, en été, le soleil brille.
Il fait chaud.
Souvent il fait très chaud.
Les enfants nagent dans l'eau et jouent avec des ballons. Ils sont très heureux.

Les arbres ont beaucoup de fruits et les fleurs sont magnifiques.

In general, in summer, the sun shines. *(Point to the sun.)*
It is hot. *(Mime that it is hot.)*
Often, it is very hot. *(Mime it being very hot.)*
The children swim in the water and play with balls. They are very happy. *(Mime swimming and playing with balls, if necessary.)*

The trees have lots of fruit and the flowers are magnificent.

Ask individual pupils, "Et toi, qu'est-ce que tu fais quand il fait chaud?" You might need to remind them of the games and sports they learned in Unit 8 or ask them to look at Sheets 8c and 8d in their folders. They might answer, "Quand il fait chaud je joue à la corde à sauter" or "Quand il fait chaud je joue au ballon."

You can also ask "Où est-ce que tu vas quand il fait chaud?" They might reply, "Quand il fait chaud je vais à la piscine" or "Je vais au parc". You can also ask "Quels fruits est-ce que tu manges en été?"

13c (i)

Hold up the picture for the autumn (on Sheet 13c(i)). Say to the pupils:

En général, en automne, il fait moins chaud.

Il fait mauvais temps car il fait du vent ou il pleut.
Les arbres sont nus car toutes les feuilles des arbres tombent.

Les enfants ramassent des champignons.

In general, in autumn, it is cooler. *(Mime putting on your coat or a jumper.)*

The weather is bad because it is windy or it rains. *(Mime windy and rainy.)*
The trees are bare because all the leaves are falling. *(Point to the picture of the tree and the leaves falling.)*
The children collect mushrooms. *(Point to the picture of the children collecting mushrooms or mime collecting mushrooms.)*

Ask the pupils: "Que fais-tu quand il pleut?" They

Vocabulaire

il fait chaud	it is hot
le soleil brille	the sun shines
nager	to swim
heureux/heureuse	happy
magnifique	magnificent
il fait moins chaud	it is cooler
il fait mauvais temps	it is bad weather
il fait du vent	it is windy
il pleut	it is rainy
les arbres sont nus	the trees are bare
tomber	to fall
les feuilles des arbres tombent	the leaves on the tree are falling
ramasser	to collect
un champignon	a mushroom
il fait froid	it is cold
il neige	it is snowing
la température	the temperature
très agréable	very nice (very agreeable)
il fait beau	it is beautiful
le ciel est souvent bleu	the sky is often blue
l'Europe	Europe
skier	to ski
un orage	a storm
le temps est orageux	it is stormy weather
l'éclair	the lightning
le brouillard	the fog

Materials

★ Sheets 13c(i)–13c(ii) (pages 266–267), photocopied onto card and cut up.
★ Sheets 8c–8d (pages 164–165) – optional.
★ Sheets 13d–13h (pages. 269–273)
★ CD, Track 25
★ CD, Track 26

might answer, "Quand il pleut je joue aux cartes" or "Quand il pleut je vais au cinéma" or "Quand il pleut je regarde la télévision."

Hold up the picture for winter (on Sheet 13c(i)). Say to the pupils:

D'habitude, en hiver, il fait froid et quelquefois il neige.	Usually, in winter, it is cold and sometimes it snows. *(Mime that it is cold and point to the snow.)*
Les enfants sont heureux car ils jouent avec la neige.	The children are happy because they are playing with the snow. *(Point to the children playing.)*

Ask the pupils: "Est-ce que tu aimes la neige?" or "Qu'est-ce que tu fais quand il fait très froid?"

Hold up the picture for spring (on Sheet 13c(ii)). Say to the pupils:

D'habitude, au printemps, il fait beau car le soleil brille et la température est très agréable.	Usually, in spring, it is beautiful because the sun shines and the temperature is very nice. *(Point to the sun.)*
Le ciel est souvent bleu.	The sky is often blue.
Les enfants jouent dans les parcs ou dans les jardins.	Children play in the parks or the gardens.

Ask the pupils: "Quelle est ta saison préférée? Pourquoi?" or "Que fais-tu quand il fait beau?"

Tell the pupils that to describe the weather, the French use an adjective such as "froid", "chaud", "beau" with the verb "faire": "Il fait froid, il fait chaud, il fait beau."

In French, the verb "faire" is used to talk about the weather because the weather is always doing something. Different types of weather with "il fait":

il fait froid	it is cold (**fr**oid like **fr**idge)
il fait chaud	it is warm
il fait beau	it is nice weather (**beau**tiful)
il fait mauvais temps	it is bad weather
il fait du vent	it is windy (**vent**ilation)
il fait du brouillard	it is foggy

Tell the class that when it is raining, the French say "Il pleut". For example, "Il pleut souvent dans le nord de l'Europe" (It often rains in the north of Europe). They do not use the verb "faire" as the verb "to rain" exists: "pleuvoir".

Then tell the class that when it is snowing, the French say "Il neige". For example, "Il neige en ce moment en Suisse" (At the moment it is snowing in Switzerland). They do not use the verb "faire" as the verb "to snow" exists: "neiger".

Other useful weather expressions that you may wish to teach the class are listed below:

un orage	a storm	(Le temps est orageux = stormy weather)
l'éclair	the lightning	
le brouillard	the fog	(Il fait du brouillard = it is foggy)
une tempête	a gale	

Memory trick

Un orage (storm): the weather is in a rage.
Un éclair (lightning): a chocolate éclair is often eaten as fast as lightning.
Une tempête (gale): Shakespeare's play is "The Tempest".

13d

Give each pupil a copy of Sheet 13d and ask the pupils to complete it.

13e

Track 49&50

Listen to Track 49 on the CD and read the words of the song on Sheet 13e. Encourage the pupils to sing along. Track 50 contains an instrumental version.

13f

Track 51&52

Listen to Track 51 on the CD and read the words of the song on Sheet 13f. Encourage the pupils to sing along. Track 52 contains an instrumental version.

13g

Give the pupils Sheet 13g and ask them to tick the correct column for each sentence. This reinforces when to use "en", "à" and "le/l'".

13h

Track 53

Listen to this report on the weather in France on Track 53 and/or read it on Sheet 13h. Pupils may want to listen to it several times. Talk about it to ensure children understand everything and ask questions, for example:

Pourquoi est-ce que les touristes vont souvent dans le sud de la France?
En France, où est-ce qu'il neige souvent?
En hiver, est-ce qu'il neige dans ta ville?
Est-ce que tu aimes quand il fait froid? Pourquoi?

In pairs, role play having a telephone conversation about the weather with a friend in France. First pairs will need to decide where the French person lives and discuss what the weather would be like there. Once they have completed the conversation, they should swap roles (encourage them to choose a new place in France as well).

Go around the room, listening to conversations and correcting where necessary. Give lots of praise. Some pairs could be asked to act out their conversation in front of the class.

Materials

★ Sheet 13i (page 274)

Hexagonie story

Give each pupil Sheet 13i. Read it with the pupils and discuss the points covered.

Essential words and phrases

At the end of this unit, give the pupils Sheet 13j, which will help them to remember essential words and phrases.

Resources

★ Sheet 13j (page 275)

Au revoir! Bonne semaine! Bon week-end!

Remember to wish the pupils a good week or weekend, depending on when the lesson takes place. Wait for them to reply, "Merci Madame/Monsieur, vous aussi!"

Nom:_____   **La date:**_____

Les mois de l'année

janvier	avril	août
juin	février	mars
septembre	mai	décembre
octobre	novembre	juillet

Nom:_____   **La date:**_____

Réponds aux questions suivantes

Answer the following questions.

1. Quels jours de la semaine vas-tu à l'école?

_____

2. Quand as-tu une leçon de français?

_____

3. Que fais-tu pendant le week-end?

_____

4. Quelle est la date de ton anniversaire?

_____

5. C'est quel jour aujourd'hui?

_____

6. Quels mois ont trente jours?

_____

7. Quelle est la date de la fête de Noël?

_____

8. Quand est la Saint Valentin?

_____

Nom:_____   **La date:**_____

Hexagonie, Part 2
© Maria Rice-Jones and Brilliant Publications

Nom:_____   **La date:**_____

Hexagonie, Part 2

Nom:_____ **La date:**_____

Regarde et écris

Look at the pictures then look at the weather sentences written at the bottom of the page. Select the correct weather expression and write it underneath the matching picture.

Exemple:

Il fait mauvais temps

_____ _____ _____

_____ _____ _____

Le temps

| Il fait mauvais temps |

| Le soleil brille | Il fait chaud | Il fait froid |

| Il neige | Il fait beau | Il fait du vent |

Nom: _____   **La date:** _____

Lis  et écoute

Read through the text of this French song and listen to it on the CD.
Sing it altogether as a class.

Il pleut, il pleut bergère

Shepherdess, it's raining

*Just after the French revolution in 1789, songs and plays about the countryside became
very popular. The singer is telling the shepherdess that it is raining and she must bring
her sheep inside. The singer can hear the noise of the rain in the trees and see the lightning
flashing.*

Il pleut, il pleut bergère,	It's raining, it's raining shepherdess
Rentre tes blancs moutons.	Bring your white sheep inside.
Allons dans la chaumière,	Let's go in the cottage,
Bergère vite allons.	Shepherdess quickly, let's go.
J'entends sur le feuillage,	I can hear on the leaves,
L'eau qui tombe à grand bruit.	The water falling loudly.
Voici venir l'orage,	Here comes the storm,
Voilà l'éclair qui luit.	Here is the lightning flashing.

Nom:_____   **La date:**_____

Lis et écoute

Read through the text of this French song and listen to it on the CD.
Sing it altogether as a class.

Gouttes, gouttelettes de pluie

Drops, droplets of rain

Refrain
Gouttes, gouttelettes de pluie
Mon chapeau se mouille
Gouttes, gouttelettes de pluie
Mes souliers aussi.

Je marche sur la route
Je connais le chemin
Je passe à travers gouttes
En leur chantant ce gai refrain.

Refrain

Je marche dans la boue
J'en ai jusqu'au menton
J'en ai même sur les joues
Et pourtant je fais attention.

Refrain

Mais derrière les nuages
Le soleil s'est levé
Il sèche le village
Et mon chapeau et mes souliers.

Dernier refrain
Gouttes, gouttelettes de pluie
Adieu les nuages
Gouttes, gouttelettes de pluie
L'averse est finie.

Chorus
Drops, little drops of rain
My hat is getting wet
Drops, little drops of rain
My shoes as well.

I walk along the road
I know the lane
I pass through drops
And to them sing this gay refrain.

Chorus

I walk in the mud
I have some up to my chin
I even have some on my cheeks
Even though I am careful.

Chorus

But behind the clouds
The sun has risen
It dries the village
And my hat and shoes.

Last chorus
Drops, little drops of rain
Farewell clouds
Drops, little drops of rain
The shower is over.

Nom:_____ **La date:**_____

Lis 📖 et complète 📝

Read the sentences and tick the correct box.

	en	à	le	l'	
Je suis né					1999.
Nous avons une leçon					mardi.
Il va à l'école					matin.
Son anniversaire est					5 mai.
Je vais skier					hiver.
Elle travaille					après-midi.
Nous habitons					France.
Nous allons					Paris.
Ils vont					vacances.
Je vais à l'école					pied.
Il va à l'école					voiture.
J'ai une leçon					14 heures.
Tu es fatigué					soir.
Il travaille					Rome.

Nom:_____   **La date:**_____

Quel temps fait-il en France?

La France a différents climats sur son territoire car on trouve des montagnes et des plaines et également deux mers: la mer Méditerranée et l'océan Atlantique. Chaque région a son climat.

Dans le nord et sur la côte ouest, il pleut souvent car la pluie vient de l'Atlantique.

Dans le centre et l'est, il y a un climat continental avec des hivers froids et des étés chauds.

En France, il y a quatre régions avec des montagnes: les Vosges, le Jura, les Alpes et les Pyrénées. Dans les montagnes, les hivers sont longs et les étés sont assez chauds.

Le midi est la région au sud de la France, sur la méditérranée. Les étés sont extrêmement chauds et les hivers sont doux. Mais quelquefois il y a le "Mistral" qui est un vent très violent et très froid.

Vocabulaire

un climat	a climate
un territoire	the territory
une montagne	a mountain
une plaine	a plain
la mer	the sea
un océan	an ocean
le nord	the north
une côte	a coast
l'ouest (m)	the west
une région	a region
assez	quite
le sud	the south
l'est (m)	the east
extrêmement	extremely
doux/douce	soft/mild
violent	violent

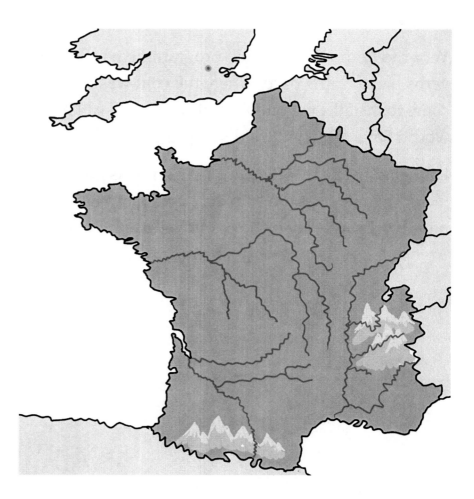

Nom:_____ **La date:**_____

The weather in action

One day while I was in Hexagonie, I was introduced
to the fairy, Faire. With her magical wand Faire could
change things in a few seconds. Inside she could tidy
a house in no time at all, but outside she was even
busier as she made the weather.

This is because, in Hexagonie, twice a year, the verbs
could decide what sort of weather they wanted to
have for special occasions, and all for free. Imagine being able to guarantee that
the weather will be nice on the day of a barbecue or a picnic outside with your
friends!

They would contact the fairy Faire who would come to their garden or to the
park to install a huge bubble underneath which the weather would be just as
they wanted. Most verbs would request an "il fait beau" or an "il fait chaud"
programme.

Very rarely the "il fait froid" programme was requested, but sometimes some
verbs had a skiing party where the cold was required. Then the fairy Faire would
come to install a big bubble and she would call Neiger (to snow). Thus the verbs
would have an "il fait froid" programme with an "il neige" programme.

I am glad to say that Pleuvoir (to rain) was not often asked because nobody,
including me, likes the "il pleut" programme. I much prefer when the weather is
nice. If only in every country I travelled, there was a fairy Faire.

Nom:_____   **La date:**_____

Essential words and phrases

The verb "faire" (to do) is used to talk about the weather because the weather is always doing something.

Quel temps fait-il?   What's the weather like?

"Il fait" is followed by an adjective:

Il fait froid/ Il fait chaud.   It is cold/ It is hot.

Il fait beau/ Il fait mauvais temps.   It is beautiful/ It is bad weather.

When not to use "Il fait"

When a verb introduces the weather:

Il pleut/ Il neige.   It is raining/ It is snowing.

How to say the months of the year

janvier	January	en janvier	in January
février	February	en février	in February
mars	March	en mars	in March
avril	April	en avril	in April
mai	May	en mai	in May
juin	June	en juin	in June
juillet	July	en juillet	in July
août	August	en août	in August
septembre	September	en septembre	in September
octobre	October	en octobre	in October
novembre	November	en novembre	in November
décembre	December	en décembre	in December

How to say the seasons of the year

les saisons	the seasons		
l'hiver	winter	en hiver	in winter
le printemps	spring	au printemps	in spring
l'été	summer	en été	in summer
l'automne	autumn	en automne	in autumn

Describe your life!

Bonjour

Say "Bonjour" to the whole class, waiting for the pupils to reply "Bonjour Madame/Monsieur." Call the register in French and expect every pupil to respond "présent(e)" when their name is called out. When you receive no answer say "absent(e)". Call out the name of a pupil and ask him/her, "Comment vas-tu?" waiting for his/her answer "Je vais bien, merci." Ask other pupils how they are. Encourage the pupil to ask you "et vous?" then answer with "Je vais bien merci", using a range of adjectives.

Recap on the weather

Ask the pupils questions about today's weather such as:
Quel temps fait-il aujourd'hui?
Est-ce qu'il pleut aujourd'hui?
Est-ce qu'il neige aujourd'hui?
Est-ce qu'il fait beau aujourd'hui?
Est-ce qu'il fait froid aujourd'hui?

Vocabulaire

une dame	a lady
une baleine	a whale
une coccinelle	a ladybird
un escargot	a snail

Materials

★ Pictures/photographs to illustrate a variety of adjectives
★ Small lined notebooks, one for each pupil

Adjectifs pour décrire

Adjectives to describe

Select from the long list below the adjectives you would like to practise with your pupils. Once you have chosen them, look at our suggestions of questions and ask similar questions.

Different ways to introduce the adjectives:

- You could mime the action while saying the adjective.

- You could show pictures from magazines to illustrate the adjectives such as: a tall man and a short man

- You could use flashcards with some expressive faces: a sad face, a happy face, an angry face, a shy face, a face with a silly expression

Some ideas for flashcards

jeune	young	a baby	Le bébé est jeune.
vieux (m)	old	an old man	Le monsieur est vieux.
vieille (f)	old	an old woman	La dame est vieille.
grand(e)	big	a whale	La baleine est grande.
petit(e)	small	a ladybird	La coccinelle est petite.
lent(e)	slow	a snail	L'escargot est lent.
rapide	fast	a sports car	La voiture est rapide.

Once you have asked some questions, you could ask your pupils to write the adjectives by alphabetical order in a notebook entitled: Mes adjectifs en français (my adjectives in French). Remember to mention that we can hardly find any adjectives starting with the following letters in French: k, q, w, x, y, and z. Then ask the pupils to illustrate their notebook by drawing or sticking a picture for each adjective chosen by them or by you. Tell the pupils that you will reward the best notebooks and tell them how important it is to keep their personal notebooks as a reference for the future years.

Here is a long list of adjectives you can choose from. We put in bold the French adjectives which are similar or quite similar to the English ones.

A

actif/active	active
affectueux/affectueuse	affectionate
agé(e)	aged/elderly
agité(e)	**agitated**
agréable	**nice/agreeable**
ambitieux/ambitieuse	**ambitious**
amusant(e)	**funny/amusing**
anxieux/anxieuse	**anxious**
attentif/attentive	**attentive**
autoritaire	**authoritarian**

B

beau/belle	handsome/beautiful
blessé(e)	injured/hurt
blond(e)	**blond**
brun(e)	brown
brutal(e)	**brutal**

C

calme	**calm**
créatif/créative	**creative**
certain(e)	**certain**
charmant(e)	**charming/very nice**
chaud(e)	hot
cher/chère	expensive
clair(e)	**clear**
compliqué(e)	**complicated**
confortable	**comfortable**
content(e)	happy
correct/e	**correct**
court(e)	short
cruel/cruelle	**cruel**
curieux/curieuse	**curious**

D

dangereux/dangereuse	**dangerous**
dégoûtant(e)	disgusting
délicieux/délicieuse	**delicious**
désagréable	**disagreeable/not nice**

différent(e)	**different**
difficile	**difficult**
doux/douce	soft
drôle	funny
dur(e)	hard
dynamique	**dynamic**

E

élégant(e)	**elegant**
énergique	**energetic**
ennuyeux/ennuyeuse	boring
énorme	**enormous**
enthousiaste	**enthusiastic**
essentiel/essentielle	**essential**
étroit(e)	narrow
excellent(e)	**excellent**
extraordinaire	**extraordinary**

F

fâché(e)	angry
facile	easy
faible	**feeble**
fantastique	**fantastic**
faux/fausse	**false**
fort(e)	strong
fou/folle	mad/crazy
fragile	**fragile**
fréquent(e)	**frequent**
froid(e)	cold
furieux/furieuse	**furious**

G

généreux/ généreuse	**generous**
gentil/gentille	kind/gentle
gourmand(e)	greedy
grand(e)	tall/big
grave	serious
gros/grosse	fat

H

handicapé(e)	disabled
haut(e)	high
heureux/heureuse	happy
honnête	**honest**
horrible	**horrible**
hostile	**hostile**
humble	**humble**

I

idéal(e)	**ideal**
idiot(e)	**idiot**
ignorant(e)	**ignorant**
impatient(e)	**impatient**

impoli(e)	**impolite/rude**
important(e)	**important**
impossible	**impossible**
incorrect	**incorrect**
incroyable	incredible
innocent(e)	**innocent**
inquiet/inquiète	worried
insolent(e)	**insolent**
intelligent(e)	**intelligent**
intéressant(e)	**interesting**
intéressé(e)	**interested**
inutile	useless

J

jeune	young
joli(e)	pretty
juste	fair

L

laid(e)	ugly
large	**large**
léger/légère	light
lent(e)	slow
libre	free
logique	**logical**
long/longue	**long**
lourd(e)	heavy

M

malade	ill
malheureux/malheureuse	unhappy
méchant(e)	naughty, nasty
mince	thin
moderne	**modern**
modeste	**modest**

N

naturel/naturelle	**natural**
nécessaire	**necessary**
nerveux/nerveuse	**nervous**
neuf/neuve	new
normal(e)	**normal**

O

occupé(e)	**busy/occupied**
ordinaire	**ordinary**
optimiste	**optimistic**
original(e)	**original**

P

pâle	**pale**
paresseux/paresseuse	lazy
patient(e)	**patient**

pauvre	poor
pessimiste	**pessimistic**
petit(e)	small
plein(e)	full
poli(e)	**polite**
positif/positive	**positive**
possible	**possible**
profond(e)	**deep/profound**
propre	clean
prudent(e)	**prudent/careful**
pure	**pure**

R

rapide	**quick/rapid**
rare	**rare**
récent/e	**recent**
responsable	**responsible**
riche	**rich**
ridicule	**ridiculous**
rond(e)	round
roux / rousse	with red hair

S

sale	dirty
seul(e)	alone
sévère	**severe**
similaire	**similar**
simple	**simple**
sincère	**sincere**
spacieux/spacieuse	**spacious**
sportif/sportive	**sporty**
stricte	**strict**
studieux/studieuse	**studious**
sûr(e)	**sure**
sympathique, sympa	nice

T

tendre	**tender, loving**
terrible	**terrible**
timide	shy
transparent	**transparent**
triste	sad

U

utile	useful

V

vieux / vieille	old
vide	empty
violent(e)	**violent**

You could ask the pupils to find some memory tricks for some adjectives. We show you some below:

There are a few tricks that might help the pupils remember some of these adjectives:

paresseux(se)	lazy	Lazy like a **para**site.
sympathique	nice	A **sympath**etic person is often nice.
cher (chère)	expensive	When something is expensive, it is better to "share" the expense.
blessé	injured/hurt	A person who is only injured in a serious accident is **blesse**d because they survived the accident.
inquiet (inquiète)	worried	When you are worried you are restless and not **quiet**

Les adjectifs féminins

Feminine adjectives

Say that if you are talking about a person or an object that is feminine then you might have to change it to a feminine form.

Masculine	*Feminine*
When it ends in a consonant	**add an "e"**
élégant	élégante
When it ends in "eux"	**"eux" changes into "euse"**
généreux	généreuse
When it ends in "if"	**"if" changes into "ive"**
actif	active
When it ends in "e"	**does not change**
calme	calme

14a

Give the pupils Sheet 14a and ask them to do the exercise on this sheet.

Put the pupils into pairs. One pupil is the interviewer. The interviewer asks the other pupil to describe themselves, their family and their teachers. For example, they could ask, "Comment est ton père?" When they have finished the pupils should swap roles.

Vocabulaire

une cicatrice   a scar

Materials

★ Sheets 14a-–14d (pages 286–289)

Suggested topics:
1. Their family (Mon père est grand, Ma mère est sympa etc)
2. Themselves (Je suis très intelligent, Je suis jeune, De temps en temps je suis paresseux etc)
3. Their teachers (Ma prof de français est gentille et intelligente etc)

Walk around the classroom listening to the pupils and correcting them when necessary. Remember to praise good work with "Très bien" or "Excellent".

 Give Sheet 14b to the pupils and ask them to write sentences underneath each picture to describe the people or animals.

 Give Sheet 14c to the pupils and ask them to look at the faces and tick the boxes as appropriate.

 Divide the pupils into groups of four and give each group a list of four adjectives to mime in front of the class (for example, grand, gros, beau, amusant, stupide, intelligent etc.). Each pupil must mime an adjective. The class has to guess which adjective it is.

 Give Sheet 14d to the pupils and ask them to design a "Wanted" poster in French.

Materials

★ Sheet 14e (page 290)

Exemples de phrases avec des adjectifs

Examples of phrases with adjectives

Use the adjectives you have taught to talk about a topic that interests your class. Below are some possible questions, together with examples of the replies that pupils might give:

Talking about the weather

Teacher:	Est-ce que tu es triste ou content quand il fait beau?
Pupil:	Je ne suis pas triste quand il fait beau mais je suis content car je joue dans mon jardin.
Teacher:	Est-ce que tu es triste ou content quand il neige?
Pupil:	Je suis content quand il neige car je joue avec la neige.
Teacher:	Est-ce que tu portes des vêtements chauds quand il fait froid?
Pupil:	Oui, je porte des vêtements chauds quand il fait froid.
Teacher:	Est-ce que le vent est violent quand il y a une tempête?
Pupil:	Oui, le vent est violent quand il y a une tempête.

Teacher:	Quand il y a du vent est-ce que la mer est calme ou agitée?
Pupils:	La mer est agitée.
Teacher:	Quand il fait chaud est-ce que tu portes ton uniforme d'hiver ou d'été?
Pupil:	Je porte mon uniforme d'été.
Teacher:	Quand il fait froid est-ce que tu portes ton uniforme d'hiver ou d'été?
Pupil:	Je porte mon uniforme d'hiver.

Talking about school

Teacher:	Est-ce que ton école est grande ou petite?
Pupil:	Mon école est ….
Teacher:	Est-ce que ton école est belle ou laide?
Pupil:	Mon école est ….
Teacher:	Est-ce que ton uniforme est confortable?
Pupil:	Oui, mon uniforme est confortable.
Teacher:	Est-ce que ton uniforme est beau ou laid?
Pupil:	Je pense qu'il est laid.
Teacher:	Est-ce que ton uniforme est classique ou moderne?
Pupils:	Il est trop classique.
Teacher:	Est-ce que ton uniforme est élégant?
Pupil:	Je pense que mon uniforme n'est pas élégant.
Teacher:	Est-ce que ton cartable est lourd ou léger?
Pupil:	Mon cartable est toujours très lourd.

Talking about the family

Teacher:	Quand est-ce que tes parents sont sévères?
Pupil:	Ils sont sévères avec moi quand je ne suis pas gentil.
Teacher:	Est-ce que tes parents ont une voiture neuve ou vieille?
Pupil:	Ils ont une voiture ….
Teacher:	Est-ce que tes parents sont sportifs?
Pupil:	Non, mes parents ne sont pas sportifs car ils sont très occupés pendant la semaine.
Teacher :	Est-ce que tes parents sont polis ou impolis?
Pupil:	Mes parents sont toujours polis.

Talking about your house

Teacher:	Est-ce que ta maison est spacieuse?
Pupil:	Oui, ma maison est assez spacieuse.
Teacher:	Est-ce que ta maison est moderne ou vieille?
Pupil:	Elle est ….
Teacher:	Est-ce que ta chambre est propre ou sale?
Pupil:	Ma chambre est souvent propre mais pas tous les jours.

Talking about television

Teacher: Est-ce que tu regardes des films intéressants?

Pupil: Oui, je regarde des films intéressants mais pas chaque jour.

Teacher: Penses-tu que le journal télévisé est ennuyeux ou intéressant?

Pupil: Je pense qu'il est intéressant.

Teacher: Penses-tu que les dessins animés sont amusants?

Pupil: Oui, les dessins animés sont très amusants.

Teacher: Penses-tu que les films d'aventure sont passionnants?

Pupil: Oui, ils sont passionnants.

Talking about yourself

Teacher: Est-ce que tu es fatigué/e quand tu étudies trop?

Est-ce que tes cheveux sont courts, mi-longs ou longs?

Est-ce que tu es paresseux(se) quand tu es fatigué(e)?

Est-ce que tu es optimiste/pessimiste? Généreux(se)? réservé(e)? timide?

Est-ce que ton chat ou ton chien est gentil ou méchant?

Give pupils Sheet 14e and ask them to complete the sentences with adjectives of their choice.

Vocabulaire

plus … que	more … than
moins … que	less … than
aussi … que	as … as
un paquet	a packet
une lettre	a letter
le Nil	the Nile
un ticket	a ticket

Materials

★ Pictures of people of varying ages (both sexes)
★ Sheet 14f (page 291)

Compare

Compare

Take two pictures, one of an old man and one of a young boy and start comparing them. First point at the picture with the old man and say:

Il est plus vieux que le petit garçon.
Il est plus grand que le petit garçon.
Il est plus gros que le petit garçon.

Then point at the picture with the little boy and say:

Il est plus jeune que le monsieur.
Il est plus petit que le monsieur.
Il est plus mince que le monsieur.

Now take two pictures, one of an old woman and one of a young girl and encourage the pupils to compare them in the same way by using 'plus….que'.

Elle est plus vieille que la petite fille.
Elle est plus grande que la petite fille.
Elle est plus grosse que la petite fille.

Then compare things around you using "plus … que" (more …

than), "moins … que (less … than) and "aussi … que" (as … as).

 You could write the comparatives on the board and tell the pupils that in order to remember "plus" they should remember the mathematical sign "plus" and for "moins", the "minus" sign. As for "aussi" the pupils could play with letters and realize that in "aussi" there are the letters "a" and "s" of "as".

Potential questions:

You could ask individual pupils to compare themselves with another person, for example: compare yourself with your father, etc.

Teacher: Est-ce que tu es plus jeune ou plus âgé que moi?
Est-ce que tu es plus optimiste que ta mère ?
Est-ce que ton père est plus ambitieux que ta mère?
Est-ce que tu es moins grand que moi?
Est-ce que tu es moins sportif que ton père?
Est-ce que la ville de Paris est aussi grande que la ville de Londres?
Est-ce qu'un autobus est plus long qu'un train?
Est-ce qu'un paquet est aussi lourd qu'une lettre?
Est-ce que la Tour Eiffel est plus haute que l'Empire State Building?
Est-ce que le mont Everest est plus haut que le mont Blanc?
Est-ce qu'une Mini est plus chère qu'une Porsche?
Est-ce que la France est aussi grande que la Chine?
Est-ce que le Nil (the Nile) est plus long que la Seine?

Ask the pupils to bring two pictures of their choice to compare for the following lesson telling them that you will ask some pupils to compare them orally in front of the class.

 Give pupils Sheet 14f and ask them to complete it.

Essential words and phrases

 At the end of this unit, give the pupils Sheet 14g, which will help them to remember essential words and phrases.

> **Materials**
> ★ Sheet 14g (page 292)

Au revoir! Bonne semaine! Bon week-end!

Remember to wish the pupils a good week or weekend, depending on when the lesson takes place. Wait for them to reply, "Merci Madame/Monsieur, vous aussi!"

Nom:_____   **La date:**_____

Les adjectifs

Adjectives

Masculine	Feminine
When it ends in a consonant	**add an "e"**
élégant	élégante
When it ends in "eux"	**"eux" changes into "euse"**
généreux	généreuse
When it ends in "if"	**"if" changes into "ive"**
actif	active
When it ends in "e"	**does not change**
calme	calme

Écris ✎ l'adjectif féminin

Write the feminine adjective:

Masculin	Féminin	Masculin	Féminin
généreux	généreu_ _	content	content_
sportif	sporti _ _	heureux	heureu _ _
sympathique	sympathiqu_	timide	timid_
calme	calm_	facile	facil_
nerveux	nerveu _ _	difficile	difficil_

Nom:_____ **La date:**_____

Régarde et écris

Ask the pupils to write or say sentences describing the things they see in each box:

Ma maison est grande.

Mes parents sont………...

Mon frère est ……………...

Ma soeur est………………...

Ma sœur est ………………...

Mon chien est ………………...

Mon chat est ………………...

Ma sœur est ………………...

Mon frère est ……………...

© Maria Rice-Jones and Brilliant Publications

Nom:_____   **La date:**_____

Regarde et écris

Look at the following faces and tick the correct expression.

Il est content ☐

Il est triste ☐

Il est fatigué ☐

Il est fâché ☐

Il est timide ☐

Il est content ☐

Il est triste ☐

Il est heureux ☐

Il est fàché ☐

Il est calme ☐

Nom:_____ **La date:**_____

Dessine et écris

Add details to the drawing on the "Wanted" poster. Then write some sentences in French describing the man, such as "He is blond," "He lives in ...."

Vocabulaire

| une cicatrice | a scar | recherché | wanted |

Nom:_____   **La date:**_____

Lis 📖 et écris ✏️

Complete the sentences below with an adjective of your choice:

1. En hiver, il fait _____.

2. La Tour Eiffel est _____.

3. Un éléphant est _____.

4. Le train express est _____.

5. Le Nil est _____.

6. Le Mont Blanc est _____.

7. En été, il fait _____.

8. Un bébé est _____.

9. Le français est _____.

10. La leçon de français est _____.

Lis 📖 et écris ✏️

Choose the adjectives that best describe yourself and write a description of yourself:

Je suis _____.

Je ne suis pas _____.

_____

vieux / vieille	sportif / sportive	blond / blonde
jeune / jeune	sérieux / sérieuse	brun / brune
gentil / gentille	amusant / amusante	roux / rousse
méchant / méchante	optimiste / optimiste	enthousiaste / enthousiaste
petit / petite	pessimiste / pessimiste	sympa / sympa
grand / grande	studieux / studieuse	paresseux / paresseuse

Nom:_____   **La date:**_____

Lis 📖 et écris 🖊

Fill in the gaps with "plus ... que/qu'", "moins ... que/qu'" or "aussi ... que/qu'".

1. Une Rolls-Royce est _____ rapide _____ une Mini.

2. Un autobus est _____ long _____ un train.

3. Une lettre est _____ lourde _____ un paquet.

4. Mon grand-père (70 ans) est _____ âgé _____ ma grand-mère
    (70 ans).

5. Le français est _____ difficile _____ l'italien.

6. La France est _____ petite _____ l'Angleterre.

7. Il fait _____ froid en hiver _____ été.

8. Un ticket de métro est _____ cher _____ un ticket d'autobus.

Regarde 👀 et écris 🖊

*Look at those two pictures and compare the two people by using "plus ... que",
"moins ... que" and "aussi que":*

La dame est _____   Le monsieur est _____

_____   _____

_____   _____

Essential words and phrases

Adjectives written in the same way in English

patient(e)	*patient*
impatient(e)	*impatient*
violent(e)	*violent*
intelligent(e)	*intelligent*
important(e)	*important*

Adjectives written in almost the same way in English

sévère	*severe*	pâle	*pale*
optimiste	*optimistic*	pessimiste	*pessimistic*
gentil / gentille	*gentle/kind*	affectueux / affectueuse	*affectionate*
généreux / généreuse	*generous*	énergique	*energetic*
dynamique	*dynamic*	calme	*calm*
difficile	*difficult*	facile	*easy*
autoritaire	*authoritarian*	curieux / curieuse	*curious*
sportif / sportive	*sporty*	tendre	*tender, loving*
créatif / créative	*creative*	ambitieux / ambitieuse	*ambitious*
nerveux / nerveuse	*nervous/irritable*	faible	*feeble/weak*
poli(e)	*polite*	impoli(e)	*impolite/rude*
élégant(e)	*elegant*	charmant(e)	*charming/very nice*
intéressant(e)	*interesting*	compétitif / compétitive	*competitive*
agréable	*agreeable/nice*	désagréable	*disagreeable*

Other useful adjectives

grand(e)	*tall/big*
petit(e)	*small*
gros / grosse	*fat/big*
mince	*thin*
jeune	*young*
vieux / vieille	*old*
ennuyeux / ennuyeuse	*boring*

Test yourself!

Bonjour...

Say "Bonjour" to the whole class, waiting for the pupils to reply "Bonjour Madame/Monsieur." Call the register in French and expect every pupil to respond "présent(e)" when their name is called out. When you receive no answer say "absent(e)". Call out the name of a pupil and ask him/her, "Comment vas-tu?" waiting for his/her answer "Je vais bien, merci." Ask other pupils how they are. Encourage the pupil to ask you "Et vous?" then answer with "Je vais bien merci" or "Aujourd'hui je suis content(e)," etc. Always try to use a range of adjectives and encourage pupils to do the same.

Test yourself

15a

Ask the pupils to complete the test on Sheet 15a, which reviews key teaching points from other units.

Guess who?

Ask a pupil to think of another person in the class, another person in the school (eg the headteacher or caretaker) or a famous person without saying who it is. The pupil then stands up and the rest of the class ask him/her questions to identify the person they are thinking of. Reward pupils who ask good questions with a Tableau d'honneur or a sticker.

Suggestions for questions:
Est-ce que c'est un garçon ou une fille?
Quel âge a-t-il/elle?
De quelle nationalité est-il/elle?
De quelle couleur sont ses yeux?
Quelle langue est-ce qu'il/elle parle?
Où est-ce qu'il/elle habite?
Est-ce qu'il/elle a des frères ou des sœurs?
Est-ce qu'il/elle a les cheveux longs?

Materials
★ Sheets 15a(i)–15a(vi) (pages 296–301)
★ Tableau d'honneur (page 314)

Materials

★ Sheet 15b (page 302) cut into cards
★ Sheet 15c (page 303)

New identity

Choose either of these games:

Divide the pupils into teams of four. Give one pupil in each team a card from Sheet 15b, which contains information about an imaginary person. The pupil now takes on this new identity. Give the other three pupils in each team a copy of Sheet 15c, where they will find questions to ask about the imaginary person. Each of the three pupils needs to choose two questions from the list (everyone should choose different questions).

Give the teams a few minutes to prepare their questions and answers before performing in front of the class. One by one, the three pupils ask the team-mate who has taken on the new identity their questions and wait for his/her reply. Do the same with other groups. At the end of this activity, you could decide which team has performed the best and reward the members of that team.

Give each pupil one identity card from sheet 15b, and ask them to imagine they are the person on the card. Give them a few minutes to prepare and introduce themselves to the rest of the class. Do the same with other pupils and at the end reward the pupils who have done well.

Vocabulaire

au bord de la mer	on the seashore
une chambre à coucher	a bedroom
près	near
rentrer	to return

Materials

★ Sheet 15d (page 304)
★ CD, Track 54

Answer a letter in French

Read the letter on Sheet 15d with the pupils and then ask them to answer it.

This can also be done as a listening activity using Track 54 on the CD.

Ma vie

Divide the pupils into groups of four and ask them to play the game on Sheet 15e, following the instructions. The game could be enlarged to A3 when photocopied. The instructions are given in French. You may want to read through them with pupils first to ensure that they understand them.

Au revoir!

Remember always to wish the pupils a good week or weekend, depending on when the lesson takes place. Wait for them to reply "Merci Madame/Monsieur, vous aussi." If it is the last lesson before the holidays you could wish them, "Bonnes vacances!"

Vocabulaire

prendre	to take
un dé	a die
un pion	a game counter
un bouchon	a bottle top
un bouton	a button
une avance	an advance
une case	a square (on a game board)
si	if
tu es éliminé	you are eliminated
un jeu	a game
le premier joueur	the first player
arriver	to arrive
une arrivée	an arrival
un gagnant	a winner
épeler	to spell
parler de …	to talk about …
un calcul	calculation

Materials

★ Sheet 15e (page 305)
★ Dice
★ Counters

Nom:_____   **La date:**_____

Réponds ✎ aux questions suivantes

Answer the following questions.

A. "l' ", "le" or "la"?

Write three words which take "le", three words which take "la" and three words which take "l' ":

_____   _____   _____

_____   _____   _____

_____   _____   _____

B. "é" or "è"?

Tick the correct words

une télévision ☐	une église ☐	un pére ☐	une régle ☐
une tèlèvision ☐	une èglise ☐	un père ☐	une règle ☐

C. Numbers

Write the following numbers as words.

27	15
42	47
19	50
56	60
28	74

D. "Ce", "cet", "cette" or "ces"?

In front of each word write "ce", "cet", "cette" or "ces".

.......cinéma   ....supermarché   ....piscine

.......école   ....boutique   ....agence

.......gare   ....aéroport   ....boutiques

.......maisons   ....rue   ....gens

.......professeur   ....directrice   ....élèves

Nom:_____   **La date:**_____

E. Adjectives

Give the opposite of each of these adjectives:

Grand   _____

Riche   _____

Petite   _____

Vieux   _____

Laide   _____

Laid   _____

Intelligente   _____

F. "être"

Translate these phrases into French:

He is   _____

They are   _____

I am   _____

We are   _____

G. "avoir"

Translate these phrases into French:

She has   _____

We have   _____

They have _____

I have   _____

H. Possessives

Put the right possessive in front of each noun :

_____ parents (my parents)   _____ leçons (his lessons)

_____ frère (my brother)   _____ leçons (her lessons)

_____ école (his school)   _____ voiture (his car)

_____ livres (your books)   _____ professeur (my teacher)

_____ livre (your book)   _____ professeurs (her teachers)

© Maria Rice-Jones and Brilliant Publications

Nom:_____   **La date:**_____

I.   Place names

1.   Fill in the gaps with "en", "au", "aux" or "à"

_____ Chine   _____ Paris

_____ Brésil   _____ Russie

_____ Égypte   _____ Italie

_____ Belgique   _____ Londres

_____ Canada   _____ Grèce

_____ Inde   _____ Angleterre

_____ Rome   _____ Écosse

_____ Japon   _____ États-Unis

_____ Pakistan   _____ France

2.   How do you remember when to use "en", "au", "aux" or "à"?

J.   "jouer", "penser" and "écouter"

1.   Write the form of the verb "jouer" that is used with "je", "tu", "il/elle", "nous", "vous", "ils/elles" in the present tense:

je   _____

tu   _____

il/elle   _____

nous   _____

vous   _____

ils/elles   _____

Nom:_____   **La date:**_____

2. Write the form of the verb "penser" that is used with "je", "tu", "il/elle",
    "nous", "vous", "ils/elles" in the present tense:

    je   _____   nous   _____

    tu   _____   vous   _____

    il/elle   _____   ils/elles   _____

3. Write the form of the verb "écouter" that is used with "je", "tu", "il/elle",
    "nous", "vous", "ils/elles" in the present tense:

    je   _____   nous   _____

    tu   _____   vous   _____

    il/elle   _____   ils/elles   _____

K. What time is it?

Write out the words in French for the times and draw the hands like in
the example.

   10.20 am   12.30 am   6.45 am   4.40 am

Il est dix heures vingt. _____   _____   _____

   2.30 pm   5.55 pm   11.00 pm   7.35 pm

_____   _____   _____   _____

Nom:_____   **La date:**_____

L. "aller"

1. Write the form of the verb "aller" that is used with "je", "tu", "il/elle",
    "nous", "vous", "ils/elles" in the present tense:

    je   _____

    tu   _____

    il/elle   _____

    nous   _____

    vous   _____

    ils/elles   _____

M. "aller à"

Fill in the gaps using "au", "à la", "à l' " or "aux":

Je vais _____ cinéma.   Je vais _____ supermarché.

Je vais _____ marché.   Je vais _____ piscine.

Je vais _____ gare.   Je vais _____ boucherie.

Je vais _____ États-Unis.   Je vais _____ poissonnerie.

Je vais _____ aéroport.   Je vais _____ église.

N. "Manger" and "boire"

1. Write the form of the verb "manger" that is used with "je", "tu", "il/elle",
    "nous", "vous", "ils/elles" in the present tense:

    je   _____

    tu   _____

    il/elle   _____

    nous   _____

    vous   _____

    ils/elles   _____

Nom:_____   **La date:**_____

2.   Write the form of the verb "boire" that is used with "je", "tu", "il/elle",
      "nous", "vous", "ils/elles" in the present tense:

je   _____

tu   _____

il/elle   _____

nous   _____

vous   _____

ils/elles   _____

O. "faire"

1.   Write the form of the verb "faire" that is used with "je", "tu", "il/elle",
      "nous", "vous", "ils/elles" in the present tense:

je   _____

tu   _____

il/elle   _____

nous   _____

vous   _____

ils/elles   _____

P. Expressions using the verb "faire"

Translate these expressions:

Faire la vaisselle   _____

Faire le ménage   _____

Faire les courses   _____

Faire la lessive   _____

Faire le repassage   _____

Nom:_____   **La date:**_____

Cartes d'identité

Identity cards

Nom:	Ditton
Prénom:	John
Nationalité:	anglais
Âge:	10
Adresse:	Londres, Angleterre
Famille:	parents, deux frères
Maison:	grand appartement, Londres
	chambre individuelle
Études:	**aime** **n'aime pas**
	anglais mathématiques
	gym sciences
Sport préféré:	rugby
Vacances:	cinq fois par an
Destination:	France: Paris, Nice
Profession des	père: docteur
parents:	mère: femme au foyer (housewife)

Nom:	Schmith
Prénom:	Konstanze
Nationalité:	allemande
Âge:	17
Adresse:	Bonn, Allemagne
Famille:	parents, 2 sœurs
Maison:	maison individuelle
	chambre individuelle
Études:	**aime** **n'aime pas**
	langues latin
	maths gym
Sport préféré:	ski
Vacances:	trois fois par an
Destination:	oncle et tante à Berlin
Profession des	père: boucher
parents	mère: caissière de supermarché

Nom:	Bartez
Prénom:	Roberto
Nationalité:	espagnol
Âge:	15
Adresse:	Marbella, Espagne
Famille:	parents divorcés, 1 frère, 1 sœur
Maison:	chambre avec frère (to share : partager)
	maison individuelle
Études:	**aime** **n'aime pas**
	français informatique
	maths sciences
Sport préféré:	football
Vacances:	une fois par an
Destination:	grande ville européenne
Profession des	père: facteur
parents:	mère: professeur de musique

Nom:	O'Connor
Prénom:	Ursula
Nationalité:	irlandaise
Âge:	14
Adresse:	Dublin, Irlande
Famille:	parents divorcés, 1 soeur
Maison:	appartement avec mère et soeur
	chambre avec sœur (to share: partager)
Études:	**aime** **n'aime pas**
	anglais français
	maths
Sport préféré:	équitation
Vacances:	deux fois par an
Destination:	avec père: Grèce ou Turquie
	avec mère: grands-parents à Londres
Profession des	père: boulanger
parents:	mère: infirmière

Nom:	Gerbino
Prénom:	Milena
Nationalité:	italienne
Âge:	12
Adresse:	Milan, Italie
Famille:	parents, 0 frère, 0 sœur
Maison:	appartement assez grand
	chambre individuelle
Études:	**aime** **n'aime pas**
	sport musique
	langues sciences
Sport préféré:	tennis, danse moderne
Vacances:	deux fois par an
Destination:	Sicile (Italie du sud)
Profession des	père: consultant en marketing
parents:	mère: femme au foyer (housewife)

Nom:	Abu-Kabi
Prénom:	Omar
Nationalité:	algérien
Âge:	15
Adresse:	Paris, France
Famille:	parents, 2 frères, 2 sœurs
Maison:	maison individuelle, banlieue de Paris (suburb of Paris)
	chambre avec 1 frère (to share: partager)
Études:	**aime** **n'aime pas**
	français anglais
	sciences mathématiques
Sport préféré:	tennis
Vacances:	une fois par an
Destination:	Algérie
Profession des	père: maçon
parents:	mère: femme au foyer (housewife)

Nom:_____   **La date:**_____

Questionnaire

Translate the following questions into French then choose two questions to ask the pupil who is pretending to be the imaginary person. Everyone in your group must ask different questions.

1.   What is your name and how old are you?

2.   What is your nationality and where do you live?

3.   Do you have brothers or sisters?

4.   Do you live in a big house?

5.   Do you have your own bedroom?

6.   Where do you go to school?

7.   What are your favourite subjects at school and what are the subjects you do not like?

8.   What is your favourite sport?

9.   How often do you go on holiday and where?

10.   What does your father do and what does your mother do?

© Maria Rice-Jones and Brilliant Publications

Nom:_____ **La date:**_____

Lis et réponds

Read this letter from a French boy called Jérôme and write a letter back to him. Remember to answer all of his questions!

Bonjour,

Je m'appelle Jérôme et je suis français. Et toi? J'ai dix ans, et toi, quel âge as-tu? J'habite à Nice dans le sud de la France. Où est-ce que tu habites? J'habite dans un appartement au bord de la mer. Il y a trois chambres à coucher: une chambre pour mes parents, une chambre pour moi et une autre pour ma sœur Estelle. Est-ce que tu habites dans une maison ou un appartement? Ma sœur a huit ans. Est-ce que tu as des frères ou des sœurs?

Je vais dans une école près de chez moi. En France, nous n'allons pas à l'école le mercredi car c'est une journée pour faire des activités. Nous allons à l'école le lundi, le mardi, le jeudi, le vendredi et le samedi matin. Quels jours est-ce que tu vas à l'école?

Pendant le week-end, je vais avec mon ami Luc à la piscine car j'adore ça. Et toi, où est-ce que tu vas pendant le week-end? J'aime bien aller à l'école car je fais beaucoup de sports. Je joue au football et au rugby. Quel est ton sport préféré?

Pendant la semaine, je mange à la cantine. La nourriture est assez bonne. Quelquefois je mange un steak avec des frites ou des légumes ou du poulet et du riz. Je ne mange pas de poisson car je n'aime pas ça. Pour le dessert, il y a très souvent des fruits. Est-ce que tu manges à la cantine? Est-ce que c'est bon?

Quand je rentre à la maison à quatre heures et demie, je mange un pain au chocolat ou un fruit puis je fais mes devoirs. Si j'ai le temps, je regarde "les Simpsons" car ils sont amusants. Et toi, qu'est-ce que tu fais quand tu rentres chez toi?

À bientôt,

Ton correspondant,

Jérôme

Nom:_____   **La date:**_____

Prend un dé (a die) et des pions (des bouchons, des boutons, etc). Avance sur les cases et fais les choses indiquées dans les cases. Si tu ne sais pas faire la chose indiquée, tu es éliminé du jeu. Le premier joueur qui arrive à la case "Arrivée" est le gagnant.

Ma vie				4. Mes parents	5. L'alphabet	16. Faire	17. L'heure
		3. Ma chambre		Parle de tes parents.	Épelle ton nom de famille.	Qu'est-ce que tu fais à la maison pour aider?	Quelle heure est-il maintenant?
		Décris ta chambre.					
1. Identité	2. Ma maison		6. Mon école	7. Ma leçon préférée	14. Les mois	15. Le week-end	18. Pas de chance!
Dis ton prénom, ton nom et ton âge.	Décris ta maison.		Décris ton école.	Parle de ta leçon préférée.	Quels sonts les mois de l'année en français?	Où vas-tu pendant le week-end?	Retourne à la case 12.
8. Traduction	9. Pas de chance!	10. Le calcul	11. La cantine	12. La cuisine	13. Le sport	19. Le déjeuner/ le dîner	20. Les vacances
How do you say "often" and "same" in French?	Retourne à la case 3.	Compte de 70 à 90 en français.	Nomme 3 fruits et 3 légumes en français.	Qu'est-ce qui contient du lait? (What is made with milk?)	Quel est ton sport préféré?	À quelle heure est-ce que tu déjeunes et tu dînes pendant la semaine?	Où est-ce que tu vas en vacances?
			Arrivée!				

Hexagonie, Part 2   **305**
© Maria Rice-Jones and Brilliant Publications

Vocabulary introduced per unit

Unit 1

à	at
accent aigü	acute accent
accent grave	grave accent
accent circonflexe	circumflex accent
allemand(e)	German
allons dans les bois	let's go to the wood
alphabet (m)	alphabet
américain(e)	American
anglais(e)	English
au revoir	goodbye
bébé (m)	baby
bonjour	hello
bravo	bravo
canadien(ne)	Canadian
château (m)	castle
chinois(e)	Chinese
cinq	five
Comment ça s'écrit?	How is that spelt?
comptine (f)	counting rhyme
consonne (f)	consonant
cueillir des cerises	to pick cherries
cuillère (f)	spoon
dans mon panier neuf	in my new basket
De quelle nationalité es-tu?	What is your nationality?
De quelle nationalité est-il/elle?	What is his/her nationality?
deux	two
dîner (m)	dinner
dix	ten
dix-huit	eighteen
dix-neuf	nineteen
dix-sept	seventeen
douze	twelve
école (f)	school
écossais(e)	Scottish
église (f)	church
éléphant (m)	elephant
elles seront toutes rouges	they will be all red
enchanté(e)	nice to meet you
espagnol(e)	Spanish
Et toi?	And you?
étoile (f)	star
français(e)	French
frère (m)	brother
feuille (f)	leaf
gallois(e)	Welsh
hélicoptère (m)	helicopter
hôpital (m)	hospital
huit	eight
il/elle s'appelle	his/her name is (he/she is called)
Il/elle s'appelle comment?	What is his/her name?
indien(ne)	Indian
irlandais(e)	Irish
italien(ne)	Italian
japonais(e)	Japanese
je m'appelle	my name is (I am called)
je suis…	I am…
je suis de…	I am from…
je suis désolé(e)	I am sorry
je ne sais pas	I don't know
Madame	Mrs/Madam
Mademoiselle	Miss
maison (f)	house
mère (f)	mother
moi	me
Monsieur	Mr/Sir
nationalité (f)	nationality
neuf	nine
Noël	Christmas
non	no
onze	eleven
où	where
oui	yes
pakistanais(e)	Pakistani
pendu (m)	hangman
père (m)	father
perle (f)	pearl
polonais(e)	Polish
portugais(e)	Portuguese
quatorze	fourteen
quatre	four
quinze	fifteen
règle (f)	ruler
seize	sixteen
sept	seven
six	six
téléphone (m)	telephone
télévision (m)	television
tête (f)	head
treize	thirteen
très bien	well done
trois	three
tu t'appelles	your name is (you are called)
Tu t'appelles comment?	What is your name?
un	one
vingt	twenty
voyelle (f)	vowel

Unit 2

à bientôt	see you soon
absent(e)	absent
appel (m)	register
avion (m)	aeroplane
bonne semaine	have a good week
bureau (m)	desk
cahier (m)	an exercise book
cartable (m)	schoolbag
c'est	it is/it's
c'est correct	it's correct
chaise (f)	chair
chat (m)	cat
chien (m)	dog
classeur (m)	folder
client(e) (m/f)	customer
cloche (f)	bell
Comment vas-tu?	How are you?
commerçant(e) (m/f)	shopkeeper
crayon (m)	pencil
dictionnaire (m)	dictionary
élève (m)	pupil
eau (f)	water
fenêtre (f)	window
gomme (f)	rubber
guitare (f)	guitar
horloge (f)	clock
je vais bien	I am well
je voudrais…	I would like…
klaxon (m)	horn
lampe (f)	lamp
limonade (f)	lemonade
livre (m)	book
magasin (m)	shop
merci	thank you
moi aussi	me too
moto (f)	motorbike

mur (m)	wall	cerise (f)	cherry	jean (m)	pair of jeans
oiseau (m)	bird	ces	these + plural	jeune	young
orage (m)	storm		noun (masculine	journal (m)	newspaper
ordinateur (m)	computer		and feminine)	jupe (f)	skirt
plafond (m)	ceiling	cet	this + masculine	laid(e)	ugly
pluie (f)	rain		singular noun	leçon (f)	lesson
porte (f)	door		beginning with	long(ue)	long
poster (m)	poster		a vowel	mais	but
présent(e)	present	cette	this + feminine	magnifique	magnificent
professeur (m)	teacher		singular noun	manteau (m)	raincoat
Qu'est-ce que	What is it?		beginning with	marron (m)	chestnut
c'est?			a consonant or	marron	brown/
règle (f)	ruler		a vowel		chestnut
réveil (f)	alarm clock	chambre (f)	bedroom	menu (m)	menu
souvenir (m)	souvenir	chapeau (m)	hat	mince	thin
stylo (m)	pen	chaussette (f)	sock	moderne	modern
stylo plume (m)	ink pen	chaussure (f)	shoe	monument (m)	monument
sur	on	chemise (f)	blouse	naturel(le)	natural
taille-crayon (m)	pencil	chemise de	nightgown	nécessaire	necessary
	sharpener	nuit (f)		nerveux(se)	nervous
train (m)	train	chou-fleur (m)	cauliflower	neuf (neuve)	new
trousse (f)	pencil case	cinéma (m)	cinema	noir(e)	black
table (f)	table	citron (m)	lemon	normal(e)	normal
vent (m)	wind	collant (m)	pair of tights	occupé(e)	occupied
verre (m)	glass	compétitif(ve)	competitive	olive (m)	olive
voilà	here it is/here	correct(e)	correct	orange (f)	orange
	they are	couleur (m)	colour	orange	orange
vous aussi	you too (to a	courageux(se)	courageous	ou	or
	group or adult)	court(e)	short	pâle	pale
		costume (m)	suit	pantalon (m)	pair of trousers
Unit 3		cravate (f)	tie	patient(e)	patient
		cuisine (f)	kitchen	pauvre	poor
abricot (m)	apricot	de quelle	what colour	personne (m)	person
accessoire (m)	accessory	couleur est...	is...	petit(e)	small
actif(ve)	active	difficile	difficult	place (f)	place
agressif(ve)	aggressive	directeur (m)/	headteacher	poli(e)	polite
ami(e) (m/f)	friend	directrice (f)		positif(ve)	positive
amusant(e)	amusing/funny	écharpe (f)	scarf	possible	possible
armoire (f)	wardrobe	élégant(e)	elegant	pull-over (m)	jumper
aussi	also/too	enfant (m)	child	pyjama (m)	pair of pyjamas
avocat (m)	avocado	excellent(e)	excellent	riche	rich
banane (f)	banana	exercice (m)	exercise	robe (f)	dress
beau/belle	handsome/	extraordinaire	extraordinary	rose	pink
	beautiful	extravagant(e)	extravagant	rouge	red
blanc(he)	white	gant (m)	glove	salade (f)	lettuce
bleu(e)	blue	gentil(le)	kind	short (m)	pair of shorts
blond(e)	blond	grand(e)	tall	simple	simple
bonnet (m)	bonnet	gris(e)	grey	sincère	sincere
botte (f)	boot	gros(se)	fat	spectaculaire	spectacular
brun(e)	brown	idéal(e)	ideal	strict(e)	strict
calme	calm	important(e)	important	stupide	stupid
carotte (f)	carrot	impossible	impossible	sur	on
casquette (f)	baseball cap	incorrect(e)	incorrect	sweat-shirt (m)	sweatshirt
ce	this + masculine	intelligent(e)	intelligent	tee-shirt (m)	t-shirt
	singular noun	intéressant(e)	interesting	terrible	terrible
	beginning with	invisible	invisible	tomate (f)	tomato
	a consonant	jaune	yellow	uniforme (m)	uniform
ceinture (f)	belt				

trop — too
université (f) — university
vendeur (m / vendeuse (f) — shop assistant
vert(e) — green
veste (f) — jacket
vêtement (m) — piece of clothing
vieux (vieille) — old
violent(e) — violent
voiture (f) — car

Unit 4

ancienne — ancient
animal domestique (m) — pet
appartement (m) — apartment
au nom de — in the name of
avoir — to have
bagage (m) — luggage
bouche (f) — mouth
bras (m) — arm
car — because
chambre (f) — (bed)room
cheveux (m) — hair
clé (f) — key
client(e) (m/f) — customer
cousin(e) (m/f) — cousin
depuis — since
des — some
devise (f) — motto
divorcé(e) — divorced
docteur (m) — doctor
doigt (m) — finger
douche (f) — shower
drapeau (m) — flag
égalité — equality
épaule (f) — shoulder
Est-ce que…? — Introduces a question
Est-ce que tu as…? — Do you have…?
Est-ce que vous avez…? — Do you have…? (plural and polite)
Est-ce qu'ils/elles ont…? — Do they have…?
Et vous? — And you? (plural and polite)
être — to be
famille (f) — family
fatigue(e) — tired
faux/fausse — false
femme (f) — woman
fille (f) — girl
fraternité — fraternity

(brotherhood)
garage (m) — garage
garçon (m) — boy
genou (m) (les genoux) — shoulder (shoulders)
grosses bises (f) — love (literally: big kisses)
homme (m) — man
hôtel (m) — hotel
ici — here
il/elle a — he/she has
il/elle est — he/she is
ils/elles ont — they have
ils/elles sont — they are
jambe (f) — leg
j'adore — I adore
j'ai — I have
jardin (m) — garden
je n'ai pas de — I don't have
je ne suis pas fatigué(e) — I am not tired
je suis — I am
je suis content(e) — I am happy
liberté — freedom
main (f) — hand
maintenant — now
maison (f) — house
malade — ill
marié(e) — married
mer (f) — sea
moderne — modern
monarchie (f) — monarchy
nez (m) — nose
nous avons — we have
nous sommes — we are
objet (m) — object
œil (m) (les yeux) — eye (eyes)
orteil (m) — toe
parapluie (m) — umbrella
parent (m) — parent
pas de — not any
passeport (m) — passport
pied (m) — foot
piscine (f) — swimming pool
poisson rouge (m) — goldfish
pour — for
pourquoi — why
président (m) — president
problème (m) — problem
radio (f) — radio
réceptionniste (m/f) — receptionist
reine (f) — queen
rendez-vous (m) — appointment
république (m) — republic

réservation (f) — reservation
restaurant (m) — restaurant
roi (m) — king
salut — hi/hello
sœur (f) — sister
superbe — superb
symbole (m) — symbol
tu as — you have
tu es — you are
valise (f) — suitcase
vous avez — you have (plural and polite)
vous êtes — you are (plural and polite)
vrai — true
vue (f) — view

Unit 5

à l'infini — forever
admirable — admirable
ainsi — that's the way
banque (f) — bank
bel — beautiful
bibliothèque (f) — library
cadet (m)/ cadette (f) — youngest
cave (f) — cellar
cent — hundred
chandelle (f) — candle
cheval (m) — horse
chez moi — at my house
chez toi — at your house
cinéma (m) — cinema
clair (m) — light
corps (m) — body
cuisine (f) — kitchen
d'origine — originally from
école mixte (m) — co-educational school
écureuil (m) — squirrel
écrire — to write
en face de — opposite
en général — in general
entrée (f) — entrance hall
gare (f) — train station
grand-père (m) — grandfather
grand-mère (f) — grandmother
grenier (f) — loft (attic)
hamster (m) — hamster
il danse — he dances
il répondit — he replied
il y a — there is/there are
je crois qu'elle y est — I think she's there

je n'ai plus de feu	I don't have any more fire		singular)	ils/elles parlent	they speak
joie (f)	joy	sujet (m)	subject	Inde	India
jumeau (m) (jumeaux)	twin (m) (twins (m,pl))	ta	your (feminine singular)	Irak	Iraq
jumelle (f)	twin (f)	tes	your (plural)	Irlande	Ireland
lapin (m)	rabbit	théâtre (m)	theatre	Israël	Israel
leçon (f)	lesson	ton	your (masculine singular)	Italie	Italy
leur	their (masculine and feminine singular)	tous	all	Japon	Japan
		uniforme scolaire (m)	school uniform	je parle	I speak
				jouer	to play
leurs	their (plural)	va chez la voisine	go to the (female) neighbour	langue (f)	language
lit (m)	bed			lion (m)	lion
lune (f)	moon	vie (f)	life	Lisbonne	Lisbon
ma	my (feminine singular)	ville (f)	town	Londres	London
		vos	your (plural)	lourd(e)	heavy
magasin (m)	shop	votre	your (masculine and feminine singular)	Malaisie	Malaysia
mairie (f)	town hall			Maroc	Morocco
matin (m)	morning			Martinique	Martinique
mes	my (plural)			Népal	Nepal
mon	my (masculine singular)			nous parlons	we speak
		Unit 6		Pakistan	Pakistan
mort(e)	dead	à	in/to	pari (m)	bet
mot (m)	word	Afghanistan	Afghanistan	parce que	because
musée (m)	museum	Algérie	Algeria	parler	to speak
nom (m)	surname	Allemagne	Germany	pays (m)	country
nos	our (plural)	Amérique	America	Pays-Bas	(the) Netherlands
notre	our (masculine and feminine singular)	aujourd'hui	today		
		avec	with	Pays de Galles	Wales
		beaucoup	a lot	peau (f)	skin
notre peuple	our people	Belgique	Belgium	penser	to think
on bat le briquet	someone lit a match	boum (f)	dance party	peu, un (m)	little, a
		Brésil	Brazil	Pologne	Poland
ouvre-moi	open for me	Bruxelles	Brussels	Quand	when
parc (m)	park	Canada	Canada	regarder	to look
peluche (f)	stuffed toy	canne (f)	cane (walking stick)	Russie	Russia
plume (f)	fountain pen			Sénégal	Senegal
poster (m)	poster	chanter	to sing	skier	to ski
poule (f)	chicken	Chine	China	Suisse	Switzerland
poupée (f)	doll	combien	how much	téléphoner	to telephone
pour l'amour de Dieu	for the love of God	cuisiner	to cook	tennis (m)	tennis
		danser	to dance	tour (f)	tower
prénom (m)	(first) name	Danemark	Denmark	tu parles	you speak
prête-moi	lend me	dessiner	to draw	Tunisie	Tunisia
quel/quelle/ quels/quelles	what	Écosse	Scotland	Venezuela	Venezuela
		écouter	to listen	vous parlez	you speak
quelquefois	sometimes	Édimbourg	Edinburgh		
sa	his/her (feminine singular)	en	in/to	**Unit 7**	
		en vacances	on holiday	à la campagne	in the country
		Espagne	Spain	accepter	to accept
		États-Unis	(the) United States of America	acteur (m)/ actrice (f)	actor
salle à manger (f)	dining room			adorable	adorable
salle de bains (f)	bathroom	Égypte	Egypt	adorer	to adore
salon (m)	sitting room	France	France	adulte (m/f)	an adult
ses	his/her (plural)	Gabon	Gabon	agréable	agreeable/ happy
si formidable	so great	Grèce	Greece		
son	his/her (masculine	il/elle parle	he/she speaks	aimer	to like/love
		île (f)	island	amusant	amusing

arbre (m)	tree	facteur (m)/	postman/	souvent	often
architecte (m/f)	architect	factrice (f)	postwoman	tente (f)	tent
avocat(e) (m/f)	lawyer	ferme (f)	farm	terminer	to terminate/
barman (m)	barman	fermier (m)/	farmer		end
beau-père (m)	step-father	fermière (f)		travailler	to work
bien sûr	of course	fleuriste (f)	florist	type (m)	type
bijoutier (m)	jeweller	habitation (f)	dwelling	vendeur (m)/	sales person
bijoutière (f)		habiter	to live	vendeuse (f)	
boulanger (m)/	baker	hôtesse de	air hostess	vétérinaire (m/f)	vet
boulangère (f)		l'air (f)		village (m)	a village
boucher (m)/	butcher	hôtel (m)	hotel	vraiment	really
bouchière (f)		igloo (m)	igloo		
cabane (f)	hut/shack	immeuble (m)	a building		
cabane pour	playhouse	individuel(le)	individual		
enfants (f)		infirmier (m)/	nurse		
cabane dans	tree house	infirmière (f)			
un arbre (f)		inviter	to invite		
caravane (f)	caravan	jardinier (m)/	gardener		
caissier (m)/	check-out	jardinière (f)			
caissière (f)	assistant	jour (m)	day		
chauffeur	taxi driver	journaliste (m/f)	journalist		
de taxi (m)		maçon (m)	builder		
chalet (m)	chalet	malade	ill		
chaque	each	mécanicien(ne)	mechanic		
château (m)	castle	(m/f)			
chef (m)	chef	même	same/even		
coiffeur (m)/	hairdresser	même si	even if		
coiffeuse (f)		musicien(ne)	musician		
commencer	to start/	on trouve	one finds		
	commence	opticien(ne) (m/f)	optician		
commerçant(e)	shopkeeper	palais (m)	palace		
(m/f)		partager	to share		
comptable (m/f)	accountant	passer	to pass (time)		
conducteur	bus conductor	pavillon (m)	villa		
de bus (m)/		pendant	during		
conductrice		pharmacien(ne)	pharmacist		
de bus (f)		photographe	photographer		
confortable	comfortable	(f/m)			
couturier (m)	dressmaker	peintre (m/f)	painter		
couturière (f)		pilote (m/f)	pilot		
cuisinier (m)/	cook	plombier (m)	plumber		
cuisinière (f)		policier (m)/	policeman/		
danseur (m)/	dancer	policière (f)	policewoman		
danseuse (f)		populaire	popular		
demi-frère (m)	step-brother	préférer	to prefer		
dentiste (m/f)	dentist	près	near		
désirer	to desire	professeur (m)/	teacher		
détester	to hate/detest	prof (f)			
donner	to give	réceptionniste	receptionist		
électricien(ne)	electrician	(m/f)			
(m/f)		refuser	to refuse		
en ce moment	at the moment	routier (m)	lorry driver		
ensemble	together	scientifique (m/f)	scientist		
étudiant(e)	student	serveur (m)/	waiter/		
(m/f)		serveuse (f)	waitress		
étudier	to study	si	if		
extérieur	exterior	soldat (m)	soldier		

Unit 8

À quoi est-ce	What are you
que tu joues?	playing?
accordéon (m)	accordion
badminton (m)	badminton
basket (m)	basketball
bille (f)	marble
carte (f)	card
cache-cache	hide and seek
clarinette (f)	clarinet
corde à sauter (f)	skipping rope
cour (f)	playground
cricket (m)	cricket
écolier (m)	pupil
élastique (m)	French elastic/
	French skipping
football (m)	football
flûte (f)	flute
flûte à bec (f)	recorder
guitare (f)	guitar
hockey (m)	hockey
instrument	musical
musical (m)	instrument
jeu (m)	game
le lundi	every Monday
Levez la main	Raise your
	hand
marelle (f)	hopscotch
orgue (m)	organ
percussions (f)	percussion
	instruments
piano (m)	piano
ping-pong (m)	table tennis
quand	when
récréation (f)	break time
rugby (m)	rugby
tennis (m)	tennis
trompette (f)	trumpet
violon (m)	violin

Unit 9

après-midi (m)	afternoon
avant	before
cantine (f)	canteen
cinquante	fifty

collègue (f/m)	colleague
commencer	to start
de quelle heure	from what time
à quelle	until what
heure...?	time...?
déjeuner	to lunch
demi(e) (m/f)	half
d'habitude	usually
dîner	to dine
durer	to last
élève (m)	pupil
en conséquence	therefore
film (m)	film
heure (f)	hour
manger	to eat
matin (m)	morning
midi	noon
minuit	midnight
Montrez-moi	Show me the
le numéro	number
moins	less
montre (f)	watch
nombre(m)	number
petit déjeuner (m)	breakfast
(la) plupart du	most of the
temps (f)	time
prendre	to take
préparer	to prepare
quarante	forty
quart	quarter
quatre-vingts	eighty
quatre-vingt-dix	ninety
Quelle heure	What time is it?
est-il?	
rapidement	quickly
seul(e)	alone
soir (m)	evening
soixante	sixty
soixante-dix	seventy
temps (m)	time
terminer	to finish
trente	thirty
trente-deux	thirty two
trente et un	thirty one
trente-trois	thirty three
vers	about
vingt	twenty
vingt-cinq	twenty five
vingt-deux	twenty two
vingt et un	twenty one
vingt-huit	twenty eight
vingt-neuf	twenty nine
vingt-quatre	twenty four
vingt-sept	twenty seven
vingt-six	twenty six
vingt-trois	twenty tree
zéro	zero

Unit 10

aéroport (m)	airport
an (m)	year
autobus (m)	bus
avion (m)	aeroplane
bateau (m)	boat
bibliothèque (f)	library
bicyclette (f)	bike
boulangerie (f)	bakery
boucherie (f)	butcher's
cheval (m)	horse
cinéma (m)	cinema
Comment vas-tu?	How do you go?
dimanche	Sunday
école primaire (f)	primary school
il/elle va	he/she goes
ils/elles vont	they go
je vais	I go
je vais à	I go to
jeudi	Thursday
jour (m)	day
lundi	Monday
manger	to eat
mardi	Tuesday
maternelle (f)	nursery school
mercredi	Wednesday
métro (m)	tube/ underground
mois (m)	month
moto (f)	motorbike
nous allons	we go
opéra (m)	opera
par	per
parfait	perfect
pharmacie (f)	pharmacy
plaisir	pleasure
pratique	practical/ convenient
rarement	rarely
samedi	Saturday
semaine (f)	week
supermarché (m)	supermarket
tante (f)	aunt
taxi (m)	taxi
théâtre (m)	theatre
train (m)	train
tu vas	you go
une fois	one time
université (f)	university
vélo (m)	bike
vendredi	Friday
vous allez	you go

Unit 11

agneau (m)	lamb
aimer	to like/love
ajouter	to add
assiette (f)	plate
aubergine (f)	aubergine
beurre (m)	butter
bœuf (m)	beef
cabillaud (m)	cod
café (m)	coffee
casser	to break
céréales (f, pl)	cereal
chocolat chaud (m)	hot chocolate
chocolat liquid (m)	chocolate sauce
confiture (f)	jam
courgette (f)	courgette
crevette (f)	prawn
croissant (m)	croissant
croquer	to crunch
cuit(e)	cooked
farine (f)	flour
fraise (f)	strawberry
fruit (m)	fruit
haricot vert (m)	French bean
huile (f)	oil
huile tournesol (f)	sunflower oil
jambon (m)	ham
jus d'orange (m)	orange juice
kiwi (m)	kiwi
lait (m)	milk
légume (m)	vegetable
liste (f)	list
mangue (f)	mango
melon (m)	melon
nourriture (f)	food
pain (m)	bread
pâtes (f,pl)	pasta
petit pois (m)	pea
poire (f)	pear
poisson (m)	fish
poivron (m)	pepper
pomme (f)	apple
pomme de terre (f)	potato
porc (m)	pork
poulet (m)	chicken
riz (m)	rice
roquefort (m)	Roquefort
saucisse (f)	sausage
saumon (m)	salmon
spaghetti (m)	spaghetti
sucre (m)	sugar
thé (m)	tea
truite (f)	trout
viande (f)	meat

yaourt (m)	yoghurt
ail (m)	garlic
brie (m)	brie
camembert (m)	camembert
coca-cola (m)	cola
du	some (+ masculine singular)
de la	some (+ feminine singular)
de l'	some (+ singular word beginning with a vowel)
des	some (+ plural)
eau (f)	water
eau gazeuse	sparkling water
frite (f)	chip
fromage (m)	cheese
je mange	I eat
lasagne (f)	lasagne
limonade	lemonade
tu manges	you eat
il/elle mange	he/she eats
ils/elles mangent	they eat
je bois	I drink
il/elle boit	he/she drinks
ils/elles boivent	they drink
nous buvons	we drink
nous mangeons	we eat
pas d'	not any (+ vowel)
pas de	not any (+ consonant)
tu bois	you drink
vous buvez	you drink
vous mangez	you eat
kilo (m)	kilo
végétarien(ne) (f/m)	vegetarian
beaucoup de	a lot of
verre (m)	glass
tasse (f)	cup
bouteille (f)	bottle
marché (m)	market
vin (m)	wine
repas (m)	meal
sel (m)	salt
saladier (m)	mixing bowl
mélanger	to mix
retourner	to turn over
poser	to put

Unit 12

à côté de	next to
acheter	to buy
aspirateur (m)	vacuum cleaner
assiette (f)	plate
autre	other
chose (f)	thing
couteau (m)	knife
cuillère (f)	spoon
faire	to do/make
faire la lessive	to do the washing (of clothes)
faire le repassage	to do the ironing
faire la vaisselle	to do the washing up
faire le ménage	to do the housework
faire les courses	to go shopping
faire une promenade	to go for a walk
femme de ménage (f)	cleaning lady
fermer	to close
fourchette (f)	fork
il/ elle fait	He/She does/makes
ils/elles font	They do/make
j'achète	I buy
je fais	I do/make
lave-vaisselle (m)	dishwasher
laver	to wash
longtemps	a long time
magasin (m)	shop
marcher	to walk
nous faisons	We do/make
ouvrir	to open
par exemple	for example
paresseux/ paresseuse	lazy
passer l'aspirateur	to vacuum
quelquefois	sometimes
tu fais	You do/make
vous faites	You do/make (plural and polite)

Unit 13

année (f)	year
anniversaire (m)	birthday
août	August
arbres sont nus	the trees are bare
assez + adjectif	quite + adjective
automne (m)	autumn

avril	April
briller	to shine
brouillard (m)	fog
célébrer	to celebrate
champignon (m)	mushroom
chaud(e)	hot
climat (m)	climate
côte (f)	coast
date (f)	date
début (m)	beginning
décembre	December
doux/douce	soft/mild
éclair (m)	lightning
est (m)	east
été (m)	summer
extrêmement	extremely
fête (f)	festival
février	February
fin (f)	end
froid	cold
heureux/heureuse	happy
hiver (m)	winter
il fait beau	it is beautiful
il fait chaud	it is hot
il fait du vent	it is windy
il fait froid	it is cold
il fait mauvais temps	it is bad weather
il fait moins chaud	it is cooler
il neige	it is snowing
il pleut	It is raining
janvier	January
jour de congé (m)	day off
juin	June
juillet	July
magnifique	magnificent
mai	May
mars	March
mer (f)	the sea
montagne (f)	mountain
nager	to swim
neiger	to snow
Noël	Christmas
nord (m)	north
novembre	November
ocean (m)	an ocean
octobre	October
orageux/orageuse	stormy
ouest (m)	west
Pâques	Easter
plaine (f)	plain
pleuvoir	to rain
(le) premier janvier	(the) first of January
printemps (m)	spring
ramasser	to collect
région (f)	region

saint	saint	escargot (m)	snail	profond(e)	deep/profound
saison (f)	season	essentiel/	essential	propre	clean
septembre	September	essentielle		prudent(e)	prudent/
sud (m)	south	étroit(e)	narrow		careful
température (f)	temperature	fâché(e)	angry	pur(e)	pure
temps (m)	weather	facile	easy	rapide	quick/rapid
territoire (m)	territory	faible	feeble	rare	rare
tomber	to fall	fantastique	fantastic	récent(e)	recent
		fort(e)	strong	responsable	responsible

Unit 14

affectueux/	affectionate	fou/folle	mad/crazy	ridicule	ridiculous
affectueuse		fragile	fragile	rond(e)	round
âgé(e)	aged/elderly	fréquent(e)	frequent	roux/rousse	with red hair
agité(e)	agitated	froid(e)	cold	sale	dirty
ambitieux/	ambitious	furieux/furieuse	furious	seul(e)	alone
ambitieuse		généreux/	generous	sévère	severe
anxieux/	anxious	généreuse		similaire	similar
anxieuse		gourmand(e)	greedy	spacieux/	spacious
attentif/	attentive	grand(e)	tall/big	spacieuse	
attentive		grave	serious	sportif/sportive	sporty
aussi … que	as … as	handicapé(e)	disabled	studieux/	studious
autoritaire	authoritarian	haut(e)	high	studieuse	
baleine (f)	whale	honnête	honest	sûr(e)	sure
blessé(e)	injured/hurt	horrible	horrible	sympathique,	nice
brutal(e)	brutal	hostile	hostile	sympa	
créatif/créative	creative	humble	humble	tendre	tender/loving
certain(e)	certain	idiot(e)	idiot	ticket (m)	ticket
charmant(e)	charming/very	ignorant(e)	ignorant	timide	shy
	nice	impatient(e)	impatient	transparent	transparent
cher/chère	expensive/dear	impoli(e)	impolite/rude	triste	sad
cicatrice (f)	scar	incroyable	unbelievable	utile	useful
clair(e)	clear	innocent(e)	innocent	vide	empty
coccinelle (f)	ladybird	inquiet/inquiète	worried		
compliqué(e)	complicated	insolent(e)	insolent		
content(e)	happy	intéressé(e)	interested		
court(e)	short	inutile	useless		
cruel/cruelle	cruel	joli(e)	pretty		
curieux/	curious	juste	fair		
curieuse		laid(e)	ugly		
dame (f)	lady	large	large		
dangereux/	dangerous	léger/ légère	light		
dangereuse		lent(e)	slow		
dégôutant(e)	disgusting	lettre (f)	letter		
délicieux/	delicious	libre	free		
délicieuse		logique	logical		
désagréable	disagreeable/	malheureux/	unhappy		
	not nice	malheureuse			
différent(e)	different	méchant(e)	naughty/nasty		
drôle	funny	modeste	modest		
dur(e)	hard	moins … que	less … than		
dynamique	dynamic	(le) Nil	(the) Nile		
élégant	elegant	ordinaire	ordinary		
énergique	energetic	optimiste	optimistic		
ennuyeux/	boring	original(e)	original		
ennuyeuse		paquet (m)	packet		
énorme	enormous	pessimiste	pessimistic		
enthousiaste	enthusiastic	plein(e)	full		
		plus … que	more … than		

Tableau d'Honneur

La date: _____

Nom: _____

Pour: _____

Signature du professeur

_____

Je suis désolé(e), Madame/Monsieur, je ne sais pas.

 © Maria Rice-Jones and Brilliant Publications

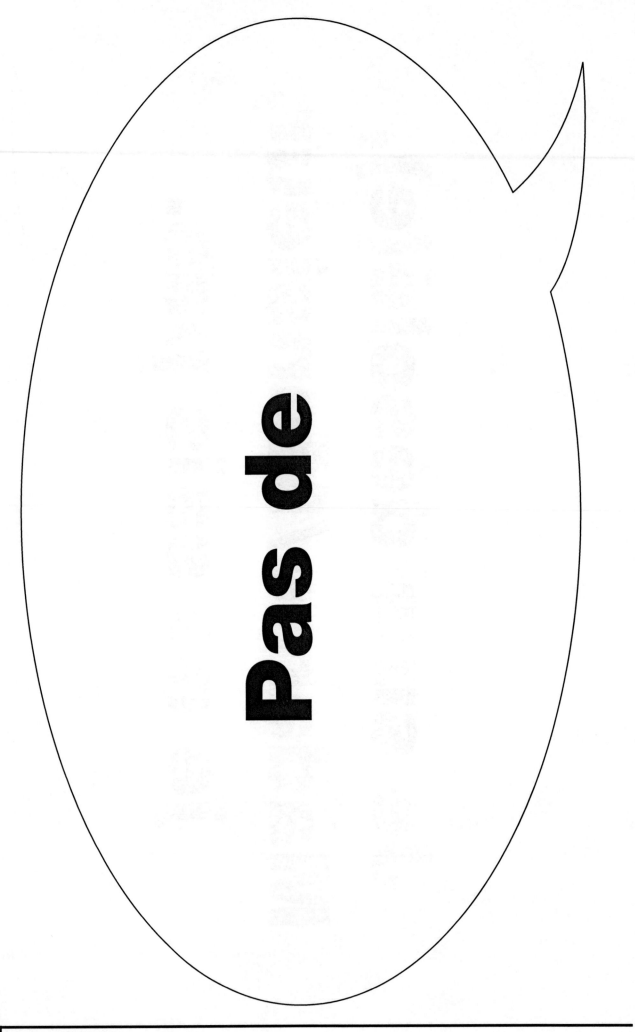

Hexagonie, Part 2
This page may be photocopied for use by the purchasing institution only.

Transcript of CD

Track 1

Alphabet song

✳

Track 2

Instrumental version of Alphabet song

✳

Track 3

On this track you will hear five names being spelt out in French. You will hear all the names twice. Write down the letters and work out the name.

1   R O B E R T … R O B E R T

2   J E S S I C A … J E S S I C A

3   M A R I A … M A R I A

4   T H O M A S … T H O M A S

5   I V O R … I V O R

✳

Track 4

1   une règle … une règle

2   un éléphant … un éléphant

3   un bébé … un bébé

4   un frère … un frère

5   une mère … une mère

6   un père … un père

7   une école … une école

8   un hélicoptère … un hélicoptère

9   une télévision … une télévision

10   une étoile … une étoile

11   une cuillère … une cuillère

12   une église … une église

✳

Track 5

Luc: Bonjour enchanté, je m'appelle Luc.

Susan: Bonjour enchantée, je m'appelle Susan.

Luc: De quelle nationalité es-tu?

Susan: Je suis anglaise, et toi, de quelle nationalité es-tu?

Luc: Je suis français. Je suis de Boulogne, et toi?

Susan: Moi, je suis de Nottingham. Au revoir.

Luc: Au revoir.

✳

Track 6

Un, deux, trois song

✳

Track 7

Instrumental version of Un, deux, trois song

✳

Track 8

Le client: Bonjour Madame.

La commerçante: Bonjour Monsieur.

Le client: Je voudrais un livre sur Paris, s'il vous plaît.

La commerçante: Un livre sur Paris. Très bien, voilà.

Le client: Je voudrais un dictionnaire français–anglais, s'il vous plaît.

La commerçante: Voilà Monsieur.

Le client: Très bien, c'est combien s'il vous plaît?

La commerçante: C'est vingt euros Monsieur.

Le client: Merci beaucoup Madame. Au revoir.

La commerçante: Au revoir Monsieur.

✳

Track 9

Rain; wind blowing; noisy storm; car horn; cat meowing; dog barking; doorbell ringing; train; aeroplane; helicopter; guitar; bird singing; telephone ringing; alarm clock ringing; motorbike revving up; grandfather clock

✳

Track 10

1   storm

2   guitar

3   (car) horn

4   bird

5   motorbike

6   alarm clock

7   rain

8   (door) bell

✳

Track 11

La cliente: Bonjour Monsieur.

Le vendeur: Bonjour Madame.

La cliente: Je voudrais un pantalon noir et une chemise blanche s'il vous plaît, Monsieur. Ce pantalon est très joli et cette chemise aussi.

Le vendeur: Je suis désolé Madame, mais cette chemise n'est pas pour vous car elle est trop grande.

La cliente: Et cette chemise verte, est-ce qu'elle est pour moi?

Le vendeur: Oui, cette chemise verte est parfaite.

La cliente: Très bien, je voudrais ce pantalon noir et cette chemise verte, s'il vous plaît.

Le vendeur: Merci beaucoup Madame.

✳

Track 12

Le client: Bonjour Madame.

La réceptionniste: Bonjour Monsieur.

Le client: J'ai une réservation au nom de Roberts, s'il vous plaît.

La réceptionniste: Voilà, vous avez la chambre dix-huit.

Le client: Est-ce que la chambre a une douche?

La réceptionniste: Oui, Monsieur elle a une douche. Avez-vous un passeport Monsieur?

Le client: Oui, voilà Madame.

La réceptionniste: Merci Monsieur. Avez-vous des bagages?

Le client: Oui, j'ai deux valises.

La réceptionniste: Très bien Monsieur. Ici vous avez la clé.

Le client: Merci beaucoup Madame. Au revoir.

La réceptionniste: Au revoir.

✳

Track 13

Salut Brigitte!

Je suis avec mes parents à Deauville. Nous sommes dans un grand hôtel moderne. Ma chambre est très grande et confortable et la vue sur la mer est superbe. J'adore être ici car il y a aussi une piscine et un excellent restaurant. Et toi, où es-tu maintenant?

Grosses bises,

À bientôt!

Ton amie

Marie

✳

Track 14

La famille Durand

Monsieur et Madame Durand sont français. Ils sont mariés et ils ont quatre enfants. Ils ont deux garçons (André et Luc) et deux filles (Estelle et Céline). André a 14 ans, Luc a 13 ans, Estelle a 10 ans et Céline a 7 ans. Monsieur Durand a 45 ans et Madame Durand a 42 ans. Ils ont une grande maison avec un grand jardin pour les enfants et un garage pour la voiture.

✳

Track 15

La France

En France, il n'y a pas de reine ou roi, mais il y a le Président de la République. La France est une République depuis la Révolution de 1789. "Marianne" est le symbole de la République Française. La devise de la France est "liberté, égalité, fraternité". Le drapeau français est: bleu, blanc, rouge.

✳

Track 16

Bonjour, je m'appelle Adeline, je suis française et j'ai dix ans. Mes parents sont français. Je n'ai pas de frère ou de sœur. Ma maison est grande. Dans ma chambre, il y a mon bureau avec mes livres, mes stylos et mes cahiers. Sur mon lit, il y a ma poupée Lucie et mes peluches. Mon ordinateur n'est pas dans ma chambre. Il est dans le bureau de ma mère.

✳

Track 17

Bonjour, je m'appelle Camel et je suis français d'origine algérienne. Mes parents sont algériens. Mon appartement n'est pas très grand mais il est confortable. Dans ma chambre, il y a mon ordinateur, mes posters et mon lit. J'ai quatre frères. Moi, je suis le cadet de la famille et j'ai neuf ans.

✳

Track 18

Bonjour, je m'appelle Manon, je suis française et j'ai neuf ans. Ma maison est très grande. J'ai des animaux à la maison: mon hamster qui s'appelle "Tony", mon chien qui s'appelle "Joker", mon poisson rouge qui s'appelle "Kity" et mes deux chats qui s'appellent "Félix" et "Lily". Dans mon jardin j'ai des animaux: des écureuils, des oiseaux et mes cinq poules.

✳

Track 19

Jean Petit qui danse song

✳

Track 20

Instrumental version Jean Petit qui danse

✳

Track 21

Au clair de la lune song

✳

Track 22

Instrumental version Au clair de la lune

✳

Track 23

Dany:	Je m'appelle Dany.
Laura:	Et je m'appelle Laura. Nous sommes jumelles. Nos yeux sont bleus, nos cheveux sont bruns.
Dany:	Nous sommes dans une école qui est dans un petit village en Normandie. Notre école est une école mixte. Dans notre école, il y a dix professeurs et deux cents élèves. Dans notre classe, nous sommes vingt-cinq élèves, seize filles et neuf garçons. Notre professeur est une femme très gentille qui s'appelle Madame Moreau.
Laura:	Dans notre classe, il y a cinq ordinateurs et une télévision. Sur les murs de notre classe, il y a des posters sur les différentes régions de France. Nos leçons sont intéressantes mais quelquefois elles sont trop longues.

✳

Track 24

Chanson d'amour d'Hexagonie

✳

Track 25

Instrumental version Chanson d'amour d'Hexagonie

✳

Track 26

Lyon sounds like the word "lion", which means "lion".

Lille sounds like the word "l'île", which means "the island".

Cannes sounds like the word "canne", which means "cane".

Tours sounds like the word "tour", which means "tower".

Sète sounds like the number "sept".

Bordeaux sounds like the red wine, "Bordeaux".

Lourdes sounds like the word "lourde", which means "heavy".

Meaux sounds like the word "mot", which means "word".

Pau sounds like the word "peau" which means "skin".

Caen sounds like the word "quand" which means "when".

Paris sounds like the word "pari", which means "bet".

∗

Track 27

Je parle français parce que je suis français. J'habite dans une maison qui a un grand salon, une petite cuisine, une assez grande salle à manger, une salle de bains et trois chambres. Je n'habite pas avec mes parents car maintenant je suis adulte.

Mes parents habitent avec leur chien "Rex" dans un appartement. Ils n'habitent pas dans une grande ville mais à la campagne près d'un petit village.

∗

Track 28

Il y a beaucoup de types de maisons en France.

À Paris, il y a beaucoup d'immeubles Haussmaniens.

Un pavillon est une maison individuelle confortable avec un jardin et un garage. En général, on trouve ces pavillons à l'extérieur des grandes villes.

Il y a beaucoup de châteaux viticoles sur la Loire.

Les maisons alsaciennes sont typiques en Alsace.

En Normandie, une maison-cour est une ferme qui est souvent une maison d'habitation.

Il y a beaucoup de chalets Savoyards dans les Alpes.

Les maisons basques sont typiques dans le Pays Basque.

En Provence, on trouve le mas provençal.

Quelle maison est-ce que tu préfères? Pourquoi?

∗

Track 29

Je suis professeur et je travaille dans une école mixte. Je travaille chaque jour avec des élèves. Il y a trente élèves dans ma classe. Je ne travaille pas pendant le week-end car je suis occupée avec ma famille.

∗

Track 30

Je m'appelle Matthieu. J'ai neuf ans et j'habite à Paris. J'habite dans un grand appartement, dans un immeuble moderne avec ma mère, mon beau-père, mon grand frère Bruno qui a onze ans et mon demi-frère Grégoire qui a cinq ans. Mes parents

sont divorcés. Mon père est professeur et même mon beau-père est professeur et ma mère travaille dans un restaurant près de la maison. En général, je passe mes vacances chez mes grands-parents à Nice. Je partage ma chambre avec mon frère Bruno. Nous passons des moments très agréables ensemble car nous avons un ordinateur pour deux et nous jouons souvent avec l'ordinateur. Et bien sûr, chaque jour, nous jouons un peu avec Grégoire qui est vraiment adorable et amusant. Et toi?

∗

Track 31

Bruno:	Bonjour Isabelle.
Isabelle:	Bonjour Bruno.
Bruno:	Comment vas-tu aujourd'hui?
Isabelle:	Je vais très bien, et toi?
Bruno:	Moi aussi. Est-ce que tu aimes le sport?
Isabelle:	Oui, bien sûr!
Bruno:	En général, à quoi est-ce que vous jouez à ton école?
Isabelle:	Les garçons jouent au football mais ils ne jouent pas au rugby et les filles jouent au volleyball.
Bruno:	Dans mon école, les garçons jouent au football, au rugby et au cricket et les filles jouent au badminton.
Isabelle:	Est-ce que tu voudrais jouer au tennis avec moi?
Bruno:	Pourquoi pas?

∗

Track 32

Twelve different times will be read out in French. Each time will be repeated and then there will be a pause for you to draw the hands on the blank clock faces on Sheet 9c.

1	Il est minuit. (pause) Il est minuit.
2	Il est neuf heures. (pause) Il est neuf heures.
3	Il est trois heures et demie. (pause) Il est trois heures et demie.
4	Il est dix heures et demie. (pause) Il est dix heures et demie.
5	Il est onze heures et quart. (pause) Il

est onze heures et quart.

6	Il est quatre heures moins le quart. (pause) Il est quatre heures moins le quart.
7	Il est une heure cinq. (pause) Il est une heure cinq.
8	Il est deux heures dix. (pause) Il est deux heures dix.
9	Il est cinq heures vingt. (pause) Il est cinq heures vingt.
10	Il est sept heures moins dix. (pause) Il est sept heures moins dix.
11	Il est huit heures moins vingt-cinq. (pause) Il est huit heures moins vingt-cinq.
12	Il est midi et demi. (pause) Il est midi et demi.

*

Track 33

Le matin à 7 heures 15, je mange. Je prends mon petit déjeuner. Pendant la semaine, je prends mon petit déjeuner seule car je mange rapidement. Pendant le week-end, je prends mon petit déjeuner avec ma famille. La plupart du temps, je prépare le petit déjeuner vers 7 heures. Je ne prends pas le petit déjeuner avec mes élèves car je ne prends pas le petit déjeuner à l'école.

*

Track 34

À midi, je mange. Je déjeune. Pendant la semaine, je travaille à l'école, je déjeune avec mes collègues à la cantine. Pendant le week-end je ne travaille pas, et je déjeune chez moi. En général, je ne déjeune pas avec mes élèves car je n'ai pas le temps.

*

Track 35

Le soir, je mange. Le soir, je dîne. D'habitude, je dîne chez moi avec ma famille. Nous dînons vers 19 heures car avant nous sommes occupés. Pendant le week-end, nous dînons souvent avec nos amis, chez nous ou chez eux.

*

Track 36

En général, je vais à l'école en voiture parce que je n'habite pas près de l'école.

Je vais au centre ville en métro parce que ce n'est pas pratique en voiture.

Je vais à pied à la boulangerie qui est près de chez moi.

Je vais aux États-Unis en avion.

Je vais à l'aéroport en taxi.

*

Track 37

Je m'appelle Philippe. Je mange, le matin, le midi, le soir. Je mange trois fois par jour.

Je m'appelle Emma. Je vais à l'école cinq jours par semaine.

Je m'appelle Matt. J'ai une leçon de français trois fois par semaine.

Je m'appelle Charlotte. Je vais en vacances quatre fois par an.

*

Track 38

L'école en France

De 3 ans à 6 ans, les petits enfants vont à la maternelle. Les enfants commencent l'école primaire à 6 ans. De 6 ans à 10 ans, ils vont à l'école primaire. Les élèves vont à l'école sans uniforme.

En général, il y a des cours le matin de 8h30 à 11h30 et l'après-midi, il y a des cours de 13h30 à 16h30. Le matin, il y a toujours une récréation de 15 minutes, de 10h15 à 10h30. À midi, les élèves déjeunent à la cantine de l'école ou déjeunent à la maison avec leurs parents.

Les élèves ne vont pas à l'école le mercredi mais ils vont à l'école le samedi matin. Le mercredi, beaucoup d'enfants ont des cours de musique ou de sport.

*

Track 39

La Marseillaise song

*

Track 40

Instrumental version of La Marseillaise

*

Track 41

Marchand: Bonjour Madame! Qu'est-ce que vous désirez aujourd'hui?

Mme Neville: Je voudrais du lait et des œufs, une douzaine d'œufs s'il vous plaît.

Marchand: Voilà Madame, autre chose?

Mme Neville: Oui, je voudrais des légumes: des carottes, un kilo de carottes. Des courgettes, seulement quatre, puis deux kilos de pommes de terre et pour finir des champignons, un kilo de champignons.

Marchand: Voilà, et avec ça?

Mme Neville: De la moutarde, de l'ail et des oignons s'il vous plaît.

Marchand: Voilà! Ça vous fait 9 euros 50, s'il vous plaît.

Mme Neville: Voilà.

Marchand: Merci beaucoup Madame! Bonne journée!

Mme Neville: Vous aussi!

*

Track 42

Le petit déjeuner

En général, les Français boivent du café noir, une tasse de thé ou un chocolat chaud. Ils mangent du pain beurré, avec de la confiture ou du miel. Les enfants mangent des céréales ou un yaourt. Puis, ils boivent un jus d'orange.

Le déjeuner

Le déjeuner est important pour les Français. Ils mangent de la viande ou du poisson avec du riz ou des pâtes ou de la salade. Après, ils mangent des fruits. Ils boivent de l'eau et, pour terminer, un café ou un thé. De temps en temps, ils mangent un croque-monsieur ou un steak avec des pommes frites.

Le goûter des enfants

Quand les enfants rentrent de l'école, ils mangent un goûter: un pain au chocolat, une barre de céréales, du pain avec de la confiture, une pomme, une orange ou des biscuits.

Le dîner

Pour commencer, les Français mangent une salade ou du jambon ou de la soupe. Pour continuer, ils mangent de la viande ou du poisson avec des légumes ou des pommes de terre, ou de la salade. Pour terminer, ils mangent du fromage et un dessert.

*

Track 43

La capucine (nasturtium dance) song

*

Track 44

Instrumental version of La capucine

*

Track 45

En général, je ne fais pas les courses pendant la semaine car je suis très occupé avec mon travail. Je fais les courses au supermarché pendant le week-end. D'habitude, je vais dans un petit supermarché près de chez moi car c'est rapide. La plupart du temps, je fais les courses pour toute la semaine. J'achète de la viande, du poisson, des légumes, des œufs et beaucoup d'autres choses.

*

Track 46

Chaque jour à la maison, après le petit déjeuner, le déjeuner et le dîner ma mère lave les assiettes, les verres, les fourchettes, les couteaux et les cuillères. Elle fait la vaisselle car nous n'avons pas de machine pour faire la vaisselle. Nous n'avons pas de lave-vaisselle. Moi, je suis encore petit, alors je ne fais pas la vaisselle mais quelquefois j'aide ma mère. Par exemple, si j'ai le temps après le petit déjeuner, je lave mon bol, mon verre, ma cuillère, et mon assiette. Ma mère est très contente quand je fais ça.

*

Track 47

Non, non, non, non, je déteste le ménage! Je ne fais pas le ménage dans ma chambre car je n'ai pas le temps. Je préfère quand ma mère fait le ménage mais elle n'est pas contente de moi. Elle pense que je suis paresseuse. Mais quelquefois, je fais des actions gentilles et j'aide ma mère car je passe l'aspirateur dans toute la maison.

*

Track 48

Pendant le week-end, je fais souvent une promenade dans le parc à côté de chez moi. Je marche longtemps et je pense à beaucoup de choses. J'adore faire des promenades. Quand je suis en vacances, je fais beaucoup de promenades car j'aime marcher.

∗

Track 49

Il pleut, il pleut bergère song

∗

Track 50

Instrumental version of Il pleut, il pleut bergère

∗

Track 51

Gouttes gouttelettes de pluie song

∗

Track 52

Instrumental version of Gouttes gouttelettes de pluie

∗

Track 53

La France a différents climats sur son territoire car on trouve des montagnes et des plaines et également deux mers: la mer Méditerranée et l'océan Atlantique. Chaque région a son climat.

Dans le nord et sur la côte ouest, il pleut souvent car la pluie vient de l'Atlantique.

Dans le centre et l'est, il y a un climat continental avec des hivers froids et des étés chauds.

En France, il y a quatre régions avec des montagnes: les Vosges, le Jura, les Alpes et les Pyrénées. Dans les montagnes, les hivers sont longs et les étés sont assez chauds.

Le midi est la région au sud de la France, sur la méditerranée. Les étés sont extrêmement chauds et les hivers sont doux. Mais quelquefois il y a le "Mistral" qui est un vent très violent et très froid.

∗

Track 54

Bonjour,

Je m'appelle Jérôme et je suis français. Et toi? J'ai dix ans, et toi, quel âge as-tu? J'habite à Nice dans le sud de la France. Où est-ce que tu habites? J'habite dans un appartement au bord de la mer. Il y a trois chambres à coucher: une chambre pour mes parents, une chambre pour moi et une autre pour ma sœur Estelle. Est-ce que tu habites dans une maison ou un appartement? Ma sœur a huit ans. Est-ce que tu as des frères ou des sœurs?

Je vais dans une école près de chez moi. En France, nous n'allons pas à l'école le mercredi car c'est une journée pour faire des activités. Nous allons à l'école le lundi, le mardi, le jeudi, le vendredi et le samedi matin. Quels jours est-ce que tu vas à l'école?

Pendant le week-end, je vais avec mon ami Luc à la piscine car j'adore ça. Et toi, où est-ce que tu vas pendant le week-end? J'aime bien aller à l'école car je fais beaucoup de sports. Je joue au football et au rugby. Quel est ton sport préféré?

Pendant la semaine, je mange à la cantine. La nourriture est assez bonne. Quelquefois, je mange un steak avec des frites ou des légumes ou du poulet et du riz. Je ne mange pas de poisson car je n'aime pas ça. Pour le dessert, il y a très souvent des fruits. Est-ce que tu manges à la cantine? Est-ce que c'est bon?

Quand je rentre à la maison à quatre heures et demie, je mange un pain au chocolat ou un fruit puis je fais mes devoirs. Si j'ai le temps, je regarde "les Simpsons" car ils sont amusants. Et toi, qu'est-ce que tu fais quand tu rentres chez toi?

À bientôt,

Ton correspondant,

Jérôme

Answer key for worksheets

Sheet 1c (page 22)

1. une règle
2. un éléphant
3. un bébé
4. un frère
5. une mère
6. un père
7. une école
8. un hélicoptère
9. une télévision
10. une étoile
11. une cuillère
12. une église

Sheet 1g (page 26)

11 onze
12 douze
13 treize
14 quatorze
15 quinze
16 seize
17 dix-sept
18 dix-huit
19 dix-neuf
20 vingt

Sheet 1h (page 27)

4 + 6 = dix
15 + 2 = dix-sept
19 – 7 = douze
3 + 3 = six
12 – 6 = six
10 + 10 = vingt
20 – 13 = sept
4 – 4 = zéro
5 + 8 = treize
20 – 2 = dix-huit

Sheet 2c (page 41)

1. un ordinateur
2. une maison
3. un élève
4. un téléphone
5. un bureau

6. une fenêtre
7. un cartable
8. une lampe
9. une fleur
10. un cahier
11. une télévision
12. un verre

Sheet 2f (page 45)

1. l'orage   storm
2. la guitare   guitar
3. le klaxon   horn
4. l'oiseau   bird
5. la moto   motorbike
6. le réveil   alarm clock
7. la pluie   rain
8. la cloche   bell

Sheet 2g (page 46)

la fleur
l'oiseau
la cloche
la maison
l'eau
le chien
le chat
la guitare
le classeur
le téléphone
la porte
l'avion

Sheet 3a (page 59)

1. cette voiture
2 ce journal
3. ces enfants
4. ce cinéma
5. cette télévision
6. ce monument
7. ces personnes
8. cette école
9. cet oiseau
10. ces professeurs
11. ce pull-over

12. cet avion

Sheet 3c (page 62)

1. De quelle couleur est ce marron?
   Ce marron est (marron).
2. De quelle couleur est cette
   cerise? Cette cerise est (rouge).
3. De quelle couleur est cette
   salade? Cette salade est (verte).
4. De quelle couleur est cette
   orange? Cette orange est
   (orange).
5. De quelle couleur est cette
   carotte? Cette carotte est
   (orange).
6. De quelle couleur est ce citron?
   Ce citron est (jaune).
7. De quelle couleur est cette
   tomate? Cette tomate est
   (rouge).
8. De quelle couleur est cet
   avocat? Cet avocat est (vert).
9. De quelle couleur est cette olive?
   Cette olive est (verte/noire).
10. De quelle couleur est cet
    abricot? Cet abricot est
    (orange).

Sheet 3g (page 66)

1. Madame Martin n'est pas vielle,
   elle est jeune.
2. Antoine n'est pas petit, il est
   grand.
3. La voiture de Marc n'est pas
   grande mais elle est petite.
4. L'exercice est incorrect ou
   correct.
5. Monsieur Rousseau est mince
   ou gros.
6. Monsieur Martin est jeune ou
   vieux.
7. La Seine (River Seine) est
   courte ou longue?

Hexagonie, Part 2
© Maria Rice-Jones and Brilliant Publications

8. Le stylo n'est pas blanc, mais il est noir.

Sheet 4a (page 80)

tu as

Luc a

nous avons

j'ai

Emma et Louis ont

vous avez

Marie a

1. Nous avons un chien.
2. J'ai un idée.
3. Ils (or elles) ont des enfants.
4. Il (or elle) a trois frères.
5. Vous avez un chat
6. Tu as 10 ans.
7. Il (or elle) a une radio.
8. Ils (or elles) ont un ordinateur.

Sheet 4c (page 82)

1. J'ai des chaussures.
2. Tu as un frère et une sœur.
3. Nous avons un rendez-vous avec le docteur.
4. Est-ce que vous avez un ordinateur?
5. Est-ce qu'elle a un chien ou un chat?
6. J'ai deux bananes.
7. Ils ont un cahier.
8. Je n'ai pas d'oranges.

Sheet 4d (page 83)

1. Non, je n'ai pas d'enfants car …
2. Non, je n'ai pas de parapluie maintenant car…
3. Non, je n'ai pas de voiture car …
4. Non, je n'ai pas d'ordinateur orange car …
5. Non, je n'ai pas de maison en France car …

Sheet 4e (page 84)

tu es

Pierre est

nous sommes

je suis

Pierre et Martine sont

vous êtes

Marie est

1. Nous sommes frères.
2. Je suis brune.
3. Ils sont vieux.
4. Elle est belle.
5. Vous êtes mariés.
6. Tu es petit.
7. Il est blond.
8. Elles sont sœurs.

Sheet 4f (page 85)

1. J'ai des chaussures car je n'ai pas de bottes.
2. Tu es content car tu as un frère et une sœur.
3. Ils sont malades car ils sont fatigués.
4. Elle est très occupée parce que la directrice est malade.
5. Nous avons un rendez-vous avec le docteur mais il est absent.
6. Est-ce que vous êtes français ou anglais?
7. Est-ce que vous avez un ordinateur?
8. Est-ce qu'elle a un chat ou un chien?
9. Est-ce qu'ils sont grands?
10. Est-ce que tu as des animaux?

Sheet 4g (page 86)

1. Faux
2. Faux.
3. Vrai
4. Vrai
5. Faux

Sheet 4h (page 87)

1. Ils sont mariés.
2. Ils ont quatre enfants.
3. Céline a sept ans.
4. Non, ils ont une grande maison.
5. Ils sont français.
6. _____

Sheet 4i (page 88)

1. Non, il y a le Président de la République.
2. C'est une femme.
3. La France est une république.
4. Le drapeau français est bleu, blanc et rouge.
5. La devise de la France est 'liberté, égalité, fraternité'.
6. _____

Sheet 5a (page 101)

2. la mère, ma mère.
3. la sœur, ma sœur
4. le frère, mon frère
5. le chien, mon chien
6. le chat, mon chat
7. l'école, mon école
8. le cheval, mon cheval
9. les amis, mes amis
10. les parents, mes parents
11. les professeurs, mes professeurs
12. les vêtements, mes vêtements
13. le grand-père, mon grand-père
14. la grand-mère, ma grand-mère
15. le cousin, mon cousin
16. la cousine, ma cousine
17. les exercices, mes exercices
18. le lapin, mon lapin
19. l'uniforme, mon uniforme
20. les livres, mes livres

Sheet 5c (page 103)

mon adresse

son école

ton prénom

ma maison

son nom

ta maison

tes parents

sa grand-mère

mes frères

sa grand-mère

Sheet 5g (page 107)

Nos yeux; nos cheveux; Notre école; notre école; notre classe; Notre professeur;notre classe; notre classe; Nos leçons

1. Leurs yeux sont bleus.
2. Non, leur école est en Normandie
3. Il y a neuf garçons dans leur classe.
4. Oui leur prof est gentille.
5. Il y a des posters sur les murs de leur classe.

Sheet 6b page 120

1. en Angleterre
2. en France
3. aux Pays-Bas
4. en Allemagne
5. au Danemark
6. en Belgique
7. en Grèce
8. en Italie
9. en Égypte
10. en Israël

1. en Amérique
2. aux États-Unis
3. au Canada
4. au Brésil
5. au Venezuela
6. en Martinique

1. en Russie
2. en Inde
3. en Malaisie
4. en Chine
5. au Japon
6. au Népal
7. au Pakistan

Sheet 6c (page 121)

Lyon

Lille

Cannes

Tours

Sète

Bordeaux

Lourdes

Meaux

Pau

Caen

Paris

Sheet 6g (page 126)

1. Elle chante.
2. Elles parlent beaucoup.
3. Il joue au tennis.
4. Elle danse.
5. Nous cuisinons.
6. Il regarde la télévision.
7. Je skie bien.
8. Je pense à mes vacances.
9. Vous parlez avec nous.

Sheet 7b (page 139)

j'habite

tu habites

il / elle habite

nous habitons

vous habitez

ils / elles habitent

j'étudie

tu étudies

il / elle étudie

nous étudions

vous étudiez

ils / elles étudient

je danse

tu danses

il / elle danse

nous dansons

vous dansez

ils / elles dansent

je pense

tu penses

il / elle pense

nous pensons

vous pensez

ils / elles pensent

Sheet 7d (page 141)

1. l'igloo
2. le château
3. la cabane
4. l'hôtel
5. la tente
6. le palais
7. la ferme
8. le pavillon
9. l'église
10. le chalet

Sheet 7g (page 145)

1. J'habite au Canada.
2. Il travaille en France.
3. Nous parlons avec nos amis en Allemagne.
4. Vous skiez en Italie
5. Je parle espagnol en Espagne.
6. Elles cuisinent dans un restaurant à Paris.
7. Ils travaillent beaucoup aux États-Unis.
8. Elle étudie au Japon.
9. Tu habites avec tes parents en Écosse.

Sheet 7i (page 150)

1. Il est fermier.
2. Elle est docteur.
3. Il est professeur.
4. Elle est serveuse.
5. Il est vétérinaire
6. Elle est conductrice de bus.

1. pharmacienne
2. infirmière
3. fermière
4. pilote
5. serveuse
6. scientifique
7. policière
8. dentiste
9. vétérinaire
10. factrice
11. électricienne
12. danseuse

Sheet 8a (page 162)

Il cuisine

Elle joue

Ils parlent

Il téléphone

Elle dessine

Elles regardent

Ils dansent

Il écoute

Elles chantent

Sheet 8c (page 164)

Je joue aux cartes.

Je joue à la marelle.

Je joue à l'élastique.

Je joue au ballon.

Je joue aux billes.

Je joue à la corde.

Sheet 8d (page 165)

Il joue au football.

Il joue au rugby.

Elle joue au tennis.

Il joue au basket.

Il joue au golf.

Ils jouent au ping-pong.

Il joue au cricket.

Il joue au hockey.

Elles jouent au volleyball.

Sheet 8e (page 166)

Elle joue du piano.

Il joue du violon.

Il joue de la guitare.

Ils jouent de la flûte.

Elle joue de la flûte à bec.

Ils jouent de la clarinette.

Il joue des percussions.

Il joue de la trompette.

Elle joue de l'accordéon.

Sheet 9a (page 183)

1. 02 78 56 12 34
2. 05 46 88 92 20
3. 01 65 33 21 55
4. 02 88 90 53 22
5. 08 45 33 26 11
6. 05 23 40 25 36

Sheet 9e (page 187)

1. 8h40
2. 17h15
3. 11h45
4. 00h10
5. 13h18
6. 14h50
7. 12h05
8. 9h55
9. 6h30

Sheet 10a (page 205)

1. Je vais à la banque.
2. Je vais à la boucherie.
3. Je vais à la boulangerie.
4. Je vais à l'aéroport.
5. Je vais au supermarché.
6. Je vais à la piscine.
7. Je vais à l'école.
8. Je vais à Paris.
9. Je vais au parc.
10. Je vais à la gare.
11. Je vais à l'église.
12. Je vais à la librairie.
13. Je vais à la bibliothèque.
14. Je vais au café.
15. Je vais au restaurant.

Sheet 10c (page 207)

1. Les enfants vont à l'école.
2. Il va au bureau.
3. Elle va à la bibliothèque.
4. L'ambulance va à l'hôpital.
5. Nous allons au cinéma.
6. Vous allez au restaurant.
7. Il va à la piscine.
8. Ils vont à l'aéroport.

Sheet 10e (page 209)

en bateau

à pied

en voiture

en avion

à moto

à cheval

à vélo

en autobus

en métro

Sheet 10f (page 210)

1. Chaque jour, je vais à l'école.
2. Chaque week-end nous allons au cinéma.
3. Tu vas en France en avion.
4. Il va à Paris en autobus.
5. Ma mère va au supermarché en voiture.
6. Ils vont au parc à pied.
7. Elle va au bureau en métro.
8. Vous allez à l'église à cheval.
9. Je vais aux États-Unis en avion.
10. Je vais à l'école à vélo.

Sheet 11a (page 226)

le café

le sucre

le beurre

le thé

la confiture

le lait

le chocolat chaud

le jus d'orange

les fruits

le yaourt

les céréales

le pain

le croissant

Sheet 11b (page 227)

La viande

le poulet

le bœuf

le porc

l'agneau

les saucisses

le jambon

Le poisson

le saumon

la truite

les crevettes

le cabillaud

Les légumes

les aubergines

les courgettes

les carottes

les tomates

© Maria Rice-Jones and Brilliant Publications

les petits pois
les poivrons
les pommes de terre
la salade

Les fruits
les fraises
les bananes
les cerises
les oranges
les kiwis
les pommes
les poires
les mangues
le melon

Les pâtes
les spaghettis
les lasagnes

Le fromage
le camembert
le Roquefort

Le riz
le riz blanc
le riz brun

Sheet 11e (page 230)

1. Le matin, je mange du pain avec du beurre et de la confiture.
2. Je bois une tasse de café avec un peu de lait chaud.
3. Le matin, il mange des œufs, des tomates et du jambon.
4. Il boit du lait et aussi un jus d'orange.
5. Elle ne mange pas de viande car elle est végétarienne.
6. À midi il boit toujours un verre de vin rouge et il mange un sandwich avec du jambon et du fromage.
7. Il mange beaucoup de légumes car il aime ça.
8. Le soir nous mangeons toujours de la salade avec du poisson ou de la viande.
9. Nous mangeons beaucoup de viande car nous aimons ça.

Sheet 11f (page 231)

Je voudrais du lait et des œufs, une douzaine d'œufs s'il vous plaît.
Oui, je voudrais des légumes: des carottes, un kilo de carottes. Des courgettes, seulement quatre, puis deux kilos de pommes de terre et pour finir des champignons, un kilo de champignons.
De la moutarde, de l'ail et des oignons s'il vous plaît.

Sheet 11h (page 233)

Je voudrais un kilo de pommes de terre.
Chaque matin, je bois une tasse de thé.
Une fois par jour, il boit un verre de vin.
Elle boit une bouteille d'eau chaque jour.
Je voudrais trois bouteilles de lait.
Je voudrais une bouteille de limonade.

Sheet 11m (page 238)

Hello to all of you.
There is a bottle of champagne in the kitchen, some Coca-Cola for the children, some lemonade, glasses and some cakes on the table. It's for you. Bon appétit and have a good holiday!

Sheet 13g (page 272)

Je suis né en 1999.
Nous avons une leçon le mardi.
Il va à l'école le matin.
Son anniversaire est le 5 mai.
Je vais skier en hiver.
Elle travaille l'après-midi.
Nous habitons en France.
Nous allons à Paris.
Ils vont en vacances.
Je vais à l'école à pied.
Il va à l'école en voiture.
J'ai une leçon à 14 heures.
Tu es fatigué le soir.
Il travaille à Rome.

Sheet 14a (page 286)

généreuse
contente
sportive
heureuse
sympathique
timide
calme
facile
nerveuse
difficile

Sheet 14c (page 288)

Il est content
Il est fâché
Il est timide
Il est triste
Il est calme

Sheet 14f (page 291)

1. Une Rolls-Royce est plus rapide qu'une Mini.
2. Un autobus est moins long qu'un train.
3. Une lettres est moins lourde qu'un paquet.
4. Mon grand-père (70 ans) est aussi âgé que ma grand-mère (70 ans).
5. Le français est plus difficile que l'italien.
6. La France set moins petite que l'Angleterre.
7. Il fait plus froid en hiver qu'en été.
8. Un ticket de métro est aussi cher qu'un ticket d'autobus.

Sheet 15a(i) (page 296)

B
une télévision; une église; un père; une règle

C

vingt-sept	quinze
quarante-deux	quarante-sept
dix-neuf	cinquante
cinquante-six	soixante
vingt-huit	soixante-quatorze

D

ce cinéma	ce supermarché
cette piscine	
cette école	cette boutique
cette agence	
cette gare	cet aéroport
ces boutiques	
ces maisons	cette rue
ces gens	
ce professeur	cette directrice
ces élèves	

Sheet 15a(ii) (page 297)

E

Petit

Pauvre

Grande

Jeune

Belle

Beau

Idiote

F

Il est

Ils sont

Je suis

Nous sommes

G

Elle a

Nous avons

Ils ont

J'ai

H

mes parents	ses leçons
mon frère	ses leçons
son école	sa voiture
tes livres	mon professeur
ton livre	ses professeurs

Sheet 15a(iii) (page 298)

I

1.
en Chine	à Paris
au Brésil	en Russie
en Égypte	en Italie
en Belgique	à Londres
au Canada	en Grèce
en Inde	en Angleterre
à Rome	en Écosse
au Japon	aux Etats-Unis

au Pakistan   en France

2. When a country ends in "e", use "en" before it. When a country ends in a letter other than "e", use "au". When a country starts with a vowel use "en". When a country is plural, use "aux". Before names of towns use "à".

J

1. je joue

    tu joues

    il / elle joue

    nous jouons

    vous jouez

    ils / elles jouent

Sheet 15a(iv) (page 299)

2. je pense

    tu penses

    il / elle pense

    nous pensons

    vous pensez

    ils / elles pensent

3. j'écoute

    tu écoutes

    il / elle écoute

    nous écoutons

    vous écoutez

    ils / elles écoutent

K

douze heures trente

six heures quarante-cinq

cinq heures moins vingt

quatorze heures trente

dix-huit heures moins cinq

vingt-trois heures

dix-neuf heures trente-cinq

Sheet 15a(v) (page 300)

L

je vais

tu vas

il / elle va

nous allons

vous allez

ils vont

M

Je vais au cinéma.   Je vais au supermarché.

Je vais au marché.   Je vais à la piscine.

Je vais à la gare.   Je vais à la boucherie.

Je vais aux Etats-Unis. Je vais à la poissonnerie.

Je vais à l'aéroport.   Je vais à l'église.

N

1. je mange

    tu manges

    il / elle mange

    nous mangeons

    vous mangez

    ils / elles mangent

Sheet 15a(vi) (page 301)

2. je bois

    tu bois

    il / elle bois

    nous buvons

    vous buvez

    ils / elles boivent

O

je fais

tu fais

il / elle fait

nous faisons

vous faites

ils / elles font

P

To do the washing up

To do the housework

To do the (food) shopping

To do the (clothes) washing

To do the ironing